WHAT'S LEFT OF ENLIGHTENMENT?

What's Left of Enlightenment?

A Postmodern Question

EDITED BY KEITH MICHAEL BAKER
AND PETER HANNS REILL

STANFORD UNIVERSITY PRESS

Stanford, California 2001

Stanford University Press
Stanford, California
©2001 by the Board of Trustees of the
Leland Stanford Junior University
Printed in the United States of America

Library of Congress Cataloging-in-Publication Data

What's left of enlightenment? : a postmodern question / edited by Keith
Michael Baker and Peter Hanns Reill.
   p. cm.
   Includes bibliographical references and index.
   ISBN 0-8047-4025-9 (alk. paper) — ISBN 0-8047-4026-7 (pbk.: alk. paper)
   1. Enlightenment. I. Baker, Keith Michael. II. Reill, Peter Hanns.

B1302.E65 W48   2001
149'.97—dc21   2001020686

This book is printed on acid-free, archival-quality paper.

Original printing 2001

Last figure below indicates year of this printing:
10 09 08 07 06 05 04 03 02 01

Typeset in 10/12.5 Galliard by John Feneron

Contents

Contributors

KEITH MICHAEL BAKER is J. E. Wallace Sterling Professor in the Humanities, Professor of History, and Cognizant Dean for the Humanities at Stanford University. He served as Director of the Stanford Humanities Center from 1995 to 2000. His publications include *Condorcet: From Natural Philosophy to Social Mathematics* (Chicago, 1975) and *Inventing the French Revolution* (Cambridge, 1990), and he has edited *The French Revolution and the Creation of Modern Political Culture*, vol. 1: *The Political Culture of the Old Regime* (1987) and vol. 4: *The Terror* (1994). His most recent work has been on the political languages of the French Revolution.

LORRAINE DASTON is Director at the Max Planck Institute for the History of Science in Berlin and Honorary Professor at the Humboldt-Universität Berlin. She is the author of *Classical Probability of the Enlightenment* and (with Katharine Park) *Wonders and the Order of Nature, 1150-1750*, which were awarded the Pfizer Prize of the History of Science Society in 1989 and 1999, respectively. Her most recent edited volume is *Biographies of Scientific Objects*. She has published numerous articles on the history of objectivity, the cognitive passions, and the emergence of the fact. She is a Fellow of the American Academy of Arts and Sciences and member of the Berlin-Brandenburg Academy of Sciences.

DENA GOODMAN is Professor of History and Women's Studies at the University of Michigan. She is the author of *Criticism in Action:*

Enlightenment Experiments in Political Writing (1989) and *The Republic of Letters: A Cultural History of the French Enlightenment* (1994) and the co-editor, with Elizabeth C. Goldsmith, of *Going Public: Women and Publishing in Early Modern France*.

DAVID A. HOLLINGER is Chancellor's Professor of History at the University of California at Berkeley. His most recent book is *Science, Jews, and Secular Culture: Studies in Mid-Twentieth Century American Intellectual History* (Princeton, 1996). His recent articles have appeared in *Daedalus, Representations, Constellations, Journal of American History, Church History*, and *Diacritics*.

LAWRENCE E. KLEIN is a lecturer in History at the University of Cambridge and a fellow of Emmanuel College. He is the author of *Shaftesbury and the Culture of Politeness* (1994) and numerous articles on eighteenth-century English intellectual and cultural history. His edition of the third earl of Shaftesbury's *Characteristics of Men, Manners, Times, Opinions* appeared in 1999.

JONATHAN KNUDSEN was professor of German history at Wellesley College before his untimely death in 1999. Knudsen was a major interpreter of the German Enlightenment. His pathbreaking book *Justus Möser and the German Enlightenment* offered an important revision of Möser, placing him squarly within the Enlightenment. Knudsen was a co-editor of the volume *Aufklärung und Geschichte: Studien zur deutschen Geschichtswissenschaft im 18. Jahrhundert* and wrote a number of excellent articles on German cultural and intellectual history. At the time of his death he was working on a cultural history of Berlin from the late eighteenth century to the mid-nineteenth.

MICHAEL MERANZE is Associate Professor of History at the University of California, San Diego. He is the author of *Laboratories of Virtue: Punishment, Revolution, and Authority in Philadelphia, 1760-1835* (1996) and editor of Benjamin Rush, *Essays: Literary, Moral, and Philosophical* (1988).

PETER HANNS REILL is professor of history at the University of California, Los Angeles, and director of UCLA's Center for Seventeenth and Eighteenth Century Studies and of the William Andrews Clark Memorial Library. His major fields of interest are the history of historical writing and the interconnections between the sciences and the humanities in the late eighteenth and early nineteenth century.

RICHARD RORTY taught philosophy at Wellesley, Princeton, and the University of Virginia before becoming Professor of Comparative Literature at Stanford in 1998. His most recent books are *Truth and Progress, Achieving Our Country: Leftist Thought in Twentieth-Century America,* and *Philosophy and Social Hope.*

HANS SLUGA is Professor of Philosophy at the University of California at Berkeley. He is the author of *Gottlob Frege* (1980) and *Heidegger's Crisis: Philosophy and Politics in Nazi Germany* (1993). He has written numerous essays on themes in both analytic and non-analytic philosophy and is currently completing a book on political philosophy.

JOHNSON KENT WRIGHT is Associate Professor of Interdisciplinary Humanities at Arizona State University. He is the author of *A Classical Republican in Eighteenth-Century France: The Political Thought of Mably* (Stanford University Press, 1997) and essays on modern historiography.

WHAT'S LEFT OF ENLIGHTENMENT?

KEITH MICHAEL BAKER

PETER HANS REILL

Introduction

It has become increasingly clear in recent years that, for all their differences, the many varieties of thinking commonly grouped together under the rubric of "postmodernism" share at least one salient characteristic: they all depend upon a stereotyped, even caricatural, account of the Enlightenment. Postmodernity, by definition, requires a "modernity" to be repudiated and superseded. And the tenets of this modernity—variously described as rationalism, instrumentalism, scientism, logocentrism, universalism, abstract rights, eurocentrism, individualism, humanism, masculinism, etc.—have invariably been assumed to be postulates of a philosophy of absolute reason identified with the so-called Enlightenment Project. The aim of this volume is to explore more critically than usual the now conventional opposition between Enlightenment and Postmodernity and to suggest some of the complications bearing upon it.

The authors of the essays presented in Part I under the rubric, "Enlightenment or Postmodernity," offer some general reflections on the way in which contemporary discussion characterizes the two movements as radical alternatives. In doing so, David Hollinger defends the epistemological heritage of the Enlightenment as a necessary foundation for the acceptance and implementation of the crucial liberal values to which it also gave rise. In his judgment, to flirt with relativism is to put rights at risk. Richard Rorty, by contrast, argues that it is both possible and necessary to disengage the political project of the Enlightenment from its outmoded epistemological base. What's left of Enlightenment, in his view, is its forward-looking aspiration to create a more decent human society through practical action, not its atavistic desire for a non-human authority embedded in such hypostatizations as "Truth" and "Reason."

Part II, "Critical Confrontations," provides a kind of archeology of the opposition between Enlightenment and Postmodernity by charting a series of critical engagements carried out by those who have demeaned or affirmed Enlightenment values in the course of the twentieth century. German thinkers played a crucial role in forming the terms of the debate. Jonathan Knudsen traces the first major critique of Enlightenment made by German historicists from the beginning of the nineteenth century, a critique that continued well into World War II with such thinkers as Meinecke, Auerbach, and Benjamin. Hans Sluga shows how Heidegger's consideration of the Enlightenment served as an entry point to the much larger critique of grounded rationality and universal reason which led to his radical rethinking of reason as embedded in history. Johnson Kent Wright, by contrast, analyzes the famous interpretation of the Enlightenment published in 1932 by Heidegger's principal philosophical opponent during the Weimar period, Ernst Cassirer. Appearing as it did on the eve of the Nazi seizure of power, and seen in its historical context, Cassirer's *The Philosophy of the Enlightenment* was at once a celebration of Enlightenment thinking and a defense of Weimar values. Its goal was the restoration of an activist conception of philosophical reason which is not merely imitative or instrumental but has the power to shape life itself.

Kant's motto, "*Sapere aude*—Dare to Know," was the epitome of the philosophy Cassirer found in the Enlightenment. Nor has he been alone in that regard. Michel Foucault's well-known confrontation with the Kantian imperative is analyzed in the essay by Michael Meranze. In Meranze's analysis, Foucault turned the Kantian injunction against the Enlightenment itself by identifying the singular, contingent, and arbitrary elements in what Kant presented as universal, timeless, necessary, and obligatory. Thus he continued the Enlightenment even as he challenged it. Meranze's Foucault, urging us to problematize all problematizations, remains, in striking ways, an Enlightenment figure.

Part III, "A Postmodern Enlightenment?," includes three essays that complicate the dichotomy between Enlightenment and Postmodernity by pointing to the existence within the Enlightenment of elements frequently seen as characteristic of Postmodernity itself. The central characteristic of contemporary thinking, as Lorraine Daston defines it, is a repudiation of devices of naturalization. Postmodernism refuses the absolutist discourse of nature and natural facts it assumes to be the legacy of the Enlightenment, instead mapping the path to emancipation through celebration of the cultural and the contingent rather than of the natural and the necessary. In Daston's analysis, however, the Enlightenment had no supreme confidence in the authority of facts or in the undisputed rule of nature. To the contrary, it exhibited enormous anxiety regarding the reliability of facts and the extent to which the rule of nature could be frustrated by human action. Its constantly reiterated fears of the powers of the imagination need to be seen as a powerful index of its sense of the fragility of facts and the unreliability of nature.

Epistemological anxiety could find practical relief in the practice of sociability, as David Hume most famously argued. It is appropriate therefore that the concluding essays of the volume turn to this aspect of the Enlightenment. Focusing on issues of gender, Dena Goodman offers us an Enlightenment which refused the choice between universality and difference and saw the latter as an essential social value. Through the civility practiced in the salons, she argues, difference—and especially a gendered difference—shaped the common good. Lawrence Klein, too, sees polite conversation as the quintessential activity of the Enlightenment, a way of fashioning self and world by the process Richard Rorty has advocated as "continuing the conversation."

Holding skepticism at bay through the effort to maintain a human conversation, seeking liberation even in the face of uncertainty, hoping for the best in human conduct even while recognizing the human capacity for the worst: these, too, are part of what's left of Enlightenment.

Earlier versions of the essays in this volume were presented at conferences held at the William Andrews Clark Memorial Library/

Center for Seventeenth- and Eighteenth-Century Studies at UCLA and the Stanford Humanities Center, Stanford University. We wish to acknowledge the excellent staffs of these two Centers and to thank them for their work in organizing these conferences. We are also grateful to Charly J. Coleman for his assistance in preparing the volume for publication.

PART I

ENLIGHTENMENT OR POSTMODERNITY?

DAVID A. HOLLINGER

The Enlightenment and the Genealogy of Cultural Conflict in the United States

In 1969, Charlie Manson and his band committed the stylized murders for which they are still remembered. Several months after these grisly events, a faculty colleague of mine at SUNY Buffalo, where he and I had just begun our teaching careers, said to me in a sober voice that if Charlie Manson was what it truly meant to not believe in God—if this cult of murder was the culmination of the historical process of secularization, was what the Enlightenment had come to— he was glad to remain a Christian believer. At first I thought my friend was joking. He was a sophisticated Assistant Professor of English, widely read, and a specialist, as it happened, in the eighteenth century. Surely, he was carrying out the kind of ironic routine that he, as a master of Fielding and Gibbon, of Hume and Johnson, could handle well. But I soon saw he was in earnest, and was trying to send a warning to me, whom he suspected of being rather too far over on the free-thinking side of the spectrum of spiritual orientations. I was nonplused by my friend's sincerity, and, without thinking, my tongue almost in cheek but not quite, mumbled something to the effect that the Catholicism so dear to him had resulted, after all, in the Spanish Inquisition.

Our friendship somehow survived, for a few years, at least. But I invoke here my memory of this private exchange because its dynamics are similar to many of the public conversations of our own time in which "the Enlightenment" is invoked. It is a discourse of warning and counter-warning, of morally portentous claims and counterclaims, a discourse in which episodes from intellectual history are manipulated and mobilized to discredit or to legitimate one program or another in contemporary struggles. The late Ernest Gellner appears to have believed that his opinions on contemporary issues were endowed with more weight if he identified these opinions with the Enlightenment, and that it discredited his critics to depict them as opponents of the entire body of rational and empirical wisdom built up over the course of two centuries.[1] In the meantime, John Gray seems to think his arguments against certain liberal political theorists are vastly strengthened, and the importance of his own arguments greatly underscored, if it is understood that at issue is the entire heritage of the Enlightenment.[2]

So, on the one side, we are told that the Enlightenment project apotheosized individuality and has left us without means of acting on the elementary communitarian truth that selves are the product of social groups. The Enlightenment project denied the constraints and the enabling consequences of history by assigning to human reason the role of building life anew from a slate wiped clean of tradition. This project tyrannized a host of particular cultural initiatives and tried to make everyone alike by advancing universal rules for identifying goodness, justice, and truth. Politically, the Enlightenment promoted absolutist and imperialist initiatives. Above all, the Enlightenment project blinded us to the uncertainties of knowledge by promoting an ideal of absolute scientific certainty.

Meanwhile, others assure us with equal confidence that the Enlightenment recognized the limits and fallibility of knowledge to a degree that pre-Enlightenment regimes of truth simply did not. This Enlightenment project brought under devastating scrutiny the prejudices and superstitions that protected slavery and a virtual infinity of other injustices. It created the historical and social scientific inquiries that enable us to speak with such confidence about the social dependence of the self. The Enlightenment promoted religious tolerance against the imperialist ambitions of conflicting absolutisms. Above all, the Enlightenment was subversive of traditional political authority, and ultimately it gave us democracy.

Thus we go on merrily, or sometimes grumpily, reenacting Maistre and Mill, just as I played Thomas Jefferson to my Buffalo colleague's Edmund Burke. And while so doing, we add the entire experience of the nineteenth and twentieth centuries to our inventory of historical vehicles that have transported things we like—or don't like—from the eighteenth century to the present. The Enlightenment led to Auschwitz, just as it had led to the Terror; or the Enlightenment led to the principles by which we judge the Terror to have been excessive, just as it led to the standards by which Auschwitz can be the most convincingly condemned today. This dynamic is displayed on shelves of books well beyond the constantly cited works of Lyotard and Habermas, ranging from Alasdair McIntyre's *After Virtue* to Stephen Toulmin's *Cosmopolis*, from Connor Cruise O'Brien's *On the Eve of the Millennium* to John Gray's *Enlightenment's Wake*.[3] I'm hot stuff because I'm not only refuting you, my puny opponent, but I am refuting every great thinker from Descartes to Popper; or, watch out, you think you are arguing against only me, but the implications of your reasoning are to deny the common sense of every humane and rational mind since the seventeenth century. Into such heroic postures we seem to fall into very quickly when we invoke the Enlightenment. One result of this dynamic in some contexts has been to turn the Enlightenment into a conversation-stopper: as soon as one's interlocutor is firmly classified as a defender or a critic of the Enlightenment, a host of associations, loyalties, and counter-loyalties are implicitly in place, and there is little to say.

This is often so in the multiculturalist debates. The Enlightenment blamed for what is said to be the excessive universalism and individualism that multiculturalists are trying to correct. The Enlightenment, it seems, has led us to suppose that all people are pretty much alike, thus blinding us to diversity. It is another mark of lingering Enlightenment assumptions, moreover, to focus on ostensibly autonomous individuals rather than the groups that provide individuals with their culture. And on the other side of the ideological coin, those who suspect multiculturalism of putting people into a small number of color-coded boxes and expecting them to stay there often voice their complaint in the name of the Enlightenment's revolt against the claims of blood and history. Yet some ideas that might be seen as extensions of an Enlightenment tradition—such as the right of an individual to choose his or her own cultural affiliations regardless of ancestry—are quite acceptable to the same audiences who will be suspicious of these same ideas if they are presented as Enlightenment ideas. A good rule of thumb in the multiculturalist debates is that a good way to get your ideas accepted is to conceal, rather than to emphasize, whatever ancestry those ideas may have in the Enlightenment.[4]

The polemical use of history is common. It would be a mistake to suggest that the case I have described is unique. The legacy of the Enlightenment, in particular, has always been contested because so many enduring religious, political, and philosophical issues were engaged in the historic episode that bears its name. But during the last quarter-century, the Enlightenment has been an extreme case of this dynamic in the United States. Why this has happened is the chief question I pursue here. I want also to comment, more tentatively, on another question: where do we go from here? What are the prospects for an honest inquiry into the long-term historical trajectories in which the Enlightenment-invoking quarrels of our own time are embedded?

~

An answer to the first question requires an understanding of how the debate over the "modern" was transformed during the 1980s by historical claims offered under the sign of postmodernism. Among Anglophone intellectuals, the term modernism was long used to refer to a cluster of revolts against the Enlightenment. Lionel Trilling's generation used the term "modernism" to refer to Nietzsche, Proust, Conrad, Yeats, Mann, Joyce, Stravinsky, Picasso, Nolde, Klimt, and William James. In a stock-taking essay of 1961, "On the Teaching of Modern Literature," Trilling himself offered a penetrating meditation on the modern canon, commenting on the moral and pedagogical problems presented by each of the texts he used in his legendary course at Columbia University.[5] *Consciousness and Society*, H. Stuart Hughes's a classic work of 1958, considered the social thought of the 1890–1930 epoch largely as a critique of the Enlightenment.[6] The modern canon, in the arts as well as philosophy and social theory, was widely understood in the 1950s and 1960s to be the work of a heroic generation of late-nineteenth and early-twentieth century intellectuals who had challenged the epistemological and political traditions of the Enlightenment, and had seen the dark side of what came to be called the modernization process.[7] What had happened during the very late nineteenth and early twentieth centuries, scholars agreed, was a revolt against the positivism, rationalism, realism, and liberalism that the Victorian intellectuals had refined from the Enlightenment of the eighteenth century. Carl Schorske's use of the word "modernism" in his *Fin-de-Siècle Vienna* of 1980 continued this firmly grounded and widely dispersed historiographical practice.[8]

During the 1980s, however, Anglophone intellectuals attended to a formidable sequence of books and articles that used the word modernism very differently, to refer not to the revolt against the Enlightenment, but to the tradition of the Enlightenment itself. Modernism came to mean not Dostoevsky, but Descartes. Anyone whose sense of modernism had been formed by Richard Ellmann and Charles Feidelson, Jr.'s massive anthology of 1965, *The Modern Tradition*,[9] and by the works of Trilling, Hughes, Schorske, Richard Blackmur, Anthony Quinton, and Irving Howe— to list only some of the most prominent discussants of modernism during the period between 1940 and 1980—had cause to wonder why the term modernism was suddenly being linked with rationalism, the Scientific Revolution, and Kant. These things, one had learned on good authority, were what modernists tried to get beyond.

This new sense of modernism was aggressively retailed in the United States under the name of postmodernism. Nietzsche, after his long career as a founder of modernism, began a new career as a precursor, if not a founder, of postmodernism. The transition can be sometimes found within the work of a single scholar. In 1983 philosopher Robert Pippin described Nietzsche as the prototypical modernist, and in 1991 described Nietzsche as the prototypical postmodernist.[10] Nietzsche's ideas had not changed. Nor had the details of Pippin's analysis of those ideas. The only thing that had changed was the history in which Nietzsche was to be placed, or, more precisely, the movement to which he was assigned. What took place between Pippin's two iterations of Nietzsche's grand historical significance was that modernism had become the Enlightenment and the revolt against it had become postmodernism. The same repackaging was afforded to William James, who, in book after book, made the switch from modernist to postmodernist.

The postmodernists virtually plundered the old modernist canon, appropriating the thinkers they liked for postmodernism and declaring the rest to be lingering echoes of the Enlightenment. In a vivid case of the classic maneuver of appropriation and effacement, some of the postmodernists appropriated the most exciting of the contributions of the canonical modernists and effaced the movement that produced them. The profound tensions within the work of the 1890–1930 generation were relaxed by a new historiography responsive to the hegemonic ambitions of persons who claimed postmodernism as their vehicle. The 1890–1930 historical moment was thus virtually evacuated in order to create a more stark and momentous confrontation between postmodernism and the old Enlightenment of Descartes and Kant. There was virtually nothing of consequence in between. Hardly anybody, it seemed, had really seen through the illusions of the Enlightenment until the postmodernists came along. All those folks who thought everything had changed on or about December 1910 were kidding themselves. There was a big break, all right, but it did not take place in Bloomsbury on the eve of World War I. It took place in Paris after 1968. One book after another carrying postmodernism in its title provided a capsule history of postmodernism, in which the generation of 1890–1930 was treated not as the group of heroic, agonistic explorers whose careers had been analyzed by Trilling and Howe, by Hughes and Schorske, but as a pusillanimous prolegomena to Foucault.[11]

Entailed in this transformation in the Enlightenment's relation to modernism was the more widespread acceptance, by American academics, of a notion of intellectual modernity that had been popular in France, and that achieved currency in the United States along with the ideas of French theorists whose names were associated with postmodernism.[12] Two autonomous revolts against two quite distinctive modernisms merged, apparently without anyone's planning it or negotiating it.[13] The first modernism was that taken for granted when the term postmodernism was first invoked by Leslie Fiedler, Susan Sontag, and Howe in the United States in the 1960s. The modernism against which these writers and their American contemporaries defined postmodernism was still the modernism of Eliot and Pound and Nietzsche and James; this was the modernism that entailed a critique of the Enlightenment and of the social and cultural processes of "modernization." Fiedler and Sontag and others thought this old modernism, as appreciated in the pages of the *Partisan Review* and the *Hudson Review*, had become academicized and stuffy. In this context, postmodernism seemed a refreshing change. It was found in the fiction of Thomas Pynchon and the music of John Cage. But a resoundingly different version of modernism, one associated with the Enlightenment, was the counter-referent for Lyotard's *Postmodern Condition*, translated into English in 1984.[14] The French conversation that produced Lyotard had been preoccupied, moreover, not with the arts, but with ideas about language, power, and the human subject that had been developed by philosophers, psychologists, and political theorists.

The authority of this French-centered conversation was facilitated by several specific features of the American intellectual scene. Active engagement with Lyotard was encouraged in the mid–80s by the antiphilosophical philosopher Richard Rorty, who briefly but portentously took for himself the label postmodernist and began to write about Proust and Nabakov shortly after having revived a pragmatic antifoundationalism for which the way had been prepared by Thomas S. Kuhn. These literary-philosophical explorations of Rorty's—grounded in James, Dewey, and Kuhn, and openly appreciative of the political tradition of American liberalism—served to enlarge and extend the postmodernist debate in the United States.[15] Another engagement was manifest in the work of Frederic Jameson, the most influential Marxist literary critic of the era. Jameson's critical studies of canonical modernists preceded his widely discussed paper of 1984, "Postmodernism, or the Cultural Logic of Late Capitalism," which addressed many genres of modernism and of postmodernism.[16] Simultaneously, Jürgen Habermas' attacks on the French postmodernists and on Hans-Georg Gadamer for betraying the Enlightenment project invited the large contingent of American followers of the Frankfurt School to engage the issues, and of course to see postmodernism's modernism as that of the Enlightenment.

Still, these two quite distinctive postmodernisms—an American, literary-artistic postmodernism defined against the canonical modernists of 1890–1930, and a French, philosophical-political postmodernism defined against the Enlightenment—might not have become part of the same discourse were it not for the quaint belief that there is but a single torch to be passed, requiring that each moment in the discourse of intellectuals be named. What is our moment? Why, the moment of postmodernism, of course. How do we know what it is? Well, we can start by scrutinizing the various things said and done under its sign. By the end of the 1980s the Anglophone world was awash with sweeping assessments of architecture, poetry, film, social theory, epistemology, fiction, and political economy, all of which were said to partake of postmodernism in the French sense of the term.[17] Older critiques of the Enlightenment that had previously attained only a tiny constituency, such as Theodor Adorno and Max Horkheimer's *Dialectic of Enlightenment*, a book published in German in the 1940s but translated into English only in 1972, gained unprecedented currency.[18]

Hence the Enlightenment made the historic transition from a distant episode long interrogated by the great modernists into a vibrant enemy of the newest and most exciting insights coming from Paris. The Enlightenment was dehistoricized, and made into a vivid and somewhat dangerous presence insufficiently criticized and transcended by previous generations of intellectuals. It was up to us, now in the 1980s and 1990s, to do the job right, to complete the anti-Enlightenment project. No wonder the tensions surrounding the name of the Enlightenment sharply increased. All of the historic layers of mediation between "us" and the Enlightenment had been put aside. The Enlightenment became more relevant to contemporary cultural conflicts because the discourse of postmodernism made it so.

࿊

Where do we go from here? One response to the ease with which discursive blacksmiths forge and shatter links between ourselves and the Enlightenment is to suspend, temporarily, at least, explicit assertions of the Enlightenment or counter-Enlightenment significance of contemporary debates. If the Enlightenment can be moved around so easily to suit contemporary doctrinal agendas, perhaps it is not worth the struggle to establish a warranted account of the Enlightenment and its consequences. We might be better off with a more relaxed attitude toward the Enlightenment, and toward history in general, accompanied by a determination to formulate contemporary issues in terms that are closer to the ground. New openings and new alliances might come about in contemporary debates if the partisans are less determined to identify their own positions with symbolically charged discursive giants of the past. Simultaneously, we might rehistoricize the Enlightenment with a vengeance. A stronger historiography of the Enlightenment might emerge from a conviction that eighteenth-century studies can flourish well enough without exaggerated claims to relevance in contemporary culture wars. Enlightenment studies might then become more like patristics and Tang sinology, worthy *Wissenschafte* whose findings are relatively removed from debates over the character and direction of our civilization.

Yet this approach, tempting as it will be to anyone who has encountered the Enlightenment in its capacity as a conversation-stopper, runs into difficulties when enacted. Consider what happens when we try this in relation to a set of ideas that were widely adhered to by American intellectuals in the 1940s and 1950s, were then brought under severe suspicion at one point or other between the late 1960s and the 1980s, and have more recently been subject to critical revision and reassertion. Before I list some of the ideas that fall into this class, let me underscore the distinctive historical destiny of these ideas. This class is quite specific; it does not include ideas that were bequeathed by the World War II generation yet were not called sharply into question by the next generation. Excluded, also, are ideas that were so bequeathed and then so challenged yet were not reasserted with noteworthy vigor. I call attention only to ideas that underwent all three experiences: popular in the 40s and 50s, then subject to widespread suspicion, and, finally, subject to critical reformulation and defense in recent years. Such ideas—argued about so earnestly, and subject to sharp reversals—are obviously important to the intellectual life of our own time. Any study of American intellectual life since 1950 needs an analytic language for interpreting these ideas.

What ideas fall into this distinctive class? Let me suggest seven, although the list could no doubt be extended:

— Nature has a capacity to significantly resist or respond to human efforts to represent it and to intervene in it.
— Humankind as a whole is a valid epistemic unit.

— Intersubjective reason has great emancipatory potential.

— Civil liberties formulated on the basis of rights ascribed to individual citizens are indispensable to a just society.

— Religion, whatever its role in past centuries, is now likely to be irrelevant, or even an obstruction, to cognitive and social progress.

— Physical characteristics such as skin color and shape of the face should not be allowed to determine the cultural tastes and social associations of individuals.

— The United States is potentially a world-historical agent of democratic-egalitarian values.

These ideas were affirmed with conviction by a great variety of voices during the 1940s and 1950s, when modernization theorists and positivists and behaviorists and liberals and integrationists of many kinds were in vogue: the Walt Rostows and the Hans Reichenbachs, the Perry Millers and the David Trumans, the Gunnar Myrdals and Cary McWilliamses of those years. Each of the seven was later brought under suspicion, often by persons identified with one or more of the following movements: communitarianism, feminism, neo-conservatism, poststructuralism, Marxism, postmodernism, and multiculturalism. These seven ideas are now situated in the classic baby-and-bathwater domain. Some say, in effect, "forget it, it's time we got beyond those ideas, let's talk about something else," and other people respond, "wait a minute, there's something here we can probably still use, if we are careful about it." And some who say "forget it" concerning one or another of the seven will switch sides about another of the seven, and say, "hold on, I like that one if we can make it non-racist, non-sexist, non-imperialist, non-universalist, non-logocentric, non-formalist, and, above all, non-European."

Accepting one of these ideas does not require one to accept the others. One of our most indefatigable skeptics about the epistemic unity of all humankind, about the capacity of nature to provide non-discursive restraints upon our representations of it, and about the emancipatory potential of intersubjective reason is at the same time a notorious defender of the American nation-state as an instrument for democratic-egalitarian values, and a scourge of the religiosity found in the likes of Stephen Carter and Christopher Lasch. I refer to Richard Rorty.

Each of the seven ideas on my little list deserves its own history within the discourse of the American academic intelligentsia since 1950. I invoke these ideas here only to render concrete the challenge of dealing with recent intellectual history in relation to the question of the Enlightenment's legacy. Are these seven ideas "Enlightenment ideas"? Of what significance is it that one thinker who accepted all of them—Ernest Gellner—called himself an "Enlightenment Rationalist Fundamentalist"?[19] Is Anthony Appiah a "neo-Enlightenment thinker" by virtue of his defense of cosmopolitanism?[20] Is Ian Hacking, by virtue of his critique of popular notions of "social construction"?[21] Is Michael Ignatieff, by virtue of his perspective on "blood and belonging"?[22] Does the critical revision and reassertion of these ideas in very recent years amount to a "neo-Enlightenment" of sorts? I state these questions not to answer them, but to suggest that if one wants to be historical at all, it is difficult to analyze some central feature of recent American intellectual life without making at least some use of the Enlightenment. The universalism and individualism prominent in the list surely owe much to Christianity, but so does the Enlightenment itself. The potential connection between the Enlightenment and these seven energetic ideas of our own time cannot be disposed of simply by pointing to a "more complicated" intellectual ancestry. At issue, rather, is whether we can get very far in explaining how these ideas have come to us, and how they acquired the hold they have on our conversations, without making extensive use of the collection of seventeenth- and eighteenth-century-centered episodes that we continue to call "the Enlightenment."

This is to suggest that if we are going to make any use at all of intellectual history in trying to understand where we are today, the Enlightenment is extremely difficult to avoid. The temptation to turn away in disgust and frustration at the polemicism of recent uses of the Enlightenment should be resisted. To give in to this temptation would be to deny our own historicity, and to shrink from searching for the sources and sustaining conditions of the ideas that animate much of contemporary intellectual life. We might save the Enlightenment from polemicism, but at a considerable cost: we might cut off too abruptly an opportunity for the cultural self-knowledge that history is supposedly in the business of providing. Historians have been relatively passive in the disputes in which the Enlightenment has been invoked; rather, the thinkers who have been most active in those disputes are philosophers, literary scholars, and political theorists. Historians have put remarkably little resistance—in venues where it counts—to the transformation of modernism from Dostoevsky to Descartes, and to the proliferation of cardboard-character representations of the Enlightenment mind.

Facing and trying to bring reason and evidence to the polemics that invoke episodes from intellectual history, then, comes with the intellectual historian's calling unless one simply wants to withdraw from the concerns of one's colleagues in other parts of the humanities and social sciences. We should not shy away from constructing the most historically sound Enlightenment we can, and from offering the best arguments we can about its consequences. If someone claims, as did the author of a recent book, *Hitler as Philosophe*, that Hitler was a follower of Rousseau on sexuality and of Ricardo on economics, that he was a Jacobin in his religious orientation, and that he was, in general, a popularizer—in the words of the *American Historical Review*'s reviewer—of "Enlightenment values" such as "optimism, progress, and human perfectibility through adherence to natural law,"[23] these claims should be confronted head-on.

This requires that those of us who work primarily in the history of the twentieth century listen to what our colleagues in Enlightenment studies have to say. I hope we can count on our colleagues in seventeenth- and eighteenth-century studies to provide us with a sound and stable sense of the Enlightenment to work with. But you never know what they will say. In a recent issue of *Critical Inquiry*, one scholar argued that the true Enlightenment, the complete Enlightenment, the one expression of the Enlightenment that did not deny its own ferocious imperative for truth, was found not in Kant, not in Rousseau, not in Locke. The complete Enlightenment, this scholar explained, was found in that most commanding of all efforts to integrate power and knowledge, the Spanish Inquisition.[24] If my Buffalo friend had understood this in 1969, he could have had the last laugh on me.

The Continuity Between the Enlightenment and 'Postmodernism'

It is sometimes said that the Enlightenment project has failed. But there were two Enlightenment projects—one political and one philosophical. One was to create heaven on earth: a world without caste, class, or cruelty. The other was to find a new, comprehensive, worldview which would replace God with Nature and Reason.

The political project has not failed, even though it is proceeding very slowly, and only by fits and starts. Now that various apparent short-cuts to utopia, such as fascism and Marxism, have turned out to be dead ends, we have had to become more patient. It now seems clear that reformist, gradualist, social democratic changes in laws and institutions provide the only way in which the Enlightenment's goal of maximal freedom and minimal humiliation will ever be reached. Despite the need for patience, however, this goal is as desirable as ever.

The second, philosophical, project is still being pursued by many philosophers. But it has, throughout the twentieth century, been criticized. Some of this criticism comes from religious philosophers, or from Heideggerians, who think that the Enlightenment was a stage in a process of intellectual decline. But most of it comes from philosophers like me, who think that the Enlightenment philosophers were on the right track, but did not go far enough. We hope to do to Nature, Reason and Truth what the eighteenth century did to God.

The slippery and misleading term "postmodernism" is sometimes used to refer to this philosophical initiative. When used in this way, it denotes a project which dates back to Nietzsche and the American pragmatists, though (as I shall be saying shortly) it is rooted in Hegelian historicism and Darwinian biology. So I sometimes find myself being called a "postmodernist" because of my pragmatist views about truth and rationality. But I am nervous about being thus labeled, since in many contexts the term "postmodernism" is used in another sense, to refer to an attitude of political hopelessness. This attitude has become widespread since the defeat of the expectations of the revolutionaries of the 1960s.

What people call "postmodernist politics" or "cultural politics" seems to me a retreat from real politics into academic politics. All the proponents of such politics offer, as far as I can see, is distrust of traditional bourgeois liberal initiatives, and of something called "humanism" with which these initiatives are supposed to be tainted. As a good bourgeois liberal, and as somebody who cannot figure what is supposed to be wrong with "humanism," I find this new-found hopelessness mysterious.

Many writers who use the term "postmodernism" without the shudder quotes in which I prefer to enfold it think that the new philosophical world-view—the one which has emerged from the work of such neo-Nietzschean philosophers as Heidegger, Derrida, Foucault and Lyotard—has political implications. This new world-view is supposed to have shown that the last two centuries' worth of attempts to achieve a heaven on earth were somehow misguided, or somehow bound to fail. I cannot see the purported connection.

So I shall be defending two theses in this paper. The first thesis is that the twentieth-century project of treating Nature and Reason as unneeded substitutes for God is continuous with Enlightenment anti-authoritarianism. Getting rid of our sense of being responsible to something other than, and larger than, our fellow human beings is a good idea. Insofar as the terms "Nature," "Reason" or "Truth" are used to refer to something of this sort, we should drop these terms from our vocabulary. We should follow through on the Enlightenment's skepticism about non-human powers. Abandoning the last vestiges of 18th-century rationalism in favor of 20th-century pragmatism would be good for our self-confidence and our self-respect.

My second thesis is that abandoning Western rationalism has no discouraging political implications. It leaves the Enlightenment political project looking just as good as ever. The only reason we could have for abandoning that project would be if we had invented a better one. But we have not. No philosophical or scientific discovery, as far as I can see, could ever give us reason for abandoning Enlightenment politics. Nothing should be allowed to displace utopian political hope except the glimpse of an even better utopia than the one previously imagined. Dismissive attitudes toward bourgeois liberal politics persist, I think, for no better reason than force of Marxist habit.

Why, one might ask, are the two Enlightenment projects—the one political and the other intellectual—so often treated as if they were indissoluble? I think that this treatment may reflect nothing more than an historical coincidence. To see this, let us rewrite history a little, and imagine a slightly different possible world. Suppose that the autocrats had been much wilier than they were, and the bourgeoisie stupider and somewhat less pushy. Imagine that the old order had lasted until the eighteen-forties, and that the middle of the 19th century, rather than the end of the 18th, was the age of the democratic revolutions.

By then Hegel rather than Locke would have been the philosopher whom every self-respecting intellectual had to have read. Darwin rather than Newton would have been the paradigmatic scientist—the scientist whose theory was at the center of philosophical reflection. Baudelairian dandyism rather than Rousseauian pastoral would have begun to dominate the literary imagination. These counterpart figures would not, to be sure, have been quite the Hegel, the Darwin, or the Baudelaire we now know, but they might have borne striking family resemblances.

In the possible world I am imagining, by the time that the democratic revolutions had filled the world with egalitarian hope, Nature had become *vieux jeu*. It had been supplanted by History. So utopian politics came to seem indissolubly connected with nineteenth-century historicism rather than with eighteenth-century rationalism. Reason had come to be thought of as manifested more clearly in the switch from autocracy to democracy than in the switch from Ptolemy to Copernicus, or from Galen to Harvey. The dream of a democratic utopia took shape only after Darwin had suggested the possibility that we may be clever animals trying to reshape the environment to our needs, rather than intellects attempting to grasp the intrinsic structure of reality.

In asking you to imagine this possible world, I am asking you to assume that changes in the vocabulary of the intellectuals are neither foundational nor superstructural in respect to socio-political changes. My own hunch is that the two kinds of change are largely independent of each other: each is governed by its own winds and tides. We have become far too ready to periodize history in overly neat ways. In particular, we are too anxious to synchronize intellectual with artistic and socio-political revolutions.

The unfortunate popularity of the exasperating term "postmodern" is one result of this unhappy eagerness for synchrony. The urge to periodize has led intellectuals to think that the rejection of what Derrida calls "the metaphysics of presence" just *must* have political implications. Heidegger's suggestion that each epoch is governed by a single Word of Being uttered by a great thinker, and Foucault's suggestion that the switch to a new *episteme* is sudden and inexplicable, have encouraged the assumption that a new philosophy means a new politics. But politics is long, and philosophy relatively short. The urge to create a world without cruelty is deeper and more enduring than any philosophical outlook.

To avoid the assumption that a new philosophy requires a new politics it helps to remember that the Derridean opposition between the play of differences and the metaphysics of presence is nothing new. Quentin Skinner has recently shown us how the tension between rhetoric and logic—between what Skinner, following Habermas, calls dialogical and monological conceptions of reason—was important for Hobbes, and for the seventeenth century generally. This tension has loomed large throughout the history of philosophy. That is why it is so easy to find striking anticipations of the latest discoveries of "postmodern" thought in ancient, medieval, and Renaissance writers.

Another way to make this point is to suggest that it may be just an historical contingency that the metaphysics of presence outlasted medieval Aristotelianism. Stephen Toulmin seems to me right in saying that if Montaigne rather than Descartes had become the founder of the modern philosophical tradition, then it would have been literature and politics rather than mathematics and physics which would have structured the attempt to replace a religious with a secular world-view. Poetic redescription of autocratic institutions and customs as vicious rather than virtuous, and of democratic ones as virtuous rather than vicious, would then have seemed the paradigmatic intellectual achievement. Descartes' paradigm, mathematical demonstration, would have been marginalized, and so would Bacon's paradigm, scientific experimentation.

My hunch that intellectual and socio-political change proceed in relative independence of one another leads me to urge that we tell two distinct stories of the emancipation of humanity rather than one. We need one story about the progress we have made so far in creating what Avishai Margalit calls "a decent society"—a society in which institutions do not humiliate people unnecessarily. We need a separate story about progress toward a satisfactory and inspiring world-view. We should have one story about people in general and a separate story about the intellectuals: one story about how people have gotten out from under various sorts of thugs and bullies, and another story about the emancipation of thought from obsolete doctrines, doctrines framed to meet the needs of more primitive cultures.

The first story might begin with such epochal events as the prudent, self-denying, decision to enslave defeated warriors and their families—to put them to work rather than using their slow death under torture as after-dinner entertainment. It could go on to cover the increasing willingness to give alms to beggars, the end of the slave trade, the Ten Hours Act, votes for women, the growing conviction that men should not rape their wives, the Norris-La Guardia Act, the creation of the welfare state, and the repeal of anti-sodomy laws.

Such a story of past accomplishments dovetails with Enlightenment fantasies of a utopian, thoroughly decent society. The overall features of that utopia have been fairly familiar for two hundred years, but our vision of it keeps being touched up with additional details. (For example, we utopians now urge legal provision for same-sex marriage—an agenda item which did not occur to most liberal reformers until quite recently.) In this utopia nobody will be humiliated by bullies—neither by slaveowners, nor by factory owners, nor by husbands. The elimination of vast social and economic inequalities will help people treat one another decently. Mankind will finally escape from the thuggery of the schoolyard, put away childish things, and be morally mature.

When we turn to the second story—the one about the intellectuals' search for wider, richer, more adequate world-views—the founding events are the first surviving canonical texts (the Platonic dialogues and the Buddhist sutras, for example). Ambitious intellectual historians tell stories about how these texts hang together with other texts: for example, Augustine's *Confessions*, Lady Murasaki's novel, Newton's *Principia*, Shelley's poems, and Marx's and Engels's *Communist Manifesto*. By telling such stories we hope to get a sense of what, taken together, all these achievements add up to. As more figures are added to the canon, we get bigger and better stories of this sort—stories which stimulate our imagination, suggest unexplored possibilities, and so lead to the creation of new canonical texts.

Thinkers who stand in the tradition of the Enlightenment tell upbeat stories of how these texts offer us a closer and closer approximation to the correct world-view. Thinkers in the tradition of the Counter-Enlightenment—the Heideggerians and the Straussians, for example—tell downbeat stories about how they have led us away from that view. Thinkers who like to think of themselves as "postmodern," and who teach courses in what they call "cultural studies" often tell stories about non-canonical texts, written by what Foucault called "local intellectuals." They do not attempt to weave these together into a continuous narrative. For they have been taught by Lyotard to be suspicious of metanarratives which try to tie all the texts, canonical and non-canonical, together.

There is a point to this suspicion, but not, I think, to the distrust which many admirers of Foucault have for the sort of story which Hegel, Macaulay and Acton told: human history as the story of increasing freedom. Foucauldians typically have the same suspicions about narratives of progress as they do about the Enlightenment political project. But both suspicions are unjustified.

My own view of narratives of progress is that of Thomas Kuhn: there is no such thing as asymptotic approach to the Truth, but there is progress nevertheless—progress detected by retrospection. Scientific progress is made when theories which solve certain problems are replaced by theories which solve both those problems and certain additional problems, those which the earlier theories had turned out to be unable to solve. On Kuhn's view, Einstein got no closer to the way reality is "in itself" than did Newton, but there is an obvious sense in which Einsteinian physics is an improvement on Newtonian physics.

Analogously, political progress is made when institutions which have made possible increased freedom and decreased cruelty are replaced with institutions which enlarge freedom still more, and mitigate cruelty still further. Foucault was right to suggest that turning over criminals to psychiatric social workers is no closer to the moral law than drawing and quartering them. But he was wrong to suggest that it is equally cruel. He was wrong to be sardonic about all the old-fashioned, boring, familiar, attempts at social reform which have sprung from the persistence of the political hopes of the Enlightenment.

An Enlightenment-style narrative of intellectual progress is still favored by anti-Kuhnians. On their eschatological account, world-views will keep changing until we finally reach Truth. This truth will include both scientific truth, truth about the underlying laws of nature, and truth about what is right, an accurate transcription of the articles of the moral law. But on the "postmodern" narratives of intellectual and moral progress which I favor, there is no such thing as Truth to be reached. Nor is there any point in raising skeptical questions like "How do we know that the increased elegance and predictive efficiency of a scientific theory is a mark of it correspondence to the way things really are?" or "How do we know that a world with more freedom and less cruelty is a better world?"

Philosophers like me, the kind who get labeled "postmodern" but do not relish the term, can imagine that human beings might some day, with a lot of luck, come to be *morally* grown-up. For they might eventually outgrow the bullying habits they form in the schoolyard, and which the species institutionalized in its infancy. But, we insist, there is no such thing as full *intellectual* maturity. There is, to be sure, intellectual growth, but there is no natural terminus to the process of intellectual advance. Stories of intellectual advance will make possible further, surprising, intellectual advances, without end.

For my sort of philosopher, there is no way the natural world or the moral law really is, so there is nothing which scientific or political progress can hope to reflect more faithfully. Science may well converge to agreement on how the world should be described in order to facilitate technological control, but this description will not be of Nature as it is in itself, but of Nature as subjected to the Baconian demand for better tools with which to improve man's estate. Politics in different countries may well converge to a single set of democratic institutions, but these institutions will not reflect moral reality as in itself. They will, like the scientists' theories, be tools for gratifying certain human desires—the desires which have become more and more prevalent in the last two hundred years.

The choice between the Enlightenment and the post-modern accounts of intellectual progress is a choice between a world-view in which inquiry aims at accurate representation of the way Nature or Morality really is and one which gives up the distinction between appearance and reality. It gives it up in favor of a distinction between less useful descriptions and more useful descriptions. This choice is of great interest to intellectuals, but seems to me no more relevant to the Enlightenment political project—the development of an egalitarian utopia—than the choice between Christian faith and atheism.

Both atheism and Christianity, we should remember, are highly adaptable creeds. Medieval Catholicism was a good vehicle for sustaining the power of the bullies. Liberal, Social Gospel-style Christianity has been a good vehicle for attempts to break their power. White atheists and black Baptists worked side-by-side in the Civil Rights Movement, hoping to realize the same dream. The differences between their world-views made no difference to their political practice. Neither should the differences between John Searle's views about truth and rationality and my own, nor those between Jürgen Habermas' and Jacques Derrida's views of the nature of discourse.

Both Enlightenment and "post-modern" philosophy are just as flexible, when it comes to politics, as is Christianity. Just as becoming a Christian is not in itself enough to make you anxious to protect your fellow human beings from being humiliated, so becoming either an Enlightenment rationalist or a "postmodernist" is not enough. The vocabulary of either movement can be used in the defense of either fascist or social democratic political initiatives. Hans Sluga has pointed out that some Nazi philosophers made a point of the need for objective, absolute values; otherwise, they said, anti-Semitism would be merely a subjective preference.

Contemporary social democrats include many people who believe, with Kant, that the moral law is there to be recognized by the unclouded intellect—and also lots of people who are as suspicious as was Dewey of everything that Kant said. Those of us in the latter camp think that questions about the objectivity of values, or about the grounds of normativity, are pointless. We see these questions as an unfortunate legacy of Enlightenment rationalism. But we think that the association between Enlightenment egalitarianism and Enlightenment rationalism is as accidental as the association between Jesus, the preacher of brotherly love, and Christ, the divinity who will, at the Last Judgment, condemn sinners to eternal torture.

This last analogy brings me back to my claim that there is an important continuity between the Enlightenment and "post-modernism." The difference between fundamentalist and liberal Christians is the difference between those who feel a need to be subject to authority and those who do not: the difference between those for whom love cannot be the only law, and those for whom it is sufficient. I interpret the difference between the Enlightenment rationalists and us "postmodernists" in an analogous way. For the rationalists Reason has authority, because Reality, the way things are in themselves, has authority. Reality deserves respect, and Reason is the faculty which puts us in touch with Reality. For us "postmodernists," on the other hand, reason is conceived dialogically. We treat it as just another name for willingness to talk things over, hear the other side, try to reach peaceful consensus. It is not the name of a faculty which penetrates through appearance to the intrinsic nature of either scientific or moral Reality. For us, to be rational is to be conversable, not to be obedient.

On the interpretation of Enlightenment rationalism prevalent among the philosophers who get called "postmodern," the very idea of such a faculty is the expression of a sadomasochistic desire to humiliate ourselves before an authority called "Nature" or "Reality." We "postmodernists" think this desire is unworthy of the heirs of the Enlightenment—the successors of the heroic figures who overthrew the power of the priests and the kings. We think that anything you can do with notions like "Nature," "Reason" and "Truth" you can do better, with such notions as "the most useful description for our purposes" and "the attainment of free consensus about what to believe and to desire." Insofar as they claim to add something to these latter notions, invocation of Truth, Nature and Reason are relics of childish fears and superstitions—new disguises for Old Nobodaddy. Such invocation is belief—the philosophical analogue of religious fundamentalism.

Carl Becker said that Locke's popularity in the eighteenth century was due to his having "demolished . . . the Christian doctrine of total depravity, a black, spreading cloud which for centuries had depressed the human spirit." Locke's doctrine that the human mind "is no more than a blank white sheet of paper," Becker continued,

> made it possible for the eighteenth century to believe with a clear con-
> science what it wanted to believe, namely that since man and the mind of
> man were shaped by that nature which God had created, it was possible
> for men, 'barely by the use of their natural faculties', to bring their ideas
> and their conduct, and hence the institutions by which they lived, into
> harmony with the universal natural order.[1]

The Enlightenment notion of reason is of a faculty which links us with nature, and brings this harmony about. The "postmodern" repudiation of that notion is part of a larger attempt to abandon the idea that there is a universal natural order. "Postmodern" philosophers treat the idea that human beings should conform to such an order as a relic of the doctrine of total depravity—a relic we can now cast aside. Their repudiation of what Derrida calls "the metaphysics of presence" is a repudiation of the idea that a social-democratic utopia would be any more *natural* or *rational* than a fascist utopia. It would simply be less cruel, and therefore more desirable. To those who ask "What's so desirable about diminished cruelty?" there is, as far as I can see, nothing to be said. Enlightenment rationalism (found in contemporary Kantian moral philosophers such as Cristine Korsgaard) insists that there is a lot to be said.

For the Enlightenment, unaided human reason could and should take the place of religious faith. For the "postmoderns," the idea of unaided human reason is only acceptable if it is purified of the picture of reason as a faculty which tracks truth—one which aligns the human mind with the intrinsic structure of reality in general or of human nature in particular. We "postmoderns" think that we shall never be quite free of the sort of sadomasochism which produces bullies until we cease to believe in such structures. We agree with Nietzsche that a stench of blood and of the lash lingers over Kant's categorical imperative. We find the notions of "Reality" and "Truth," understood in the old rationalistic way, as obnoxious as Voltaire found the notion of "God," understood in the old fundamentalist, fideistic, way. Voltaire could respect Christ as a prophet of loving kindness, but not as a divinity with the power to punish him. Postmodern philosophers are willing to respect reality as presenting us with problems to be dealt with, but not as an authority to be obeyed.

The first stage in discarding the idea that rational inquiry is an attempt to grasp the intrinsic nature of things was Hegel's critique of the idea, common to Plato and Kant, that philosophy should imitate mathematics by finding pure, simple, elegant structures which would remain unaffected by time and chance. In Hegel's view, the Greeks could not have known what human nature or human reason are. For they did not have enough concrete material to go on. They lived in a primitive stage of civilization. The world-spirit had not yet progressed very far. Hegel thought that it would always be unsafe to think that one has grasped an abstract and general truth about the relation between human beings and the rest of the universe. For one's favorite abstract generality will at best be just a summary of the human race's experience so far, and so its apparent necessity may be only a temporary one. You never know when your purported necessity may not be *aufgehoben*—made obsolete by a new vocabulary, in which it can no longer be stated.

For writers of the nineteenth century who took over from Hegel what they called "the evolutionary view of things," reality does not have a permanent structure, nor does the human mind. So, although sentences do not change their truth-values as time goes by, there is nevertheless no quasi-object called Truth, which stays the same for all eternity. Rather, as time goes by, old structures dissolve and new ones emerge. Reason is to be thought of as dialectical and context-bound, rather than as mathematical and attuned to the eternal.

Hegel, however, retained a good deal of eighteenth-century rationalism, and it was not until Darwin that historicism could be peeled off from the conviction that something like the World-Spirit was in charge of history, and that philosophy of history should therefore take the place of metaphysics and physics as a guide to political life.

Darwin's model of evolutionary progress as made through the accidental congruence of genetic modifications with environmental niches had the effect of de-rationalizing historicism. The attempt to synthesize Hegel and Darwin into a syncretic evolutionary and historicist world-view led philosophers away from Marx and Spencer in the direction of what Peirce called "tychism"—an emphasis on the role of chance in determining the course of both biological and cultural evolution. The analogy between the two sorts of evolution helped make evident what Popper was later to call "the poverty of historicism."

On a tychistic view of evolution, you cannot extrapolate from the past to the future. You cannot do with History what the Enlightenment tried to do with Nature. You cannot get it right, once and for all. All you can do is use the tools available in the present to make the future different than it might have been. You can practice utopian politics but you cannot back up your politics by reference to what History dictates. You cannot use philosophy to underwrite your utopia. The attempt to use a philosophy of history for underwriting purposes is as hopeless as the eighteenth century's attempt to use Nature for such purposes.

This de-rationalized and tychistic version of evolution produced, at the end of the nineteenth century, the great forerunner of "postmodernism": Nietzsche. It also produced the founders of American pragmatism: James and Dewey. One reason it has been assumed that if you abandon Enlightenment rationalism you abandon Enlightenment egalitarianism is that Nietzsche denounced both. He suggested that they were signs of the same failure of nerve: the same inability to stand on one's own feet, to be content to say "thus I will it" rather than "this is what God [or Nature, or Reason] dictates to me." Nietzsche's popularity has obscured the fact that James and Dewey agreed with him about the need to get rid of the Enlightenment's notions of Truth, Reason and Nature, while disagreeing with his politics. They were equally anti-authoritarian, but less individualistic.

James and Dewey wanted to substitute "Thus *we*, we free citizens of a democratic community, will it" for "this is what Reason dictates." They heartily endorsed the Enlightenment's political project while abandoning its intellectual project. Like Nietzsche, they wanted a new world-view, one which would take Darwin to heart as the Enlightenment had taken Newton to heart, and they used Darwin to buttress Hegelian doubts about Kantian universalism. But they found Bergson's "élan vital" a better way of describing Darwinian evolution than Nietzsche's "will to power." Their version of anti-authoritarianism was communitarian rather than individualistic.

Habermas's substitution of "communicative reason" for "subject-centered reason" is a contemporary counterpart of the American pragmatists' communitarian version of anti-rationalism. Foucault's suggestion that the Enlightenment attempt at emancipation has merely shackled us more tightly is an echo of Nietzsche's aristocratic disgust with bourgeois Europe. The Habermas-Foucault debate has often presented itself in the guise of "the Enlightenment vs. postmodernism." But I think that it should instead be seen as a reprise of a debate that might have taken place around 1910, but in fact did not: a debate between the American pro-democratic form of anti-rationalism and the Nietzschean anti-democratic form.

Despite what I regard as his unfortunate insistence on preserving the rationalists' notion of "universal validity," Habermas' theory of "communicative reason" makes the same crucial move as Dewey and James made: Habermas follows Peirce in identifying the truth with the outcome of free inquiry, rather than with something which antedates such inquiry. He moves us from objectivity as correspondence to the intrinsic nature of reality to objectivity as intersubjectivity.

~

So far I have been outlining, in a rather abstract and sketchy way, my view of the relation between the Enlightenment and various ideas commonly referred to as "postmodern." By way of conclusion, I want to discuss two contemporary political theorists — John Gray and Slavoj Zizek. Both men see a tighter connection between the Enlightenment's political project and its philosophical project than I do. Gray and Zizek are convenient for my purposes because both explicitly discuss my own attempt to peel off Enlightenment liberalism from Enlightenment rationalism, and both suggest that this attempt is misguided.

In his recent book *Enlightenment's Wake*, Gray recapitulates some of the arguments made by Horkheimer and Adorno in their *Dialectic of Enlightenment*, and also some of Heidegger's arguments about the fatal consequences of adopting a Baconian, technocratic, attitude toward Nature. He says that "even if they try to dispense with universalist claims, liberal cultures cannot do without a philosophy of history in which they are accorded a privileged status in modern history, but to say this is to say that liberal cultures depend on the Enlightenment project, and its illusions, for their very identity."[2]

Gray develops this theme by commenting on my own position, which I once jokingly called "post-modernist bourgeois liberalism," and which is frequently denounced as fatuous American chauvinism. In the following passage, Gray gives an accurate account of my strategy:

> For Rorty . . . an ironical self-reflective awareness of the contingency of liberal discourse, subjecthood, and community constitutes an enhancement of the liberal form of life, not a depletion of it . . . indeed, in Rorty's somewhat Nietzscheanized Deweyanism, the search for foundations itself betrays a lack of self-confidence on the part of liberal cultures. (170)

Gray thinks that this strategy of seeing the development of a sense of contingency as a way of encouraging human beings to stand on their own feet will only work if backed up by a philosophy of history. He goes on to say:

> Rorty's post-modern liberalism differs from other forms of contemporary US liberalism in the candour and explicitness of its anti-foundationalism, but not in its content, which is an idealized version of the United States, conceived as the model for a "cosmopolitan world-society," a universal civilization. It is only if the US experience can plausibly be represented as more than a singularity that its practices can have more [than] local authority.[3] Rorty's historical defense of liberal culture, like Hegel's and Dewey's, requires the support of general propositions about historical development . . . (174)

Gray goes on to argue that John Stuart Mill and Isaiah Berlin would reject my liberalism on the ground that political institutions are grounded in cultural identity, and that US institutions cannot survive outside of American culture. In particular, they cannot survive if culture is privatized, as I would like to privatize it. For I want to carry multiculturalism to the limit by saying that, ideally, every citizen of a democracy should have his or her own self-created form of cultural life in addition to his or her sense of participation in the public, political, project of building an egalitarian utopia. I want every such citizen to have two separate stories: one about his or her own relation to contemporary culture, and another about his or her responsibilities as a citizen. My emphasis on the public-private distinction is a way of urging that there is no need to synthesize these two stories into one. Gray thinks that my "post-modern perspectivism" is bound to undermine the public culture of countries such as the US. It will, he says,

> result in . . . disenchantment in regard to the local practices of liberal cultures, even more than those of others, precisely because the universalist claims of liberal philosophy have become embedded in the public culture of liberal societies. In removing from liberal practice the support of any universal narrative, disenchantment leaves liberal practices as particular practical expedients or strands in specific cultural traditions . . . . (175)

I agree entirely with Gray when he says, "For liberalism to become merely one form of life among others would involve as profound a cultural metamorphosis as Christianity's ceasing to make any claim to unique and universal truth" (177). But I see the latter metamorphosis as presently taking place. As evidence of progress already made, I would cite President Eisenhower's much cited dictum: "America is firmly founded on religious belief, and I don't care what religion it is." Analogously, I should hope that Gray's claim that liberalism cannot survive without philosophical backup will be falsified. I hope that Christian believers, Enlightenment rationalists, and neo-Nietzscheans like myself will prove as tolerant of each other's world-views as Eisenhower thought Americans should be of each other's religions.

It is true that we neo-Nietzscheans stand out from our fellow-citizens by being the only ones who insist that liberalism is "merely one form of life among others." But my kind of neo-Nietzschean then goes on to express his or her devout conviction that it is the best form of political life yet invented. We hope that profession of faith will be enough to satisfy our religious and our rationalist fellow-citizens.

There is no way to know in advance whether the "postmodern" world-view will be among the many world-views which can be tolerated among future collaborators in the Enlightenment political project. It may be that Gray will be proved right: that a culture cannot survive without either God or some substitute for him. Maybe human beings are incapable of as much self-confidence as we postmodernists hope that they may be able to achieve. So my reply to Gray really boils down to saying that his empirical predictions are needlessly pessimistic. Maybe he is right that political hope cannot survive in a post-modernist intellectual climate. But maybe it can. Only experiment will tell. If it turns out that it cannot, however, we should say "so much the worse for postmodernist philosophy," rather than "so much the worse for the Enlightenment political project." Philosophy is a good servant of political liberalism, but a bad master.

Whereas Gray thinks that we need a philosophy of history to back up political liberalism, Zizek thinks we need psychoanalytic theory. The sort of theory which Freud developed in *Beyond the Pleasure Principle* and *Civilization and its Discontents*, and which Zizek finds restated in Lacan, has a lot in common with the great nineteenth-century philosophies of history. Both sorts of theories purport to tell us, in advance, what the outcome of various future social experiments will be.

In his book *Looking Awry*, Zizek accurately describes me as wanting "to build a liberal-democratic ethic after the failure of its universal-rationalistic foundations" and as hoping to build this ethic around our respect for what Zizek calls "the fantasy space of the other."[4] As he says, my "ideal utopian society" would be one "in which the domains of 'public' and of 'private' are clearly differentiated" (159). But, he goes on:

> The problem with this liberal dream is that the split between the public and private never comes about without a certain remainder . . . . the very social law that, as a kind of neutral set of rules, should limit our aesthetic self-creation and deprive us of a part of our enjoyment on behalf of solidarity, is always already penetrated by an obscene, "pathological," surplus enjoyment . . . . the flaw of Rorty's "liberal utopia" [is that] it presupposes the possibility of a universal social law not smudged by a "pathological" sense of enjoyment, i.e., delivered from the superego dimension. (159–160)

Zizek's belief in Lacan's theory of the *"objet petit a*, the object-cause of desire embodying surplus enjoyment" (167) leads him to argue that "democracy is possible only on the basis of its own impossibility; its limit, the irresistible "pathological" remainder, is its positive condition" (166).

I can certainly agree with Zizek that there is an element of sado-masochistic enjoyment in the sacrifices of private pleasure to the general welfare which are required by the ethics of Mill's *On Liberty*. But my reaction is "so what?" I cannot see why my utopia presupposes either a smudgeless social law, or an absence of pathological enjoyment of my social bondage. Sadomasochistic pleasure is always a matter of more or less. There is a lot less of it involved in obeying Mill's mild commandments than in obeying those of a fierce father-figure, one who can decree eternal punishment.

My willingness to say "so what?" is strengthened by Zizek's apparent willingness to say the same thing. For he goes on to say that a "postmodernist" approach would "require us . . . to assume this constitutive paradox of democracy" (168). "The democratic attitude," he says

> is always based upon a certain fetishistic split: *I know very well* (that the democratic form is just a form spoiled by stains of "pathological" imbalance) *but just the same* (I act as if democracy were possible). Far from indicating its fatal flaw, this split is the very source of the strength of democracy: democracy is able to take cognizance of the fact that its limit lies in itself: in its internal "antagonism." (168)

Zizek here seems to say that the impossibility of liberal democracy is just a *theoretical* impossibility—a problem for theorists but not for citizens. That seems to me right, and to be a good reason for saying that we should relegate theory to the private realm, and not let it affect our sense of public responsibility. It is also a good reason for telling one story about political progress and a separate story about intellectual progress. It is a good reason to think that though we need to come to an agreement with our fellow-citizens about what story of the former sort to tell, it is as unnecessary that we all share the same philosophical outlook as that we share the same religious faith.

This distinction between the theoretical and the practical point of view is often drawn by Derrida, another writer who enjoys demonstrating that something very important—meaning, for example, or justice, or friendship—is both necessary and impossible. When asked about the implications of this paradoxical fact, Derrida usually replies that the paradox does not matter when it comes to practice. More generally, a lot of the writers who are labeled "postmodernist," and who talk a lot about impossibility, turn out to be good experimentalist social democrats when it comes to actual political activity. I suspect, for example, that Gray, Zizek, Derrida and I, if we found ourselves citizens of the same country, would all be voting for the same candidates, and supporting the same reforms, as would Searle and Habermas.

Postmodernist philosophers have gotten a bad name because of their paradox-mongering habits, and their constant of terms like "impossible," "self-contradictory" and "unrepresentable." They have helped create a cult of inscrutability, one which defines itself by opposition to the Enlightenment search for transparency—and more generally, to the "metaphysics of presence," the idea that intellectual progress aims at getting things clearly illuminated, sharply delimited, wholly visible.

I am all for getting rid of the metaphysics of presence, but I think that the current rhetoric of impossibility and unrepresentability is counter-productive overdramatization. It is one thing to say that we need to get rid of the metaphor of things being accurately represented, once and for all, as a result of being bathed in the light of reason. This metaphor has created a lot of headaches for philosophers, and we would be better off without it. But that does not show that we are suddenly surrounded by unrepresentables; it just shows that "more accurate representation" was never a fruitful way to describe intellectual progress.

Even if we agree that we shall never have what Derrida calls "a full presence beyond the reach of play," our sense of the possibilities open to humanity will not have changed. We have learned nothing about the limits of human hope from metaphysics, or from philosophy of history, or from psychoanalysis. All that we have learned from "postmodern" philosophy is that we may need a different gloss on the notion of "progress" than the rationalistic gloss that the Enlightenment offered. We have been given no reason to abandon the belief that a lot of progress has been made by trying to carry through on the Enlightenment's political program. Since Darwin we have come to suspect that whether such progress is made is largely a matter of luck. But we have been given no reason to stop hoping to get lucky.

PART II

CRITICAL CONFRONTATIONS

JONATHAN KNUDSEN

The Historicist Enlightenment

German historicism, in all its variety, constitutes one central cultural strand of the revolution in historical consciousness of the nineteenth century. Since historicism was formed out of the Enlightenment and against it, historicism and Enlightenment share a conceptual asymmetry similar to other pairings, such as *Gemeinschaft* and *Gesellschaft* or modernism and postmodernism. These terms describe a theoretical position and a movement unfolding in time where one term in the pair emerged in perceived emancipation from the other. From the perspective of full-blown historicism, the Enlightenment was inextricably tied to notions of progress, secularization, natural law, and a one-dimensional and shallow utilitarianism. For the offspring of the Enlightenment, historicism became linked to the Romantic counterrevolution, forms of irrational subjectivity, a Gnostic attitude toward texts, the glorification of the state, and relativism leading to nihilism. This conceptual opposition has led to persistent efforts to reevaluate both movements with respect to each other. The contents of the terms thus continued to alter over the nineteenth and twentieth centuries, becoming the negatively charged *Other* to the practitioners, critics, and heirs of these traditions. Consequently, it is quite striking to see how diverse in meaning the terms have been, for they too often functioned as conceptual markers to locate participants in an increasingly cloudy methodological debate.

When Enlightenment and historicism became the subject of renewed controversy during the Weimar Republic and then again during the postwar period, the structure of that controversy was once again highly ideological and diffuse. At the end of the century it would appear that debate over postmodernism has now rendered the struggle between historicism and Enlightenment more or less obsolete.

Historicism, the belief that all reality is historical and that explanation lies in understanding life in its becoming, was a movement discontinuous in its sensibility with the Enlightenment but often continuous with it in method. This continuity was not readily recognized or admitted by the founders of historicism. Nineteenth-century historicists, despite their differences, shared the desire to deny their affinities with Enlightenment historiography. Moving within an intellectual universe shaped by a highly reflective philosophical system, that was itself conditioned by idealist philosophy, by the new humanistic study of antiquity, and by a Romantic hermeneutics, they mounted a sustained effort to construct a discontinuous prehistory of historicism, a position that colored much of modern German intellectual life. For the past thirty years, however, historians of Germany have invested great intellectual effort to reconstruct continuities between Enlightenment and historicism, particularly in the realm of method.[1]

Historicism originated by emptying the Enlightenment of a sense of history, which it then appropriated exclusively to itself. Most recent historians—and Peter Reill has been foremost in this effort—have rightly abandoned the view that the Enlightenment was an ahistorical movement. In exploring the range, depth, and character of the historical sensibility and writing in the period, more often than not they have now denied historicism its claims to methodological uniqueness. The commitment to a history based on documents, the use of a critical philological method, and even genetic explanation—these claims by Ranke and his school to innovation—are all present by the later eighteenth century. The discovery and application of laws of development, for instance, can be widely found in humanist historiography and in the jurisprudential histories of the German Empire (*Reichshistorie*).[2] If historicism means abandoning cosmopolitan history on the model of Adam Ferguson, Isaac Iselin, or Immanuel Kant in favor of the local or the individual, such a local or provincial perspective has been shown, quantitatively and qualitatively, to be fundamental to historical writing during the Enlightenment.[3] If historicism means reappropriating classical Greek and Roman patterns of thought, such patterns can also be seen as surviving within humanist and civic republican modes of historical explanations.[4] Finally, if historicism is linked to certain key eighteenth-century historians who are thought to be anti-Enlightenment figures — Justus Möser or Johann Gottfried Herder, for example — they have been shown in methodological and historiographical terms to be much more unambiguously within mainstream Enlightenment traditions.[5] Thus the lines between the older Latin humanism, Enlightenment historiography, and historicism have been eroded to become part of a continuum of refinement in methods and techniques. For this reason it has become difficult to take at face value the filiation of ideas traced in influential works from the early part of the twentieth century, such as those by Dilthey, Meinecke, or Srbik.[6]

One of the most substantial conclusions generated by recent research on the Enlightenment has been to restore the central place of history to it. Interest in subjects historical occurred within and outside the university. Recent works have rightfully emphasized the growing professionalization of historical writing, especially within the German university. The later eighteenth century witnessed an enormous rise in the prestige of history and the interest in historical explanation. The number of chairs and lectures in history grew substantially over the century at both Protestant and Catholic universities: theology, public law, and "statistics" all came to be taught as historical subjects.[7]

The development of a critical philological method, one of the hallmarks of nineteenth-century historicism, was also well advanced. The methods of textual analysis were not taught in one place in the university, but spread throughout the various faculties of the liberal arts, jurisprudence, and theology. Though much scholarly emphasis has been placed on the special achievement of the Göttingen classicists — e.g., the importance of Christian Gottlob Heyne for Friedrich August Wolf, Barthold Georg Niebuhr, and Wilhelm Humboldt — we can see that the historicizing of hermeneutics was well underway by the mid-eighteenth century in each of the traditional faculties.[8] Furthermore, it was advanced by figures otherwise clearly associated with enlightened values. The categories of contingency and historical empathy emerge from Wolffian principles in J. C. Gottsched's *Erste Gründen gesammten Weltweisheit* [*First Principles of Complete Philosophy*] published in 1733.[9] And in the work of the theologian Johann Martin Chladenius, especially his *Allgemeine Geschichtswissenschaft* [*General Historical Science*] published in 1752, the historical standpoint associated with historicism seems to be fully articulated. Chladenius stressed the distinction between original accounts [*Geschichte*] and their historical reconstruction [*Historie*]. He discussed the place of historical reconstruction within the moral order, the necessity for histories to be coherently ordered around a central subject, and finally, the proposition that history constituted a different kind of human truth than offered by classical mathematical physics.[10] The interest in history outside the university, moreover, was part of a broader process by which the German reading public established itself as a secular moral and political community. Historical-political information was necessary to the development of the separate identity of civil society. It is striking how much history the German public read in the eighteenth century. About ten percent of all German book production fell into the category of history. About fifteen percent of all journals specialized in historical subjects. Except for literature, no other category seems to have grown so rapidly after the Seven Years' War. Local reading societies subscribed to a surprisingly large number of historical-political and cameralist journals. More than eighty percent of these journals dealt with contemporary matters. Over the century, moreover, they gradually abandoned a focus on the court and became more materialist in orientation. Increasing emphasis was placed on geographical, demographic, economic, and "statistical" explanation, and, in general, their themes became more tightly tied to the broad program of enlightened reform.[11]

II

Indeed there seems to have been a direct correlation between the political radicalization and spread of the Enlightenment and the intensified interest in history, for the growing historical sensibility went together with a resurgence in natural rights theory.[12] Moreover, this so-called "younger" natural rights tradition of the later eighteenth century deployed historical argumentation. Linked to history by its attempt to examine the historical legitimacy of existing institutions or to legitimate civil society, it gave to the public realm that "critical" or "emancipatory" dimension typical of the seventeen-seventies, eighties and nineties. We see this fusion of history and natural rights argumentation in the speculative histories of the period (e.g. Iselin, Kant), but also in those essays and works attacking the historic rights of the nobility or the development of monarchical power.

If historicism shared methodological principles with the Enlightenment, Enlightenment attitudes toward history did differ substantively from historicism. For this reason I wish to stress both their continuity in method and their discontinuity in sensibility. The commitment to a fusion of history and speculation was misinterpreted by historians in the historicist tradition who looked back into the eighteenth century and saw this position as ahistorical. In contrast to historicism, Enlightenment history was concerned with the legal points of origin in their own civilization. Their Latin education, particularly the reading of Tacitus, also gave German Enlightened thinkers an anthropological interest in the pre-Carolingian past. They showed relatively little interest in medieval life, especially as reflected in the journal literature, except in so far as it concerned questions of contemporary reform. Justus Möser, for example, was remembered by historicists for the relatively few essays he published on medieval institutional life. But he wrote predominantly about contemporary matters. His historical works were conceived as commentaries on burning constitutional issues, and his explanatory patterns still moved within the world of contract theory and natural rights speculation.[13] The conservative strand of historicism elevated the study of the Middle Ages, broke the link between history and natural rights speculation, and substituted neo-corporatist and Romantic assumptions about the monarchical state for emancipatory arguments about rights. The support of the Restoration and a focus on the monarchical state by Ranke and others, however, reveal these historians to have been no less presentist in intent.

Enlightenment historians appear to have had a more open model of human experience than did nineteenth-century historicists. This seems a rather paradoxical assertion given that the category of "personality" and "individuality" were so central to nineteenth-century idealism. Still, historical writing in the late eighteenth century was impressively flexible and experimental—far more than it would be under the Restoration. Its range was formidable. Besides the historical journals, we see a flood of travel literature with historical materials, urban histories, historical biographies, and social-political fiction with a historical perspective.[14] As with journal literature, these works often emphasized current matters. They were also immersed in the material world. Enlightenment historians sought to integrate all aspects of human experience into their inquiries, attempting to evolve a form of "total history." This effort explains their fascination with structure or what was then called "statistics" or "constitutional history."

Eighteenth-century German historians were committed to a critical rationality, to explanation as demystification [*Entzauberung*], and to a world of facts. Möser, for instance, formulated an aesthetic of "totality" [*Totaleindrücke*], but he continued to distrust historians— he named Montesquieu—who placed an emphasis on structure over erudition. Möser, like other historians—August Ludwig Schlözer, for instance—opted for an open narrative as the best means to sustain a dialogue with his readers. In this way the historian could explain the known and the unknown. The very breadth of their interests, coupled with the attempt to convey large amounts of information, often caused a loss of focus and synthetic power. This dilemma is clear in the urban histories of the period, as in the history of Berlin and Potsdam written by the publisher and author Friedrich Nicolai.[15] Nicolai combined great efforts at precision in the gathering of statistical materials with a fairly loose mode of presentation, because he and his lay audience were filled with wonderment about the everyday world and were engaged in an ongoing, communal act of discovery.[16] Form was less significant than a Baconian interest in the world. The contrast between this view of history and that of early Romanticism was made evident in Fichte's evaluation of Nicolai's historical writing. For Fichte, Nicolai was "the most complete example of mental derangement in our age" because, among other reasons, he "scraped together

... all kinds of facts and opinions without any relationship or purpose."[17]

This point leads me again to stress the aesthetic divide that separated the world of the Enlightenment from that of historicism. Ranke was perhaps the first professional historian in Germany to write at the level of great literature and, perhaps with Johannes Müller, among the very first to write in this manner for a large public. With the exception of Schiller and perhaps Arnold Heeren, he was the first to attain the international stature of Hume, Robertson, Voltaire, and Gibbon. Ranke placed aesthetic demands on his work that did not exist among earlier historians (with the possible exception in Germany of Winckelmann, Möser, and Schiller). Unlike his Enlightenment predecessors, Ranke was committed to concealment and illusion through an essentially closed narrative, one that chose political experience and the contest between states as primary and one that pushed his own methodological reflections to his working papers and to the periphery of his work (prefaces, methodological introductions, appendices). As he wrote in a famous passage, "I wished to be able to extinguish myself and to allow the things to speak, to allow the mighty forces to appear for themselves" [Ich wünschte mein Selbst gleichsam auszulöschen und nur die Dinge reden, die mächtigen Kräfte erscheinen zu lassen].[18] Ranke also employed a German language that had become much more supple and rich in the long generation from Kant, Lessing and Goethe to Jean Paul and Heine. It was a "meaning-laden" language, one that saw the word in romantic terms akin to A. W. Schlegel's idea that "The letter is the true magic wand" [der Buchstabe ist der wahre Zauberstab].[19] It did not separate literary form from intellectual discovery.[20] The commitment to aesthetic requirements was not simply a narrative choice: it was inseparably bound to a complex epistemological position in which all reality had become dynamic, historical, and immanent. Ranke's meaning-laden language became an integral part of the cultural inheritance of the German educated elite.

Differences in cultural sensibility intensified over the course of the nineteenth century. A sense of cultural superiority in the German educational establishment became tied to a view of exceptionalism in German history, and these assumptions permeated all of the intellectual classes, from conservatives to liberals, and even those on the left. The neo-humanist curriculum in the secondary schools and the university system was rooted in the belief that German culture had superseded the Enlightenment. Lessing, Kant, Möser, and Herder were all interpreted as figures of transcendence out of which had emerged German neo-humanism, idealism, and historicism.[21] It was largely left to outsiders—young Hegelians like Bruno Bauer, liberals like Georg Gervinus, Karl Biedermann, and Hermann Hettner, and socialists like Franz Mehring—to keep alive another more dynamic interpretation of the German Enlightenment.[22]

By the end of the century the concern with defining historicism was a cultural phenomenon not unlike the earlier concern with defining Enlightenment in the last decades of the eighteenth century.[23] Wolfgang Mommsen, Georg Iggers and others have examined this ground with care, tracing the development of historicism as a cultural worldview and the formation of the neo-Rankean school and the hegemony of historicism within the historical profession from the end of the century through the Weimar Republic.[24] I cannot add much to their account within the framework of this brief essay.

III

In conclusion, I wish to indicate how pervasive was the negative historicist interpretation of the Enlightenment, even during the crisis years of the Weimar Republic and during the immediate post-war period. As other authors in this volume argue, the Enlightenment can stand as an important foundational moment for the ideas of tolerance, rights, the rule of law, etc. We also tend to construct a narrative that links Romanticism, nationalism, and racism to the barbarisms of the twentieth century. The German historicist tradition, however, looks to the nineteenth century as achieving a deeper notion of personality, a more profound understanding of culture, and a richer intellectual life based on intellectual merit. This tradition—and here it shared values with the left—saw the Enlightenment as a period of manipulation and mobilization.

This German tradition thus created a different narrative that linked the Enlightenment to instrumental reason, mass democratic mobilization, and political terror tying it directly to the barbarisms of the twentieth century.[25] The pairing of historicism and Enlightenment is thus a surprisingly good entry into the work of key intellectuals of the period, ranging from the political right to the left. For this purpose I have made soundings into the work of Friedrich Meinecke, Karl Löwith, Rudolf Bultmann, Erich Auerbach, and Walter Benjamin. My tentative conclusion is that the Nazi accession to power, and even the barbarism of World War II, did not cause those who survived the war to rethink their understanding of the German Enlightenment. I will briefly consider Meinecke, Auerbach, and Benjamin in this intellectual context (Löwith and Bultmann are too complicated for brief mention).

Friedrich Meinecke spent much of the Weimar Republic as editor of the *Historische Zeitschrift* and engaged, at the same time, in studies for his influential work on historicism, *Die Entstehung des Historismus* [*The Rise of Historism*], which was published in 1936.[26] In this work, Meinecke identified historicism as a German intellectual revolution, albeit one with European roots. He argued that it was built on the twin principles of historical individuality and development, which transcended the shallow utilitarianism of the Enlightenment. Nazism did not cause Meinecke to abandon his critical opposition to the Enlightenment or to return to the eighteenth century in search for different sources of renewal.[27] In fact, Meinecke debated with those writers of the late Weimar Republic who had returned to the eighteenth century precisely in order to study German continuity anew. For example, in a review of Alfred Stern's book on the impact of the French Revolution on German intellectual life, published in 1929, Meinecke spurned Stern's view that the French Revolution was a "deep source" in the transformation of the German spirit. Instead, he argued that the Revolution had only accelerated tendencies which might otherwise have emerged "alone." This review, not incidentally, sparked a sharp commentary for its one-sidedness from Hedwig Hintze, a gifted historian of the French Revolutionary period as well as the leftist wife of Meinecke's colleague Otto Hintze.[28] We see a similar attitude in Meinecke's substantial review of Ernst Cassirer's *Die Philosophie der Aufklärung* [*The Philosophy of the Enlightenment*]. This review, published in 1934, is noteworthy for its detailed understanding and praise of the work of his German Jewish colleague's "brief for the Enlightenment." Meinecke acknowledged that "in the future the continuity between enlightenment, idealism, and romanticism must be recognized in a much more open and generous manner." He judged the work to be a "masterpiece." But despite this positive evaluation, Meinecke's critical effort in the review was to relativize Cassirer's assessment of the Enlightenment's achievements.[29] Even the war experience did not change Meinecke's view. In one of his last books, *Die deutsche Katastrophe* [*The German Catastrophe*],[30] published a year after the war's end, Meinecke ascribed the rise of Nazism to the excesses of mass democracy, and by implication to the dangers of the Enlightenment. In no way did he implicate his form of historicism in the rise of Nazism. In Meinecke's view, historicism was best embodied in Goethe's writings and Meinecke's post-war clarion call was for a return to Goethe.

Erich Auerbach's position is equally straightforward. All but one chapter of his classic work *Mimesis* was written during the years of exile between 1942 and 1945. The questions of reality and imitation, fact and objectivity, central categories to the Enlightenment, are completely determined by a historicist rendering of the eighteenth century. The allegiance to Friedrich Meinecke's *Entstehung des Historismus* is fundamental. According to Auerbach, it is "the finest and most mature work that I know."[31] After the war he returned to work on Vico and Herder as a continuation of studies he had undertaken during Weimar Republic. These, too, were completely conceived within the framework of historicism.[32]

Walter Benjamin is the most idiosyncratic of the three, for he transmuted the terms of the debate concerning historicism and the Enlightenment in a unique manner.[33] Benjamin's hostility to the Enlightenment had a variety of impulses: the Jewish youth movement, a flirtation with Marxism, his long study of Romantic aesthetics, his studies on Baudelaire. In his 1938 doctoral thesis on the philosophy of history, Benjamin attacked the Enlightenment for its supposed teleological principles. He condemned the idea of progress as empty, linear time and argued for the cultural discontinuity of the species since culture, and by extension progress, are linked to political domination. Functionally, the Enlightenment appears to him to approximate forms of German Social Democracy, which he criticized from the perspective of a redeemed historical materialism.

However, Benjamin also criticized historicism from the perspective of the cultural left, linking historicism to the neo-Rankean tradition of Prussianism, militarism, and German nationalism. He also clearly assaulted historicism from a neo-Romantic sensibility. He accused historicism of being committed to immediacy at the expense of retaining the memory of oppression and the weak hopes of the losers for a utopian liberation; of course, this had also been the hope of the Enlightenment with its visions of political emancipation through law and institutions of civil society. Against this position Benjamin argued that the historian should understand the past as a series of historical monads, as saturated moments of time. This methodological principle, moving from Leibniz and Wordsworth's "spots of time," is also a Romantic and historicist variation of empathy, yet one informed by a fervent awareness of *Jetztzeit* or "now time"—ever aware of present moments of danger.

Because Benjamin in these last years was applying German cultural assumptions to French materials, he was able to conceal his own links to the conservative speculative tradition. For this reason, among others, Benjamin has become part of a movement, like Nietzsche, that has sought to shatter the old oppositions between Enlightenment and historicism. The murkiness and lack of conceptual clarity evident in his position has been a boon to postmodernist misreadings of the German intellectual tradition. Historicism's attack on the "shallowness" of the eighteenth century continued a critique of the Enlightenment that had been contained within the Enlightenment itself. It is therefore not possible to adhere to the Enlightenment tradition without at the same time recognizing the self-critique that was embedded in it.

Heidegger and the Critique of Reason

"Thinking begins only when we have come to know that reason, glorified for centuries, is the most stiff-necked adversary of thought."[1] Perhaps no other statement by Heidegger has provoked as much outrage as this one. Does it not mark him as wholly dissociated from the pursuit of reason begun by the Greeks and brought to fulfillment in modernity? And are there not links between such an irrationalism and Heidegger's political errors of the 1930s?

⁓

Relying on statements like the one just quoted, Michael Zimmerman has recently drawn a picture of Heidegger as a resolute enemy of the Enlightenment and all that it stands for. In *Heidegger's Confrontation with Modernity*, he writes that for Heidegger "the rational ideal of the Enlightenment was nothing but an ideological screen for the 'logic of domination'."[2] Heidegger's political orientation, according to Zimmerman, involved "contempt for Enlightenment values" (38). He "had no confidence in the Enlightenment vision of 'progress'" (255). He "saw only the 'dark side' of the Enlightenment project and ... discounted the possibility of human freedom" (256). He "assailed the Enlightenment doctrine of 'universal rights,'" holding, as Zimmerman puts it, that "the Enlightenment's proclamation of universal rights and truths was itself the political manifestation of the metaphysical subjectivism at work in the power-hungry French and English" (262). Heidegger, therefore, rejected "Enlightenment guarantees of individual human rights" and "the widespread human longing for material well-being and political liberty" (92). Adopting a term coined by Jeffrey Herf, Zimmerman speaks of Heidegger as an ally of a "reactionary modernism" (xviii), which triumphed in Germany as the result of a "romantic counterrevolution to the Enlightenment" (47).[3] He endorses, moreover, Herf's judgment that "National Socialism can be understood as the political fulfillment of reactionary modernism" (92). No wonder, then, that in 1933 Heidegger should have ended up on the side of the Nazis.

Zimmerman also subscribes to Herf's critique of Horkheimer and Adorno, whose *Dialectic of Enlightenment* sought to account for National Socialism by identifying an element of "unconstrained human Will to Power" in the emancipatory rhetoric of the Enlightenment. Their explanation is not only misguided but embodies "a curious kind of apology for Germany's misadventure: National Socialism was, allegedly, merely the German version of what was happening throughout the West" (48). Zimmerman finds similar fault with Heidegger's ultimate judgment on National Socialism, which "interpreted National Socialism as a German version of the consequences of Enlightenment metaphysics" (Ibid.). There is a surprising confluence with the Horkheimer-Adorno view, but both views are to be rejected since "far from being the consequence of the Enlightenment, National Socialism resulted from insufficient Enlightenment" (Ibid.). Zimmerman's picture may strike us as plausible and, indeed, as familiar.[4] It is, however, curiously at odds with Heidegger's own words. For neither in *Being and Time* nor in the writings of the decades that follow does he reveal a substantive interest in the Enlightenment or any of its French or British protagonists.[5] The Enlightenment is for him rather just one of the possible embodiments of modern consciousness. This is spelled out most clearly in Heidegger's Nietzsche lectures, where we read:

> The securing of supreme and absolute self-development of all the capacities of mankind for absolute domination over the entire world is the secret goal that prods modern man again and again to new resurgences ... What is consciously posited as binding appears in many guises and disguises. What binds can be human reason and its law (Enlightenment), or the real, the factual, which is ordered and arranged by such reason (positivism).

What binds can be humanity harmoniously joined in all its accomplish-ments and molded into a beautiful figure (the human ideal of classicism). What binds can be the development of the power of self-reliant nations, or "the proletariat of all lands," or individual peoples and races. What binds can be the development of humanity in the sense of the progress of human rationality. What binds can also be "the hidden seeds of each indi-vidual age," the development of the "individual," the organization of the masses, or both. Finally, it can be the creation of a mankind that finds the shape of its essence neither in "individuality" nor in the "mass," but in the "type."[6]

For Heidegger, in other words, the Enlightenment is not of sin-gular significance but marks a moment in a larger history. It is one of many resurgences, guises, or disguises of modern consciousness, but these are all produced around a notion of reason which incorporates at once the ideals of self-development and domination. Though a domi-nating concern with reason is for Heidegger characteristic of the modern age, a belief in the priority of reason extends at once beyond these historical limits. It encompasses, indeed, the whole history of Western metaphysics: "Western metaphysics ... determines beings in advance and for its entire history as what is conceivable and definable in the respects of reason and thinking ... Western metaphysics is based on this priority of reason."[7] Heidegger adds that "we must not con-ceive of trust in reason and the powerful *ratio* one-sidedly as rational-ism, for irrationalism too belongs within the scope of trust in reason. The greatest rationalists are most likely to fall prey to irrationalism, and conversely, where irrationalism determines the worldview, ra-tionalism celebrates its triumphs. The dominion of technology and susceptibility to superstition belong together."[8] Reflection on the Enlightenment is thus replaced by a critique of reason which ranges over the entire history of Western thought and which strives to main-tain equal distance from rationalism and irrationalism. The results of this critique—with its rejection of absolute norms and definitive truths, with its wariness towards instrumentalist and technocratic embodiments of reason—no doubt bears directly on Enlightenment claims. Even so, the Enlightenment itself is present in Heidegger's thought only as a distant trail in the long, tangled history of reason.

⌒

This brings us back to Heidegger's initial statement and the adversarial relationship it poses between reason and thinking. The sentence is no casual remark, for it summarizes an extended reflection on the concept of reason. It concludes, in fact, the important essay "The Word of Nietzsche: 'God is Dead'" which Heidegger drafted around 1943 but continued to revise and extend to the time of its publication in 1950. His initial work on the essay marked, in turn, the conclusion of a series of lectures he had given on Nietzsche in the preceding years. Heidegger's controversial statement forms thus the terminal point of a close study of Nietzsche's thought, and we must therefore read his critique of reason as being at all times informed by Nietzsche's, possibly indebted to it—though not necessarily identical with it.

But let us approach Heidegger's statement with caution. What has been said has already made evident that the questions it raises extend from the farthest ends of philosophy into the finest filigrees of Heidegger's thinking. Given the political context, these questions are also now shrouded in doubts raised by critics, scholars, and journalists who have attached themselves in one way or other to "the Heidegger case." It is enough for us on this occasion to concentrate on a few modest points, and to see our task accomplished when the air is cleared for a more "enlightened" debate about Heidegger's thought and politics.

Let us ask first what Heidegger actually said in the sentence that has caused such furor, for the Lovitt translation generally quoted is not altogether on target. We can render the sentence more accurately as: "Thinking begins only when we have come to experience that reason, made master for centuries, is the most tenacious adversary of thinking."

Our translation differs from Lovitt's in three significant ways. First, it makes clear that Heidegger was not denigrating reason as "stiff-necked" but was speaking instead of its enduring resistance to that which is here called "thinking." Second, our rendering also brings out that Heidegger was not deploring an empty glorification of reason, but rather the fact that over centuries reason has become dominant over us, that it has become our "Herr" or master. Third, our version finally brings to light that for Heidegger it is not sufficient to "know" of the opposition of reason and thinking in a more or less theoretical fashion; thinking begins for him only when one has come to "experience" (*erfahren*) that opposition.

◌

These changes provide, however, at best only marginal clarifications; they do nothing to elucidate the critical concepts of reason and thinking and their supposed opposition. "Reason" is, of course, a familiar term in the philosophical vocabulary. For all that, however, it is a peculiarly slippery concept. Geoffrey Warnock has therefore rightly warned us in *The Encyclopedia of Philosophy* that "in English the word 'reason' has long had, and still has, a large number and a wide variety of senses and uses, related to one another in ways that are often complicated and often not clear."[10] We must ask, then, in which of these possible senses Heidegger may have used the term in his pronouncement, or, rather, in which sense he used the term we have now translated as reason.

Heidegger's actual word is *"Vernunft,"* a term whose uses and connotations do not exactly match those of the English word "reason." Still, there is no alternative to rendering *"Vernunft"* as "reason." Kant's *Kritik der reinen Vernunft* becomes in English inevitably a *Critique of Pure Reason*. In order to understand what Heidegger means by the opposition of *Vernunft* and thinking, we must, however, remember that he is always attuned to the connotations and etymologies of his terms. *"Vernunft,"* a word familiar already in Old High German, has its root in the verb *"vernehmen,"* which means initially to take something before oneself [*vor-nehmen*] and thereby to bring it to notice. *"Vernehmen"* might, thus, be rendered as "to perceive" [*percipere*]. More specifically, the German word has come to mean to perceive with one's ears, to hear. *"Vernunft"* is literally, then, the ability to hear. But from early on it also has signified the capacity of cogitation by means of which we reflect on the objects of which we have taken notice. The related noun *"das Vernehmen"* carries with it, moreover, the connotation of something learned by word of mouth, and even of mere unfounded hearsay.[11] All this is indubitably significant for Heidegger. Already in *Being and Time* he speaks of *"logos,"* *"ratio,"* and *"Vernunft"* as related in meaning and yet having different connotations. He claims there that the term *"logos,"* as Plato and Aristotle employ it, means "to make manifest what one is 'talking about' in one's discourse ... The *logos* lets something be seen ... namely what the discourse is about" (32). To this he adds: "And because the function of *logos* lies in merely letting something be seen, in letting entities be perceived [*im Vernehmenlassen des Seienden*], *logos* can mean *Vernunft*" (34). Later on, in *The Principle of Reason* he writes that *"ratio* is a kind of hearing and is hence *Vernunft.*" Then reminding us that *"ratio"* means also calculation, he adds: "This calculation in the widest sense, is the manner in which man takes things up, takes them before himself, and takes them on, that is, the manner in which he takes them in or hears [*ver-nimmt*] them."[12]

The crucial point here is that the manner in which man takes things in or in which entities let themselves be perceived, naturally, fluctuates over time. By finding that *logos*, *ratio*, and *Vernunft* all refer to a *Vernehmen* or *Vernehmenlassen*, Heidegger discovers in them an inherently temporal dimension. Reason becomes historicized. In Heidegger's own terminology we can say that Being reveals and hides itself over time in various ways and that what we call reason at any given moment is the way that Being lets itself be perceived at that point. There is in Heidegger's account, then, no absolute, timeless reason of the sort that Plato and Aristotle sought to discover in their *logos* and that the moderns sought to uncover in mathematical-scientific rationality. While Western metaphysics may throughout assume the priority of reason, it "does not define man in every epoch simply and in the same sense as a creature of reason."[13] The idea has been appropriated more recently by Michel Foucault who argues in *Madness and Civilization* that reason and madness are reciprocal notions and that historical change in our social conception of madness also signals changes in our conception of reason. Coming at the same issue from a different direction, Ludwig Wittgenstein has expressed a kindred thought by arguing that the logic of our language may change over time. In his final notes he writes that the propositions we consider philosophically certain, the assumptions that define our system of belief and its logic, the rules through which our reasoning proceeds, may alter: "The mythology may change back into a state of flux, the river-bed of thoughts may shift ... And the bank of that river consists partly of hard rock, subject to no alteration or only to an imperceptible one, partly of sand, which now in one place now in another gets washed away, or deposited."[14]

↩

Heidegger's conclusion that reason has an inherently historical nature is conjoined to a second conviction according to which the appropriate form of reason of a particular age is determined by how things let themselves be perceived at that moment (that is, in Heidegger's terms, how Being reveals itself at that moment) and not simply by prevailing opinion. While ours is the age of technology, not everyone living is likely to think in technological terms. It is not even important—or likely—for Heidegger that the majority think in terms of the appropriate form of reason of their age. The majority may claim to speak the voice of reason, but the reason of the age may in reality manifest itself only in the words of the few, the outsiders, those considered to be exceptional or mad.

This thought is indebted to Nietzsche, who expressed it most vividly in a passage of *The Gay Science* entitled "The Raving Man" ["*Der tolle Mensch*"]. Heidegger's essay "The Word of Nietzsche: 'God is Dead'" is, in fact, built entirely around this passage that has also served as inspiration for Foucault's *Madness and Civilization*. Nietzsche's "madman"—modeled on Diogenes the Cynic, who ran through Athens carrying a lantern in broad daylight in search of a single honest man—is consumed by the momentous consequences of the death of God. "Whither are we moving now?," he cries. "Away from all suns? Are we not plunging continually? Backward, sideward, forward, in all directions? Is there any up or down left? Are we not straying through an infinite nothing?"[15] But the madman quickly discovers that the death of God is of no great concern to the men in the marketplace: "As many of those who do not believe in God were standing around just then, he provoked much laughter" (125). Nietzsche accounts for this in a related aphorism from *The Gay Science* in which he writes:

> After Buddha was dead, his shadow was still shown for centuries in a cave—a tremendous, gruesome shadow. God is dead; but given the way of men, there may still be caves for thousands of years in which his shadow will be shown. And we—we still have to vanquish his shadow, too. (108)

He goes on to enumerate the places where the shadow of God still lingers: in the belief, for instance, that the universe is an organism or a machine rather than chaos (109); in the conviction that reason is "a completely free and spontaneous activity" capable of attaining to absolute, timeless truths (110); in the failure to see that we ourselves are the makers of ever new tables of values which we always accept for a time as eternal and unconditional (115). Given such residues of our old belief, Nietzsche asks: "When will all these shadows of God cease to darken our minds?" (109).

Nietzsche's madman seeks to remind us that with the death of God these shadows must eventually fade away. But the reaction of the crowd in the marketplace reveals that his message is neither welcome nor as yet understood. The madman discovers that the men in the marketplace have as yet no ears for him and remain perplexed by his words.

> Here the madman fell silent and looked again at his listeners; and they, too, were silent and stared at him in astonishment ..." I have come too early," he said then; "my time is not yet. This tremendous event is still on its way, still wandering; it has not yet reached the ears of men. (125)

In juxtaposing average common sense and the madman's ravings, Nietzsche seeks to reveal that reason is on the side of the latter. What the crowd regards as reason and reasonable is nothing but an inability to hear, to perceive. The reason claimed by the crowd is reducible to what it has learned as common opinion; it represents, then, nothing more than hearsay. *Vernunft* becomes *Vernehmen*, and it is left for madness to say what needs to be said. Taking off from this thought, Foucault concludes *Madness and Civilization* by noting,

> [R]use and new triumph of madness: the world that thought to measure and justify madness ... must justify itself before madness, since in its struggles and agonies it measures itself by the excess of works like those of Nietzsche, of Van Gogh, of Artaud. And nothing in itself ... assures the world that it is justified by such works of madness.[16]

The concluding sentence of Heidegger's essay "The Word of Nietzsche: 'God is Dead'" (the sentence with which we began) must be read in this same light. Heidegger's words suggest the need to separate two sharply distinct states of mind: one that deems itself sane and rational but is, in truth, an attending to everyday hearsay and is therefore incapable of real insight, and another that inevitably appears to the crowd as mad but is authentically open and resolved to the world at the moment when God is dead. The latter calls into questions what commonsense takes for granted. There are insights that only such madness delivers.

Looking at Heidegger's statement with this in mind, one is tempted to put its use of the word "reason" in quotation marks. "Thinking begins only when we have come to experience that 'reason,' made master for centuries, is the most tenacious adversary of thinking." Reason, so understood, is precisely that which exerts mastery and persists as such over centuries; reason is here consensus and commonsense, what is generally heard and perceived. It is to such reason that Nietzsche opposed his madman. In attacking such reason and reasonableness Nietzsche himself was driven insane. But his madness reveals what reason cannot perceive. Nietzsche experienced in his life and madness the opposition of reason and thinking. Nietzsche thereby initiated the thinking called for in the present age, after the loss of God. Heidegger's statement concerning the opposition of reason and thinking is, thus, no mere formula; it refers us concretely to Nietzsche as the beginning of a now necessary thinking. It speaks of Nietzsche as the starting point of Heidegger's own reflections. "My thinking," Heidegger seems to say in the sentence in question, "begins only with Nietzsche's experience of the opposition of reason and thinking."

～

What is upheld as reason is often just deafness to the way things let themselves be perceived. But who and what upholds reason in such a manner as commonsense and consensus? Who are the men in the marketplace deriding the voice of the madman? Both Nietzsche and Heidegger consider the philosophers to be among these men. In his notebooks Nietzsche writes of them:

> Philosophers are prejudiced against appearance, change, pain, death, the corporeal, the senses, fate and bondage, the aimless. They believe first in: absolute knowledge, (2) in knowledge for the sake of knowledge, (3) in an association between virtue and happiness, (4) in the comprehensibility of

human action. They are led by instinctive moral definitions in which former cultural conditions are reflected.[17]

Unable to believe any longer in an absolute, personal God, the philosophers have put an absolute, impersonal reason in his place. Or, as
Heidegger puts it in his essay: "Into the position of the vanished
authority of God and of the teaching office of the Church steps the
authority of conscience, obtrudes the authority of reason."[18] When
Hume's radical naturalism threatened to pull down this edifice, Kant
shored it up again by appeal to a supposed transcendental authority of
reason and, thus, the ideal of reason was transmitted to Hegel and
Marx, to be revived later on by the Neo-Kantians, Nietzsche's contemporaries and the distant forebears of analytic philosophy.

There are, these philosophers tell us, truths that remain valid at all
times, absolutely and necessarily. Nietzsche rejects such absolutes as
shadows of God, as remnants of an older view in which this temporal,
changing, contingent world is seen as embedded in a truly existing,
unchanging reality. The belief in God, reason, universal truth, and absolute value all imply a distinction between two worlds. They all de-
value this world as deficient, incomplete, and eventually nothing.
They deny what really is and uphold what really is not. They are, thus,
all concealed forms of a profound and desperate nihilism. Insofar as
the conjunction of a belief in reason, in universally valid truths and
objective values is also at the heart of Enlightenment thought,
Nietzsche's attempt to dispel the shadows of God contains an implicit
critique of the Enlightenment. That critique can be summarized in
one sentence: the Enlightenment was, unbeknownst to itself and certainly against its will, a stage in the evolution of modern nihilism.

～

In these judgments Heidegger declares himself to be at one with
Nietzsche. In his essay he attacks, in particular, the philosophical doctrine that there are absolute, universal values. Value-philosophy, he
writes, has been arrived at "through scholarly preoccupation with
philosophy and through the reconstructions of Neo-Kantianism"
(70). However, "The frequency of talk about values is matched by a
corresponding vagueness of the concept" (71). Following Nietzsche,

he argues that the assumption of a realm of objective values, against which reality is measured, obstructs any real access to Being itself. "When the being of whatever is, is stamped as value and its essence is thereby sealed off, then within this metaphysics ... every way to the experiencing of Being is obliterated" (103). The result is that "value does not let Being be Being, does not let it be what it is as Being itself," and in this way, value-philosophy turns out to be "above all the consummation of nihilism" (104).

Heidegger voiced this criticism initially in *Being and Time*, where he insisted that human action and choice would be impossible if there were fixed goals and standards. He returned to this theme in his Nietzsche essay for both philosophical and political reasons. For the philosophy of value was at the time still a significant force in German philosophy and a significant counter-force to the Nietzschean tradition with which Heidegger identified. After 1933 a group of philosophers, moreover, promoted value-philosophy as the appropriate ideology of the Nazi system. The Neo-Kantian philosopher Bruno Bauch, their leader, argued then that Nazi racism and anti-Semitism, with their division of races into those of higher and lower value, would be untenable, because it was merely subjective, unless there existed absolute, objective, eternal values. Bauch wrote of these values: "Without their nontemporal, nonhistorical validity the whole of temporal life would fall prey ... to individualism, to a radical relativism, to a complete nihilism of meaning."[19] He saw such nihilism at work in the existential tradition stemming from Kierkegaard, and in which he no doubt included Heidegger. He and his associates contested, therefore, Heidegger's place in the political world of Nazi Germany. Heidegger, in return, declared in a famous and notorious passage in 1935, at a moment when he still believed in the possibility of a higher, purified National Socialism:

> The works being peddled about nowadays as the philosophy of National Socialism—but have nothing to do with the inner truth and greatness of this movement (namely the encounter between global technology and modern man)—have all been written by men fishing in the troubled waters of "values" and "organic unities."[20]

Heidegger's Nietzsche essay of 1943 continues this earlier attack on the dubious fishermen. Against Bauch and his cohort, Heidegger writes in the essay that the word "nihilism" is "often used only as a catchword and slogan and frequently also as invective intended to prejudice" and, one might add, intended to do political damage.[21] He continues that not everyone — such as himself — "who troubles himself with thoughts about Nothing and its essence is a nihilist" (Ibid.). The political context, thus, illuminates Heidegger's use of the Nietzsche passage at the heart of his essay. He clearly identifies himself with Nietzsche's madman in questioning the authority of reason and the existence of absolute values. The men in the marketplace represent, on the other hand, his philosophical opponents. Of these adversaries he writes: "Those standing about in the market place have abolished thinking and replaced it with idle babble that scents nihilism in every place in which it supposes its own opinion to be endangered" (112). Bauch and his Neo-Kantian friends may seek to advance themselves politically and philosophically by claiming to speak with the authority of reason. To this Heidegger opposes the claims of a genuine thinking.

‍⌐

We have asked: who are those men in the marketplace who believe reason is on their side and dismiss any radical questioning as madness? We must ask now what supports and maintains them in their attitude. Why do they turn to the authority of reason and values once the authority of God and the Church has diminished? Why do they insist on the need for some authority or other?

Heidegger locates the source of that need in the very concept of reason on which the tradition of Western metaphysics is built. Our modern concept of reason has its philosophical roots in the Greek *logos*. But it was the Romans who translated *logos* as *ratio* and from this our notion of 'reason' is linguistically derived. Heidegger is convinced that by rendering *logos* as *ratio*, the Romans made visible something already hidden in the original Greek term but made evident only in the modern conception of reason. In a set of lectures from 1955/56 he writes:

> *Ratio* means "reckoning" in the broadest sense, and accordingly we say "one reckons on something with something for something"; we also say "counts," without numbers coming into the picture. In reckoning, something is imputed, not arbitrarily and not in the sense of a suspicion; what

is imputed is that due to which a matter is the way it is. What is thus imputed, computed, is that upon which something rests, namely what lies present before us, ... *ratio* is therefore the basis, the footing, that is, the ground ... This representing of something as something is a bringing-before-oneself that deals with some particular thing that lies present ... Reckoning, *ratio* as such a perceiving [*Vernehmen*], is reason [*Vernunft*]. *Ratio* is as reckoning: ground and reason.[22]

Ratio attains in this manner the meaning of 'deduction' and 'justification,' of 'providing grounds,' of 'determining causes and effects.' How all this is embedded in our concept of reason, Heidegger argues, has become evident only since Leibniz stated his *principium rationis* in the early seventeenth century, which states *nihil est sine ratione*. Western metaphysics, so Heidegger asserts, has always implicitly relied on that principle; the history of metaphysics is, in fact, a slow unfolding of the multiple meanings embedded in words like *logos*, *ratio*, and *Vernunft*. In Leibniz's formulation these meanings have finally become explicit.

According to Heidegger, reason itself is historical in nature, for the way in which things let themselves be perceived fluctuates over time. But the history of reason in the West is not a series of discontinuous understandings of things. "Initially, as well as later Being cleared and lit itself, though in different ways ... Nevertheless, there is a legacy from epoch to epoch" (91). The history of Western metaphysics unfolds what is implicit in the concept of reason on which all metaphysics is based. That conviction provides Heidegger with a key for understanding modernity:

> By Leibniz's giving the little, barely thought principle *nihil sine ratione*—nothing without reason—the complete and strict formulation of the powerful fundamental principle, the incubation period of the principle of reason in one respect ended. Since then, the exacting claim reigning in the fundamental principle has displayed an authority of which no one before ever had an inkling. This brings to fruition nothing less than the innermost, and at the same time most concealed, molding of the age of Western history we call "modernity." (121)

Both modern science and modern technology operate under Leibniz's principle. "What approaches, already a long time under way, is the unconditional claim of the principle of reason in the form of complete rationality" (80). Under its sway, "what effects and is effected, what grounds and is grounded, is in our eyes, the whole of what is real" (59). Under its sway, our thinking is reduced to a mere, calculating, instrumental ratiocination.

To think, as Heidegger demands in his controversial statement, outside the experience of an opposition between reason and thinking means three things: first, to realize that modern rationality is merely a historical condition, that it has no absolute, timeless authority; second, to understand that this rationality has now reached its historical fulfillment and that what lies beyond calls for radically new forms of thought; third, to attempt to initiate such a thinking beyond the historical confines of the Western tradition.

If philosophers still persist in their search for ultimate grounds, it is because they remain in the grip of the metaphysical tradition which has told them since the beginning of Western thought that reason means ground. Thus the Neo-Kantian value-philosophers remain, in Heidegger's view, in the grip of the *principium rationis*; the secure ground they hope to attain in the realm of absolute values, the authority they hope to attain by their appeal to these values is, however, at best a historical ground and authority. To think the opposition of reason and thinking is to think beyond the limits of that tradition; it is to think outside traditional, metaphysical philosophy, for such a philosophizing always has reason on its side. It is to experience the loss of absolute grounds and absolute authorities.

In his essay on Nietzsche, Heidegger says two important things about this new mode of thinking. The first is that "to be preparatory is the essence of such thinking," and the second is that such thinking "maintains itself necessarily within the realm of historical reflection."[23] Later on, when speaking of the *principium rationis* he invites us, in this sense, to reflect on the principle rather that follow it along its normative paths. We discover then, he says, how mysterious the principle is. For, if everything has a ground, where would the ground of that principle itself be; and if it has a ground, where, in turn, would the ground of that ground be discovered? We find, according to Heidegger, that underneath all these grounds lies an unfathomed abyss, an *Ab-grund*. The *principium rationis* tells us that Being means ground, but thoughtful reflection on the principle forces us to conclude, instead, that Being is an abyss. "Nothing is without ground.

Being and ground: the same. Being as what grounds has no ground; it plays as abyss [*Ab-grund*] the play that, as historical destiny, plays being and ground into our hands."[24] Such reflexive thinking finds itself thereby outside the confines of the principle of sufficient reason. And as such it is then empowered to view adherence to Leibniz's principle as a contingent, historical fact, not one necessitated by what there is. Coming from different and yet related concerns, Wittgenstein seems to have reached similar conclusions. Our "language-game," that is, the way we think and speak, Wittgenstein writes, "is so to say something unpredictable ... It is not based on grounds. It is not reasonable (or unreasonable). It is there—like our life."[25] "What kinds of grounds have I for trusting text-books of physics?" he asks himself and answers: "I have no grounds for not trusting them. And I trust them. I know how such books are produced—or rather, I believe I know. I have some evidence, but it does not go very far and is of a very scattered kind. I have heard, seen and read various things" (600). The appeal to reason is never self-validating, according to Wittgenstein. But all validation, all "justification must come to an end," and the end of all our justification is not a self-validating truth but an ungrounded action. Wittgenstein concludes: "The difficulty is to realize the groundlessness of our believing" (166).

⤿

Nietzsche was, perhaps, the first to diagnose the groundlessness of human reason, and both Heidegger and Wittgenstein may have learned of it with his help. Nevertheless, Nietzsche himself ultimately failed to live up to his insight. That, at least, is what Heidegger argues in his 1943 essay.

At the heart of his critique lies Nietzsche's doctrine of the will to power. That doctrine, according to Heidegger, seeks to characterize the nature of Being itself. Will to power is meant, as Nietzsche himself declares, to be "the innermost essence of being."[26] The doctrine is, thus, on Heidegger's account strictly metaphysical in character. Though no longer a metaphysics of an other world, like Platonism, Christianity or Neo-Kantian value-philosophy, Nietzsche's doctrine remains metaphysical in the sense that it seeks to advance a universally valid account of what being is. Nietzsche remains, thus, despite his protests, within the horizon of Western metaphysics. Nietzsche, the philosopher with the hammer, proves to be the most recent architect of a system of metaphysics.

All this reveals itself, as far as Heidegger is concerned, most clearly in Nietzsche's attempt to replace the old values he subverts with a brand new set defined in terms of the will to power. Nietzsche's positive value is to live in accordance with the will to power. Far from undermining value-philosophy as such, Nietzsche must therefore be considered the latest exponent of this discredited type of thinking, and the criticism he has launched against this type of philosophizing must eventually fall back on his own thought. For Nietzsche, "the will to power is, as soon as it comes expressly to appearance in its pure essence, itself the foundation and realm of value-positing."[27]

This notion shows itself with special clarity in the fact that despite Nietzsche's attack on the traditional notion of value, and despite his apparent questioning of why we want truth rather than falsehood, he remains essentially attached to the assumption that truth constitutes, in an ahistorical way, an absolute value. Heidegger writes that for Nietzsche, "truth is a necessary value precisely out of the essence of the will to power" (85). Nietzsche's conception of truth as a kind of artistic fiction remains, for all its radical pretensions "a derivative of the former essence of truth" (89). The former account had held truth to be a correct representation of what is. In Nietzsche, as Heidegger puts it, "the correct no longer consists in assimilation to something present that is unthought in its presence. Correctness consists now in the arranging of everything that is to be represented" (Ibid.). And that arranging is to be brought about in accord with the will to power. The surprising conclusion for Heidegger, then, is that Nietzsche fails to escape the nihilism that he has diagnosed. His philosophy

> has brought down and slain beneath itself—and has therefore killed as that which *is* for itself—all that *is* in itself. This ultimate blow in the killing of God is perpetrated by metaphysics, which, as metaphysics of the will to power, accomplishes thinking in the sense of value-thinking. (107f.)

And "the value-thinking of the metaphysics of the will to power is murderous in a most extreme sense, because it absolutely does not let being itself take rise, i.e., come into the vitality of its essence" (108).

We must conclude that Nietzsche himself did not fully grasp the significance of the madman passage from *The Gay Science*. According

to Heidegger, it is evident that "Nietzsche can indeed experience nihilism metaphysically as the history of value-positing, yet nevertheless cannot think the essence of nihilism" (93). Nietzsche failed to
grasp that the death of God means the death of all metaphysics, of all
totalizing accounts of the nature of what is. Nietzsche failed to see
that, in the face of this, the madman proposes not another metaphysics, that of the will to power, but a new state of mind altogether, an attitude of radical seeking. Hence, the madman's initial
call: "I seek God! I seek God!" In the surprising turns of Heidegger's
essay, Nietzsche remains in the end associated with the men of reason in the marketplace. Heidegger's call for a new thinking with
which he concludes the essay so dramatically is then to be understood
also as a call for a thinking beyond Nietzsche. Heidegger's critique of
reason, which has stirred such controversy, is above all a critique of
Nietzsche.

～

To think beyond Nietzsche means, for Heidegger, to think the doctrine of the will to power from within the realm of historical reflection. It means to understand that will to power is not the essence
of Being but simply a specific historical manifestation of Being. In
characterizing Being as will to power, Nietzsche has succeeded in
capturing how Being is understood in this modern age. While this
age is often called an age of reason, it is more properly characterized as
the age of the domination (*Verherrlichung*) of reason. But such domination is a characteristic of the will, for "to will is to will-to-be-
master"—it is will to be *Herr*, that is will to domination (77). And,
thus, Nietzsche has properly recognized the modern age as that of the
will to power. As such it is also a time of a "struggle for unlimited
exploitation of the earth as the sphere of raw materials, and the re-
alistic utilization of 'human material' in the service of the unconditional empowering of the will to power in its essence" (101). It
is the age of modern science and modern technology, of the ex-
ploration of grounds and causes with the goal of controlling and sub-
jecting what is.

Whereas Heidegger had earlier defended "the inner truth and
greatness of National Socialism" against those fishing in the muddy
waters of value and organic unity, he now proceeded in 1943 to a more

encompassing judgment on the political movement he had once so rashly joined. His critical confrontation with that movement did not restrict itself now to an attack on Neo-Kantian value-philosophy that that had become rather incidental and preparatory for Heidegger's larger purpose. His confrontation with Nazi doctrine now took the form of a destruction of Nietzsche's philosophy as the essence of National Socialism.

That political movement, he now concluded, was part of the large historical concern with reason that had turned over time to a concern with will to power. Heidegger now saw National Socialism as one element in this wide-ranging historical process. His critique of Nietzsche's doctrine of the will to power became for him the means of rethinking his earlier political commitments. National Socialism, he argued now, was as much a part of the modern age as were modern capitalism and Communist socialism, or Enlightenment rationalism, Neo-Kantian value-philosophy, and Nietzsche's doctrine of the will to power. All these movements and doctrines agreed on an unspoken and unthought consensus concerning the nature of what is, a consensus brought to voice in Nietzsche's philosophy; all these movements adhered in this way to a kind of common sense. National Socialism, with its striving for global and total power, with its exploitation of the resources of science and technology, and with its planned destruction of peoples and races remained, thus committed itself in Heidegger's eyes to the authority and power of reason. Enlightenment rationalism and National Socialism proved to have common ground. And thus, in what is surely the most surprising turn in Heidegger's Nietzsche essay, his critique of reason and his call for another kind of thinking reveal themselves as a devastating critique of National Socialism.

⸎

Against all these burdens, against the whole history of the West, Heidegger saw himself engaged in the search for a new kind of thinking. Much of what he said on the way might be taken to constitute a critique of the Enlightenment: his rejection of an absolute, timeless notion of reason, his refusal to take as reason what is generally thought now to be reasonable, his critique of instrumental rationality, his repudiation of objective values. But for all that Michael Zimmerman has given us a misleading account. The proper frame of Heidegger's thought is neither the Enlightenment nor the modern age; it is the history of the West and the attempt to rethink its metaphysical foundations.

To depict him as an absolute enemy either of modernity or of the Enlightenment is misleading for another reason as well. For in charting the course of a new thinking, Heidegger does not call for the abolition of reason. He urges us, instead, to break the hold that the reliance on such thinking has over us in the form of science and technology. We get a first inkling of what he means when we read in the essay on Nietzsche: "To think in the midst of the sciences means to pass near them without disdaining them" (56). We get another clue when he writes later in the *Discourse on Thinking*: "It would be foolish to attack technology blindly. It would be shortsighted to condemn it as the work of the devil. We depend on technical devices; they even challenge us to ever greater advances."[28] And then he adds: "We can affirm the unavoidable use of technical devices, and also deny them the right to dominate us, and so to warp, confuse, and lay waste our nature" (54). There is here no wholesale rejection of reason, science, technology. We are, instead, called upon to resist being dominated by them. Heidegger wants us to acknowledge the uses and products of reason, but also wants us to resist their *Verherrlichung*, their domination and glorification. It is to this point that the final sentence of his Nietzsche essay addresses itself.

Heidegger's conception of a thinking beyond the *principium rationis* has remained controversial. For one thing, he gives various names to it at different points. In the Nietzsche essay he calls it madness and a seeking of God, but also preparatory thinking and historical reflection. Elsewhere he has spoken of it as meditative or as poetical thinking, as questioning or as waiting and letting-be. Heidegger's critics have complained that such thinking is mysticism and an invitation to passivity; they have derided it as determinedly irrationalist, and have sought to connect it with his political errors of the 1930s. But all such invective cannot obscure the profound significance of what Heidegger tried to say. For the important question is not what exact form a thinking outside the horizon of the *principium rationis* might take. The important question is whether there are such modes of thinking and how they might relate to the now dominant mode of rational thinking.

One is tempted to say that the question is whether and in what sense there can still be philosophical thinking. For philosophy has been, from the beginning, among other things also a madness, a preparatory thinking, and a questioning of our stories concerning the nature of things. At the same time, however, philosophy has always possessed a normalizing and rationalizing function. Today, in particular, philosophers are for the most part content to be tolerated at the feast of reason. They have set aside all pretensions to be radical, skeptical, subversive, destructive thinkers and have adopted instead the modest role of handymen to scientists, linguists, and computer technicians. Because of this, the real question may now be whether there is a thinking outside the normalizing confines of philosophy, and where such a thinking would find its place in an increasingly rationalized and administered world.

In asking such questions, Heidegger joins other radical thinkers of our age. In *Dialectic of Enlightenment* Horkheimer and Adorno write:

> From the beginning, the Enlightenment in the most encompassing sense of a progressive thinking has had the aim to take fear from men and to make them masters. But the fully enlightened earth shines in the sign of triumphant disaster.[29]

Determined to face these disasters, they call for a thinking that "forbids itself the least naiveté concerning the habits and directions of the spirit of the age" (5). Against the power of a fully instrumentalized rationality, they seek to activate the force of a critical reasoning. Michael Zimmerman is surely right in discerning an affinity between the pessimism of the Horkheimer-Adorno view and Heidegger's sense of a darkening age, even though these thinkers diverge on how to respond to the diagnosed condition. We may also, once again, recall Wittgenstein who speaks just as despondently of his time and sees himself engaged in the search for a new kind of thinking outside the parameters of traditional philosophy. In the *Tractatus* he speaks of science as firmly positioned within the world and as proceeding according to reason and logic. In philosophy properly understood, on the other hand, he says there are no theories, no deductions. The philosophical self sees the world as a whole, from without, *sub specie aeter-*

nitatis. To this he adds that what matters, the meaning of life, cannot be grasped in the terms of science and logic. The solution of the problem of life reveals itself for him in a philosophical silence that remains when all scientific problems have been resolved. Later on, he identifies such thinking as descriptive of what is always there but never seen because it is always too close to us. And later still he speaks of it as therapeutic, as liberating us from riddles in which the mind has been caught, and even as a destructive clearing of the ground on which we stand.

Heidegger, Horkheimer, Adorno, and Wittgenstein belonged to the same culture and the same generation. Living through the disasters of the first half of this century, they experienced instrumentalized reason in its most destructive form. One might say that the terms in which they responded are less important than the fact that they searched for modes of thinking beyond the horizons of instrumental, scientific, and technological reason. What matters is their concern that without such alternatives we may be caught in the endless spiral of the insatiable demands of reason, ensnared in ever more frantic pursuits of goals that prove always illusive. Heidegger may be said to summarize their common concern when he asks at the end of his lectures on Leibniz's principle of reason:

> Does the already given characterization of man as an animal rationale exhaust the essence of man? Is the final word to be said about being that being means ground? Or does the essence of man and his belonging to being still remain something in need of thought and this always more urgently? And if that should be so, are we permitted to abandon what is in need of thought for the rage of an exclusively calculating thinking and its gigantic successes? ... That is the question. It is the ultimate question of thinking. Its answer determines what will become of the earth.[30]

"A Bright Clear Mirror": Cassirer's
The Philosophy of the Enlightenment

Among the classics of historical writing on eighteenth-century Europe, Ernst Cassirer's *The Philosophy of the Enlightenment* occupies a unique position. Has any other book had so central and so enduring an impact on the field? First published in 1932, on the eve of its author's exile from Germany, it received a warm welcome in Cassirer's native land and elsewhere in Europe, and has continued to command respect there. But it is in the United States above all that the book has enjoyed its greatest success. Koelln's and Pettegrove's lucid translation, published by Princeton in 1951, rode the high crest of the wave of enthusiasm for Cassirer that began with his arrival in New York and his turn to writing in English. Thus launched, *The Philosophy of the Enlightenment* soon attained a canonical status within eighteenth-century studies that it has never really lost. It eventually reached a mass audience via paperback, and remains vigorously in print to this day. Even such criticism as the book has received has tended to enhance rather than detract from its magisterial reputation. By the end of the sixties, for example, *The Philosophy of the Enlightenment* seems to have become the chief pole of comparison *against* which the emergent "social history" of the Enlightenment defined itself. The practice actually began with Peter Gay, who is sometimes regarded as a "disciple" of Cassirer.[1] But he was soon trumped in this regard by Robert Darnton, for whom *The Philosophy of Enlightenment* was the finest achievement of a traditional history of ideas, one that confined its attention to a "High Enlightenment" of canonical texts, merely recatalogued by Gay; the most urgent task for historians in the present was an assault on the archives, where the true social history of the Enlightenment, high and low, lay buried.[2] Today, however, it is Darnton himself who is taxed with failing to break free from Cassirer's spell, in the most commanding work of the new feminist scholarship, Dena Goodman's *The Republic of Letters: A Cultural History of the French Enlightenment*. Ultimately, *c'est la faute à Rousseau*, the original source of the misogyny that, in Goodman's eyes, has obscured our understanding of the central contribution of the *salonnières* to Enlightenment sociability. But the chief advocate of Rousseau's outlook in our time has indeed been Cassirer, "who did more than anyone else to make the Enlightenment the subject of serious scholarship."[3]

If anything, the result of this kind of critical tribute "from below" has been to reinforce the status of *The Philosophy of the Enlightenment* as the quintessential history of the Enlightenment "from above." The essay at hand will not try to overturn that judgment. Goodman is no doubt correct in her assessment of the pivotal role played by Cassirer's text in twentieth-century scholarship on the Enlightenment, indeed, in constituting the field as an object of study. For precisely that reason, however, a serious reappraisal of *The Philosophy of the Enlightenment* — an attempt to examine the substance of its argument, rather than criticize the limits of its vision — seems overdue. For Cassirer's book appears to have enjoyed the privilege of launching a very durable research program in its field, one that may not yet be spent. What accounts for the lasting impact of *The Philosophy of the Enlightenment*? Why should it have proven difficult for different kinds of revisionism to move beyond it? If this is an opportune moment to pursue such questions, then our first task must be to take a closer look at the background from which the book emerged. Whatever elective affinity there may have been between Cassirer's study and the academic world of post-world America, *The Philosophy of the Enlightenment* was produced in a very different cultural and political context — in fact, has something of the character of a message in a bottle, from a lost intellectual world.

Context: Symbolic Forms and Weimar Liberalism

Above all, it is no accident that the book that did more than any other to restore the Enlightenment to philosophy should have been the work of a major philosopher, not a historian. There is neither space nor competence here to attempt a general profile of Cassirer as a thinker. Not only was he the author of one of the most ambitious, even extravagant philosophical projects of the twentieth century, but his thought has in fact proven very difficult to categorize, eluding any easy capture. The central puzzle of Cassirer's intellectual career is that of determining his precise relation to the Marburg "school" of neo-Kantianism in which he was formed. Was the centerpiece of his mature thought, *The Philosophy of Symbolic Forms*, the culmination and fullest expression of the neo-Kantianism of his Marburg teachers, Hermann Cohen and Paul Natorp? Or did it amount to a mutation in some novel direction, and if so, which—a turn to Hegel, to phenomenology, to pragmatism? The relations between Cassirer and such key corespondents and interlocutors as Husserl and Heidegger remain to be fully documented and interpreted; the same applies to fascinating affinities between his thought and major figures of American pragmatism, Peirce and Dewey above all, and to his considerable influence on later thinkers such as Merleau-Ponty. At all events, the most that can be attempted here is to suggest a periodization of Cassirer's intellectual career down to the publication of *The Philosophy of the Enlightenment*—if only to give us a sense of where it fits into his enormous and very complicated oeuvre.[4]

Cassirer was born in 1874, in Breslau (today Wrocław), Silesia, to a Jewish family whose wealth was drawn primarily from the manufacture of industrial chemicals. Cassirer's own generation, however, was characterized by remarkable intellectual and cultural achievement. The circle of his first cousins, with whom he maintained extremely close relations during his young adulthood in Berlin, included the composer and musicologist Fritz Cassirer; Bruno Cassirer, whose publishing firm played a key role in German intellectual life; the art dealer Paul Cassirer, famous for promoting French Impressionism and other schools of modernist painting in Germany; and the pioneer of gestalt psychology, Kurt Goldstein. At university, Cassirer's interests shifted from law to literature, and finally to philosophy. The turning-point in his intellectual life, by all accounts, was a lecture on Kant by Georg Simmel, in which the latter described Hermann Cohen's interpretation of Kant as at once authoritative and incomprehensible. The discovery of Cohen was a revelation for the young Cassirer, who soon moved to Marburg, where he completed a doctorate in 1899 under Cohen's direction. His earliest work revealed all of his most characteristic philosophic concerns, blending epistemology and history in an original fashion. Cassirer's dissertation was a study of Descartes's critique of the philosophy of mathematics and natural science of his time. This in turn became the introductory chapter in his first book, *Leibniz' System in seinen wissenschaftlichen Grundlagen* (1902), which not only contributed to the striking wider revival of interest in Leibniz at the turn of the century, but also showed Cassirer's characteristic penchant for bridging the French and the German intellectual traditions. From this starting-point, he launched a major project in historical epistemology, whose production stretched over the next two decades, *Das Erkenntnisproblem in der Philosophie und Wissenschaft der neueren Zeit*. Its first two volumes, extending from Nicolas of Cusa to Kant, appeared in 1906 and 1907, and established Cassirer's claim to be heir apparent to Cohen and Natorp within the Marburg "school." Cassirer in fact went on to assume the editorship of the ten-volume edition of Kant's works published by Bruno Cassirer between 1912 and 1923; the intellectual biography he added to the edition, *Kants Leben und Lehre* (1918), has of course enjoyed a long life in print on its own.[5]

There was a lag in winning academic recognition for these intellectual achievements, perhaps owing not a little to the darkening shadow that anti-Semitism cast over German academic life in these years. In 1912, Cohen's and Natorp's efforts to secure the former's professorship at Marburg for Cassirer failed; he had already assumed a position as *Privatdozent* at the University of Berlin, where he remained until 1918. Lack of preferment did not stem his intellectual energies. In 1910, Cassirer published *Substanzbegriff und Funktionsbegriff*, in which for the first time he staked out an independent philosophical position—in this case, a defense of "logical idealism" against empiricist epistemology. Here, too, however, the foundation of Cassirer's argument was narrative in form. Tracing the history of concept-formation in mathematics and natural science from the Greeks to modernity—with explicit reference to the advances of Schroeder, Peirce, and Russell in logic—Cassirer described the gradual replacement of a metaphysics of "substance" by a science of "relations," in which "function" had now became the touchstone of the veridical. The war years in turn provided the opportunity for Cassirer to make an initial excursion beyond epistemology, into the domain of culture. Ineligible for combat, Cassirer was eventually drafted into the "War Press Office," where his linguistic skills were put to work surveying the French press for the purposes of generating political propaganda. As his wife recounted in her memoir, Cassirer found the experience deeply demoralizing.[6] His response was to produce a remarkable survey of German cultural history, *Freiheit und Form: Studien zur deutschen Geistesgeschichte* (1916). From the Renaissance to the Enlightenment, Cassirer argued, German culture had been defined by a dialectical tension between freedom and form; the greatest figures in the national past, Goethe and Kant above all, were those who had managed to maintain these two principles in a creative, if precarious equilibrium. As these names also suggested, German culture was at its characteristic best when it rejoined, rather than departed from, a common European tradition. An attempt to define national identity in wartime, the politics of *Freiheit und Form* were quiet yet firm—its liberal cosmopolitanism at the opposite end of the spectrum from, say, Mann's notorious *Betrachtungen Eines Unpolitischen*. Assuming a milder nationalist position between the two, Ernst Troeltsch in fact charged Cassirer with having ignored the medieval roots of German freedom, which indeed rendered it distinct from Anglo-French conceptions.[7]

The end of the war and the advent of the Weimar Republic considerably improved Cassirer's academic fortunes, and in fact ushered in the most creative and productive period of his intellectual career. In June 1918 he was appointed professor in the *geisteswissenschaftliche* faculty at the University of Hamburg, a "republican" institution brought into existence just one month earlier. By happy accident, Hamburg also possessed an institutional resource that proved to be decisive for Cassirer's intellectual development in these years, the Warburg Library for Cultural Studies. Cassirer soon formed a close relationship with Aby Warburg's successor as director of the library, Fritz Saxl, and it was here that he first made the acquaintance of Erwin Panofksy. The library's holdings, especially in the areas of mythology and historical philology, provided many of the primary sources that formed the background to the emergent philosophy of "symbolic forms." Older intellectual concerns were by no means abandoned. In 1920, Cassirer published the third volume of *Das Erkenntnisproblem*, which pursued post-Kantian epistemology, from Hegel to Schopenhauer; the next year, he produced a study of Einstein's theory of relativity and the problems it posed for the philosophy of science—in effect, a striking attempt to coordinate the epistemology of "critical idealism" with the findings of the new physics. It was in fact in the latter work that the term "symbolic form" appeared in print for the first time. The idea, according to family legend, first occurred to Cassirer while boarding a bus in Berlin in 1917. By the time of his first years in Hamburg, it had become the linchpin of a massive project of philosophical totalization, which came to fruition with impressive speed. The first volume of *The Philosophy of Symbolic Forms*, entitled *Language*, came out in 1923, the second, *Mythical Consciousness*, two years later, and the third, apparently culminating volume, *Phenomenology of Knowledge*, appeared in 1929.

How should the "philosophy of symbolic forms" be described? Its background seems to have lain in a gradual realization on Cassirer's part—going back at least as far as *Substanzbegriff und Funktionsbegriff*—that his defense of an idealist epistemology in science required foundations in a deeper theory of intersubjective *meaning* itself. By 1921, Cassirer had arrived at a stable definition of the concept that would stand at the center of such a theory: "Under a 'symbolic form' should be understood every energy of mind [*Energie des Geistes*] through which a mental content of meaning is connected to a concrete, sensory sign and made to adhere internally to it."[8] The originality of this definition should not be exaggerated. If Cassirer always gave pride of place to Humboldt in tracing its genealogy, the echoes of contemporaries such as Peirce and Saussure are evident, if unintentional. Unlike these thinkers, however, Cassirer then set out to try to map both the variety and the development of the entire world of "symbolic forms," in an effort to establish, as he put it in the foreword to the opening volume of *The Philosophy of Symbolic Forms*, a "morphology of the human spirit." Although the first volume was devoted entirely to just one form, that of *language*, it also advanced a more general schema for understanding the development of all "symbolic forms," which could be expected to pass from "mimetic" through "analogical" to "symbolic" forms of expression, in a gradual movement from the concrete to the abstract. The progress of language, in particular, was traced from its initial "sensuous" expression, in the gestural and immediately aural, to more "intuitive" forms, which made use of more abstract conceptions of space and time, to a culminating state in which it had developed concepts of "pure relation," objective and self-referential. For all that, however, language never entirely loses its anchorage in sensuous and material media of expression—a feature of "symbolic forms" in general. From here, Cassirer in a sense moved backwards, historically and logically, in the second volume of *The Philosophy of Symbolic Forms*, which provided a similar theory of the development of "mythical thought." Rejecting all theories of myth as "primitive science," Cassirer portrayed it as a radically distinct form of consciousness, rooted in social ritual, more archaic, immediate, and concrete than language itself; it was in fact the instability and disenchantment of "mythic consciousness" over time that paved the way for the emergence of language as an independent symbolic form.

Four years later, the third volume of *The Philosophy of Symbolic Forms* integrated these analysis of myth and language into a systematic attempt to account for the emergence and development of scientific thought proper. *Phenomenology of Knowledge* offered more than a general epistemology, however. For the theory of symbolic forms was now for the first time grounded in something close to a full-scale philosophical anthropology, pointing to Cassirer's later definition of human beings as "symbolic animals." The key theoretical innovation was his concept of "symbolic pregnance," designed to situate the phenomenon of meaning in the very process of perception itself, prior to any intellectual or cultural moment: "By symbolic pregnance we mean the way in which a perception as a 'sensory' experience contains at the same time a certain nonintuitive 'meaning' which it immediately and concretely represents.'" Here, Cassirer suggested, lay the solution for the oldest problem of philosophical anthropology: "The relation between body and soul represents the prototype and model for a purely symbolic relation, which cannot be converted either into a relationship between things or into a causal relation . . . a genuine access to the body-soul problem is possible only if we recognize as a general principle that all thing connections and all causal connections are ultimately based upon such relations of meaning. The latter do not form a special class *within* the thing and causal relations; rather they are the constitutive presuppositions, the *condition sine qua non*, on which the thing and causal relations themselves are based."[10]

With this theory of the anthropological priority of *meaning*, Cassirer seems to have left any narrow form of neo-Kantianism well behind him. Where should *The Philosophy of Symbolic Forms* be located on the wider philosophic map? Cassirer himself was in fact quite candid about the general inspiration for his philosophical program. In the "Introduction and Presentation of the Problem" in the first volume, he paid tribute to Kant as a pioneer, each of the *Critiques* having opened up a new terrain for exploring the work of spirit, in science, ethics, and art. Yet the real model for his project was to be found elsewhere, in Hegel's attempt at a systematic, totalizing narrative in the *Phenomenology of Spirit*: "More sharply than any thinker before him, Hegel stated that we must think of the human spirit as a *concrete* whole, that we must not stop at the simple concept but develop it in the totality of its manifestations."[11] The gesture of assimilation to Hegel was repeated in the second volume of *The Philosophy of Symbolic Forms*—"That myth stands in an inner and necessary relation to the universal task of this phenomenology follows directly from Hegel's own formulation and definition of the concept"[12]—and then finalized in the third: "In speaking of a phenomenology of knowledge I am using the word 'phenomenology' not in its modern sense but with its fundamental signification as established an systematically grounded by Hegel."[13] In point of fact, however, the differences from any conventional form of Hegelianism are bound to leap out at the reader. Above all, Cassirer's presentation of the development of "symbolic forms" across time turns out to be both less linear and more plural than the model of *The Phenomenology of Spirit* would suggest. As Krois puts it in his study of Cassirer's thought, the real shape of his conception of development is *centrifugal*—a plurality of relatively autonomous "symbolic forms" exfoliating from the common matrix of mythical thought, itself a rather different starting-point from Hegel's.[14] It is worth stressing that *The Philosophy of Symbolic Forms* was very much an unfinished project: in later works, the "forms" analyzed by Cassirer included philosophy (in his essays in intellectual history), technology (a striking anticipation of certain Frankfurt School themes), morality (his study of Axel Hägerström), and art (a famous chapter in *An Essay on Man*). Not surprisingly, Cassirer's system also tends to lack any strong conception of an end-state, to match Hegel's notion of the domination of "absolute" philosophic knowledge. Indeed, for all of Cassirer's appeals to Hegel, it does not seem difficult to glimpse in his philosophic vision the inspiration of another figure standing behind both Hegel and Kant—that of Leibniz, whose thought had been the starting-point in Cassirer's own intellectual itinerary. It may not be entirely inaccurate to see in *The Philosophy of Symbolic Forms* the outline of a kind of *cultural* monadology, projecting a plurality of autonomous spheres of "meaning," traversed by a pre-established harmony and unity.

Neo-Kantian, Neo-Hegelian, or Neo-Leibnizian—in any case, Cassirer's mature thought involved a creative recovery and development of the central themes of classical German Idealism. As such, he had long since begun to contrast his own thought with an alternative tradition of continental philosophy, descending from Kierkegaard to Nietzsche, Bergson, and Scheler, whom he tended to group under the dismissive label of *"Lebensphilosophie."* By the mid-twenties, however, this tradition had produced a major new figure, capable of doing battle on the most sophisticated terrain of academic philosophy. Cassirer and Heidegger seem to have met as early as 1923, in Hamburg; a series of critical exchanges, marked by a combination of respect for and dissent from one another's philosophical positions, followed down to 1931. In 1928, Heidegger published a generous review of the second volume of *The Philosophy of Symbolic Forms*, to which he also alluded in a significant footnote in *Being and Time*.[15] Cassirer recognized the originality and importance of Heidegger's masterpiece; his most extended comment, however, was a long and insightful review of Heidegger's *Kant and the Problem of Metaphysics* in 1931. Between these dates, the two participated in a series of public lectures and discussions in Davos, Switzerland, during March and April 1929—encounters that have, in retrospect, taken on an almost legendary status as marking a profound parting of the ways in modern German thought. The exact terms of the "debate" between Cassirer and Heidegger have had to be reconstructed from onlookers' notes.[16] The terrain was the interpretation of Kant, whom Heidegger sought to rescue from the extreme cognitivism of the "neo-Kantians" by restoring what he saw as Kant's supreme emphasis on human *finitude*—the ground for his own understanding of *Dasein*. Cassirer's response was to concede the moment of finitude in Kant—thus rejecting the stark antithesis drawn by Heidegger—while also insisting on a transcendental moment as well, the opening onto a world of "objective spirit" rooted in intersubjective language. Lacking this anchor, Heidegger's interpretation ran the risk of endorsing a romantic irrationalism and relativism. Two years later, Cassirer contrasted the thought of Kant and Heidegger in these pregnant terms: "Heidegger's fundamental ontology, which is grounded in the interpretation of care as the being of the existent and which sees a primary revelation of the existent in the fundamental mode of fear, must put all of Kant's concepts from the very beginning—however much Heidegger attempted to do justice to their purely logical mode—into a changed atmosphere and thus, as it were, cover them up. Kant was and remained a thinker of the Enlightenment, in the most noble and beautiful sense of this word. He strove for illumination even as he thought about the deepest and hidden grounds of being."[17]

At all events, much of the drama attached retrospectively to the Davos "disputation" has to do with the ultimate political fates of the two thinkers. What in fact were Cassirer's own politics? As the legal liberalism of Jellinek and Kelsen and the ethical socialism of Hermann Cohen suggest, the neo-Kantianism in which he was formed was capable of inspiring strong and original programs. There is no doubt that Cassirer's chief inclination from the outset was toward a moderate version of the former. The most overt political statement of the early part of his intellectual career was *Freiheit und Form*, which projected a cosmopolitan liberalism onto the screen of German cultural history. The advent of the Weimar Republic naturally brought opportunities for more forward kinds of political expression. Cassirer observed the Revolution coolly, from a distance, but actively identified with the Republic from the start. We have seen that he accepted a professorship at the "republican" University of Hamburg in June

1919; in the same month, he joined the center-left protest against the trial and execution of Eugen Leviné for his role in the Bavarian Soviet. Cassirer seems to have voted with the DDP consistently throughout the twenties. Nevertheless, it was not until 1928 that he produced a major political statement of his own. The occasion was Hamburg's celebration of the ninth anniversary of the Weimar constitution in August. Cassirer's speech, *Die Idee der Republikanischen Verfassung*, published the following year, made a passionate defense of the Republic, by tracing its founding ideas to an interlocking set of German, English, and French thinkers—Leibniz, Wolff, Blackstone, Rousseau, and Kant, whose sober defense of the French Revolution Cassirer echoed and endorsed. In the spring of 1929, he reached the apex of his academic career, being elected Rector at Hamburg, for 1929–30—the first Jew to head a University in Germany. By this point, of course, the centrist liberalism for which Cassirer stood had begun to expire as a political force in Germany. Nevertheless, his public interventions on behalf of the Republic continued, as if in increasingly anxious compensation. Cassirer's last major political statement before his exile from Germany was the speech, "Vom Wesen und Werden des Naturrechts," delivered in February 1932—a survey of the history of the modern natural rights tradition from Grotius onwards, with special emphasis on the eighteenth-century elaboration of the concept of inalienable rights. Cassirer ended his remarks by calling for a revival of the notion in the contemporary world. Hitler's assumption of the Chancellorship a year later brought his career at Hamburg to an end. In May 1933, the same month that Heidegger delivered his own inaugural address as Rector at Freiburg, Cassirer led his family into exile in Vienna, and reached Oxford in the fall, never to return to Germany.

Text: Totalization and Nostalgia

Such were the circumstances in which *The Philosophy of the Enlightenment* was produced. As it happened, the book formed the last part of an unintentional trilogy of studies in European intellectual history, having been preceded by *Individual and Cosmos in the Renaissance* in 1927, and *The Platonic Renaissance in England*, published earlier in

1932. Cassirer spent much of the summer of 1931, just after stepping down from the Rectorship at Hamburg, reading in the Bibliothèque Nationale in Paris. The research trip also produced the two overlapping studies of Rousseau that might well be seen as extended appendices to *The Philosophy of the Enlightenment*—*Das Problem Jean-Jacques Rousseau*, which has of course become a classic in its own right, and "L'unité dans l'oeuvre de Jean-Jacques Rousseau," first delivered (in French, a matter of some pride to Cassirer) at a conference in Paris in February 1932. As for *The Philosophy of the Enlightenment* itself, it reached print at the very end of that year, and proved to be Cassirer's last publication in Germany before his exile.

At first glance, the text hardly seems to register the turbulence and drama of this background. In the Preface, Cassirer explicitly disavowed any "polemical intentions" in writing *The Philosophy of the Enlightenment*. Nor did he aim at an exhaustive treatment of the subject. On the one hand, limitations of space constrained him to approach the Enlightenment "in its characteristic depth rather than its breadth . . . in light of the unity of its conceptual origin and of its underlying principle rather than of the totality of his historical manifestations and results."[18] On the other, the Enlightenment was itself only one episode in a larger drama, the process "through which modern philosophic thought gained its characteristic self-confidence and self-consciousness," which could only be gestured at in this book. Here Cassirer referred the reader to his two earlier works of intellectual history: like *The Philosophy of the Enlightenment*, these were only "preliminary studies" for a more comprehensive "phenomenology of the philosophic spirit," which Cassirer doubted he would ever complete. As for the work at hand, his chief purpose was to emphasize the *originality* of eighteenth-century philosophy within this larger story. Its keynote was the restoration of philosophical reason to its "classical" vocation as both unifying medium of all intellectual endeavor and active shaper of the world. No less a thinker than Hegel had, on occasion, dismissed the Enlightenment as a passive "philosophy of reflection"— even though his own *Phenomenology* shows that Hegel the metaphysician knew better. For the Enlightenment set out not merely to interpret but to change the world: "[T]he fundamental tendency and the main endeavor of the philosophy of the Enlightenment are not to observe life and to portray it in terms of reflective thought . . . Thought consists not only in analyzing and dissecting, but in actually bringing about that order of things which it conceives as necessary, so that by this act of fulfillment it may demonstrate its own reality and truth."[19] It was this novel fusion of cognition and agency that lay at the core of the philosophical outlook of the Enlightenment and thus provided the chief focus of Cassirer's study. Only at the end of the Preface did he make any allusion to the intellectual and political context in which he wrote, expressing two larger hopes for the book. One was that it might succeed in overturning "the verdict of the Romantic Movement" on eighteenth-century thought, silencing once and for all the slogan of "the shallow Enlightenment." Beyond this, the unavoidably *critical* character of reflection on the history of philosophy suggested that contemporary conceptions of "progress" might appear differently when glimpsed in "that bright clear mirror fashioned by the Enlightenment": "Instead of assuming a derogatory air, we must take courage and measure our powers against those of the age of the Enlightenment, and find a proper adjustment. The age which venerated reason and science as man's highest faculty cannot and must not be lost even for us. We must find a way not only to see that age in its own shape but to release again those original forces which brought forth and molded this shape."[20] As a political gesture in 1932, this was characteristically modest, even oblique—but unmistakable nonetheless.

What shapes appeared to Cassirer in the "bright clear mirror" of eighteenth-century thought? *The Philosophy of the Enlightenment* is made up of seven chapters. The first of these, "The Mind of the Enlightenment," serves as a kind of general introduction, elaborating the portrait of the new philosophical reason of the epoch already sketched in the Preface. In point of fact, it seems that the Enlightenment, at least at the outset, may have been of *two* "minds," since the chapter is divided into two unequal parts. Cassirer began by recalling D'Alembert's own portrait of the French Enlightenment, at the moment of its self-discovery, in his "Elements of Philosophy": the eighteenth century was the century of philosophy *par excellence*, and its centerpiece was indeed a novel conception of reason. But there have been many "ages of reason"—what was the *differentia specifica* of Enlightenment rationalism? Cassirer's answer was to construct its genealogy, tracing its roots to the first philosophical system of the modern world, Cartesianism, and the subsequent impact on it of the emergence of Newtonian natural science. For the result of the success of Newton's "analytic" method, with its emphasis on empirical induction, was to modify rather than destroy Cartesian rationalism, by effecting an alteration and relaxation in its guiding ideals. Here Cassirer invoked— to lasting effect—the contrast drawn by D'Alembert and echoed by Condillac, between the *"esprit de système"* of Cartesianism and the *"esprit systématique"* of the French Enlightenment, the modulation from noun to adjective suggesting the more expansive conception of reason of the latter, now set free from any strictly mathematical or logical basis. Paradoxically, what "reason" thus lost in rigor and certainty was more than made up for by a dramatic extension of its powers, now reaching beyond abstract shape and number to govern the physical and moral worlds as well. The result was the discovery of the *formative* powers of philosophical reason that constituted the unique contribution of the Enlightenment. Having thus returned to the central theme of the Preface, instead of ending the chapter, Cassirer made an abrupt change of scene, devoting a short second section entirely to Leibniz. Despite appearances, the rationalism of the latter was in fact utterly distinct from that of Descartes—*pluralist* rather dualist or monist, with a specific accent on the *continuity* of monads, instead of a more properly Cartesian obsession with identity and difference. The result was two-fold. On one hand, the concept of *totality* or the whole had for Leibniz a far greater significance than for any French thinker. On the other hand, since the monad, in contrast to the material atom, was conceived in terms of a unique "force," Leibniz's system also enshrined a certain kind of *individualism*—in his system, "an inalienable prerogative is first gained for the individual entity." What was the upshot of Leibniz's philosophy for the "mind of the Enlightenment"? Cassirer ended the chapter reminding his readers that, according to legend, Leibniz tended to be either ignored or ridiculed in France. But the example of *Candide* was misleading. In fact, in "this fundamental opposition"—between the "classical Cartesian form of analysis and that new form of philosophical synthesis which originates in Leibniz"—"lay the great intellectual tasks which eighteenth century thought had to accomplish, and which the century approaches from different angles in its theory of knowledge and in its philosophy of nature, in its psychology and in its theory of the state and society, in its philosophy of religion and in its aesthetics."[21]

The rest of *The Philosophy of the Enlightenment* was devoted to surveying those topics, in precisely that order. In the second chapter, on "Nature and Natural Science," Cassirer turned first to a more detailed account of the emergence and triumph of Newtonianism, which, among other things, completed the long process, begun two centuries earlier, of permanently separating cosmology from religion. In physics proper, the result of the turn to empiricism was to open the door to a new kind of skepticism, which found its ultimate expression in the philosophy of Hume; the seventeenth-century concept of "substance" was a major casualty of this line of thought. The biological sciences, on the other hand, which found their major popular representation in Diderot and made their greatest advance with Buffon's *Natural History*—the biological counterpart to Newton—were far less affected by epistemological doubt, since this field of knowledge remained subject to the continued dominance of Cartesianism. Cassirer then concluded the chapter in the same way that he did the first, by looking beyond French borders. In England, the Cambridge neo-Platonists kept alive a Renaissance conception of the "dynamism" of nature. Natural science in Germany, on the other hand, was dominated by the similar heritage of Leibniz, and it was in this domain that his impact was first felt in France, above all through the efforts of Maupertuis, who happened to be the major native exponent of Newtonianism as well. The ultimate fate of science in the eighteenth century was in any case inseparable from psychology, the subject of the third chapter of *The Philosophy of the Enlightenment*. Here, the destruction of the rationalist conception of "innate ideas" by the English empiricists was the counterpart to the dethronement of metaphysical "substance." This left, however, a "core problem," that of the relation between the various fields of sensation, whose solution was necessary to ward off the threat of Berkeley's "subjective idealism." Hints of a way out of this impasse could be found in Condillac's novel emphasis on *will* in his own philosophical psychology, echoed by Rousseau. Not suprisingly, another possible solution was implied in Leibniz's monadology, which dominated the German scene. But the ultimate resolution of the problem was to be found in Kant, building on the work of Lambert and Tetens: "When these two separate streams of thought of the German Enlightenment joined in Kant, their relative goal was achieved, and with achievement the goal vanished to be supplanted by a new principle and new problems."[22]

From here, Cassirer turned in his fourth chapter to religion, in regard to which the Enlightenment could lay claim to three major achievements. One was to complete the destruction of the dogma of original sin, bringing the process of secularization begun with the Reformation to its climax. This move left a "problem" in its wake as well, that of theodicy, or the explanation of evil, whose challenge was to be seen in Voltaire's tormented life-long struggle with the ghost of Pascal. The solution was only finally reached with Kant's ethics, which stripped pleasure and pain of all moral significance—though Kant was anticipated in this respect by both the aesthetics of Shaftesbury and the social thought of Rousseau. Kant also gave full expression to a second major achievement of Enlightened thinking on religion—the erection of *toleration* as a central ethical demand of religious thought itself. Another German thinker, finally, was responsible for a third major advance in theology: it was Lessing's *Education of Humanity* that first suggested the means for overcoming the potential contradiction, introduced by Spinoza, between religion and history. In fact, Lessing's achievement pointed beyond theology to the wider domain of historical understanding, the subject of the fifth chapter of *The Philosophy of the Enlightenment*. Here Cassirer set out specifically to overturn the Romantic verdict that the Enlightenment was somehow "unhistorical"; on the contrary, it was the Enlightenment that established the conditions of possibility for Romantic historicism itself. The true pioneer here was Bayle, whose destruction of one "fact" of historical dogma after another constituted a veritable "critique of historical reason." The terrain cleared by Bayle was then occupied, in the first instance, by the incomparable Montesquieu, whose conception of "ideal types" and explanatory pluralism have formed the solid basis of all subsequent social science. Voltaire received rougher treatment at Cassirer's hands: his historiography tended to be flawed by his commitment to an all-too-static conception of human nature, sign of the dominance of the "analytic spirit" in his writing. Among other narrative historians, only Hume resisted this spirit—though he, too, lacked the "buried treasure" of Leibniz's thought, which alone possessed the means of assigning individuality its true philosophic weight in historical explanation. It was in Germany that the "treasure" of Leibniz's conception of substance was finally released into circulation by Herder, whose philosophy of history thus broke the spell of analytical thinking once and for all. Indeed, Herder had in one sense simply surpassed the Enlightenment altogether. However, Cassirer insisted, his break with the immediate past was not total: "The conquest of the Enlightenment by Herder is therefore a genuine self-conquest. It is one of those defeats which really denote a victory, and Herder's achievement is in fact one of the greatest intellectual triumphs of the philosophy of the Enlightenment."[23]

In the sixth chapter of *The Philosophy of the Enlightenment*, on "Law, State, and Society," Cassirer reproduced the themes of his contemporary writings on natural law and Rousseau. An opening section examined the doctrine of inalienable rights as it emerged in the eighteenth-century—Cassirer admitted that the notion rested on insecure foundations, in evident tension with the consensual rejection of "innate ideas." From here he turned to the adjacent field of contract theory in political thought, where Rousseau turned out to play a role analogous to that of Herder in the philosophy of history, anchoring his own conception of inalienable rights in the communal terrain of the state: "Rousseau did not overthrow the world of the Enlightenment; he only transferred its center of gravity to another position. By this intellectual accomplishment he prepared the way for Kant as did no other thinker of the eighteenth century. Kant could find support in Rousseau when he came to build up his own systematic edifice—that edifice which overshadows the Enlightenment even while it represents its final glorification."[24] Cassirer then concluded *The Philosophy of the Enlightenment* with by far the longest chapter in the book—a close analysis, extending across nearly a hundred pages of text, of the emergence of aesthetics as an independent philosophical discipline. His starting-point here, as elsewhere, was with the disintegration of an essentially Cartesian program, in this case the classical aesthetics of Boileau, which duly fell prey to a variety of subjectivist attacks, beginning with Bouhours and Dubos, and culminating with Hume. The triumph of these psychological theories of art was all too complete: "In no other field was the transition from the psychological to the transcendental approach, by which Kant finally resolved this alliance, so hard to realize and burdened with so many systematic difficulties as in that of the fundamental problems of aesthetics."[25] Cassirer then described the gradual resolution of these "difficulties," first in English thought, with Shaftesbury's reconstruction of Plotinus's conception of "intelligible beauty" and Burke's recovery of the category of the "sublime," both pointing beyond the limits of classical aesthetics; then in the neo-classicism of Gottsched and the response of various of his Swiss critics; and finally, in Baumgarten himself, who used Leibniz's doctrine of the degrees of knowledge to found the philosophical autonomy, perhaps even priority, of aesthetic judgment. At the start of the chapter, Cassirer had declared that the emergence of the new discipline of aesthetics had owed a good deal to the "pre-established harmony" between thought of the greatest philosopher and the greatest poet of the age: "Kant's philosophy and Goethe's poetry form the intellectual goal toward which this movement prophetically beckons."[26] *The Philosophy of the Enlightenment* concluded, however, with neither Kant nor Goethe, but with the figure of Lessing: "It is above all because of him that the century of the Enlightenment, to a very great extent dominated by its gift of criticism, did not fall prey to the merely negative critical function—that it was able to reconvert criticism to creative activity and shape it and use it as an indispensable instrument of life and of the constant renewal of the spirit."[27]

Now what even such a stenographic summary of the book makes clear, in the first instance, is the extent to which Cassirer made good his effort to present eighteenth-century thought "in the unity of its conceptual origins and of its underlying principle." Elsewhere in the Preface, he insisted that the Enlightenment, "which is still usually treated as an eclectic mixture of the most diverse thought elements, is in fact dominated by a few great fundamental ideas expressed with strict consistency and in exact arrangement."[28] This is a perfect description of the book itself, which is in fact structured around a single narrative form, which is then presented at *two* successive levels in the text, the first subsumed into the second. The narrative form is, of course, a familiar one: the dialectical development from an initial state of undifferentiated unity to one of rupture and fragmentation, in order to arrive at an end-state in which unity has been restored in a higher, "differentiated" shape. As for the content of the form, the prior state is always some variety of Cartesianism, whose certainty is then shaken or destroyed by a species of "analytic" or "psychological" thought, most often English in inspiration, whose "problems" then find their solution in the emergence of "synthetic" or "transcendental" philosophy—the privilege, of course, of German thinkers above all. Each of the six substantive chapters of *The Philosophy of the Enlightenment* tells the same tale, in effect. Thus Cassirer's account of eighteenth-century science began with the challenge posed to Cartesianism by Newtonian "analysis," whose empiricism turned out to lack stable foundations, risking a collapse into Hume's skepticism; the solution was to be found in Kant's "Copernican Revolution," whose origins were traced to the pluralist metaphysics of Leibniz. In psychology, the reign of Descartes's "innate ideas" was cut short by Locke and his successors; the resulting slide toward incoherent subjectivism was stayed by the rediscovery of "will" in Condillac and Rousseau, which in turn inspired Kant's restoration of psychic objectivity and wholeness, in the "transcendental unity of apperception." It was the dogmatism of Pascal, rather than the rationalism of Descartes, that formed the target of Enlightened "analysis" in the domain of religion; but the solutions to the moral and intellectual "problems" thus unleashed were, again, owing to the efforts of German thinkers— Kant's "practical reason" and defense of toleration, Lessing's reconciliation of religion and history. As for historiography, it was here a French Protestant, Bayle, who challenged the rule of dogmatism, Cartesian or Catholic; but the story again ended in Germany, where Herder, reaching back once more to Leibniz, definitively ended an unstable period dominated by an "analytical" understanding of history. Cassirer's account of political thought traced a similar path, moving from the rationalist rights theories of the seventeenth century to the liberal doctrine of inalienability in the eighteenth, and then from Rousseau to Kant. Aesthetics, finally, showed the same trajectory: the Cartesian classicism of Boileau gave way to the "psychologisms" of Dubos or Hume; Shaftesbury and Burke then paved the way for the consolidation of a fully modern aesthetic theory in

Baumgarten and Kant, which emerged in "pre-established harmony" with the artistic practice of Lessing and Goethe.

At the same time, these are not simply discrete case-studies of topics in eighteenth-century thought, nor is the order of their presentation an accidental one. For taken together, the separate chapters of *The Philosophy of the Enlightenment* reproduce precisely the same narrative at a higher level of generality. Here the first chapter, depicting the "Mind of the Enlightenment," plays a crucial enabling role. For as we have seen, far from attributing a single, stable outlook to the Enlightenment, Cassirer instead produced an elaborate description of what was essentially the *French* version of it, caught in a long moment of disequilibrium—in transition, that is, from the reign of the *"esprit de système"* to that of the *"esprit systématique."* The chapter then concluded by shifting abruptly to a snapshot of Leibniz, sitting offstage. It was the essential "task" of the Enlightenment as a whole, Cassirer insisted, to bridge the gap between the "analytic" outlook of the one and the "synthetic" project of the other—to combine, as it were, a French melody and a German counterpoint. As the succeeding six chapters pursue this project, the center of gravity of the narrative gradually shifts from the French to the German scene, with English thinkers, again, serving as mediators—of the "vanishing" variety, one is tempted to add—between the two. Thus the chapters devoted to science and psychology are still dominated by accounts of French thought, ending with mere gestures in the direction of Leibniz or Kant. The gap begins to close in the next three chapters, each of which concludes with descriptions of German resolutions to French "problems," in Kant, Lessing, and Herder. The story then reaches its climax in the last chapter, with its astonishingly detailed account of the emergence of German aesthetics; indeed, the weight of this chapter in *The Philosophy of the Enlightenment*, which lacks any conclusion proper, lies in its presentation of Baumgarten's aesthetic theory as in some sense the climax and end-point of the European Enlightenment as a whole.

In point of fact, this is unlikely to surprise any reader who knows that Cassirer was in some sense a "neo-Kantian" philosopher. For the basic shape of the narrative at this level faithfully reproduces the order of topics of Kant's three *Critiques*: Cassirer's chapters move from the scientific and epistemological terrain of the first to the religious and moral topics of the second, and then conclude at the doorstep of the *Critique of Judgment* itself. Moreover, there was a precedent for the emphasis placed upon the aesthetic in this design. For Cassirer emphatically belonged to the camp of those interpreters of Kant who see his aesthetic theory as the capstone of the critical system as a whole—the chapter on the *Critique of Judgment* in *Kants Leben und Lehre* occupies roughly the same position and weight as the chapter on aesthetics in *The Philosophy of the Enlightenment*. At the same time, there *is* an evident problem for any attempt to read the book as a "Kantian" account of eighteenth-century thought *tout court*. This is the fact that Cassirer quite clearly excluded Immanuel Kant himself from the Enlightenment. The plan of *The Philosophy of the Enlightenment* echoes that of Kant's critical philosophy; and Kant is referred to continually in its pages—the place he occupies in its index puts him in the same rank as Diderot and Voltaire. Yet there is no extended discussion of a major work of Kant's anywhere in the book, even where it is most to be expected. Over and over Cassirer's chapters lead the reader in a direction for which one work or another of Kant's would seem to be the logical end-point, only to stop short, concluding with discussions of what come to seem to be so many substitutes or "precursors"—Lessing, Herder, Rousseau, Baumgarten. Behind these, there is the figure of one other German thinker, whose works *do* receive extended discussion in *The Philosophy of the Enlightenment*, and who in fact looms as a far larger presence in the book than Kant—Leibniz, surprisingly enough. The paradox here looks acute: the one major German thinker of the epoch to align himself self-consciously and unequivocally with the Enlightenment appears to have been excluded from Cassirer's study, in favor of a philosopher who died a half-century before the movement can plausibly be said to have arrived in Germany. What is the explanation for this?

In a fascinating political reading of Cassirer's intellectual career down to the moment of his exile, David Lipton has suggested that Cassirer's treatment of Kant, or lack thereof, in *The Philosophy of the Enlightenment* was in effect an "evasion" in the face of wrenching philosophical and political pressure. Both the implosion of Weimar liberalism and the intellectual challenge posed by Heidegger ought to have led Cassirer to a new, more profound engagement with Kant. His study of the Enlightenment brought him to the threshold of just such a project; but in the end, he nervously swerved away: "Under these circumstances Cassirer undoubtedly felt that to re-examine the nature of reason would only further undermine the cause of human freedom."[29] Lipton's suggestion is to be respected; we will return in a moment to the character of *The Philosophy of the Enlightenment* as a political statement. But it may explain too much. For Cassirer's handling of Kant in the text is not only a good deal more coherent and nuanced than it appears at first glance; but it in fact becomes still more intelligible when the book is restored to the context of his mature philosophical thought as a whole. As we have seen, the Preface alerted the reader to the fact that the text was to be regarded as one more "preliminary study" for a much larger project, that of a "phenomenology of the philosophic spirit." Philosophy, in other words, was here understood as another "symbolic form," in Cassirer's technical sense of the term, in whose history the Enlightenment was only one specific moment. Indeed, it is one of the great rhetorical achievements of *The Philosophy of the Enlightenment* that Cassirer was able to present the "dramatic action" of eighteenth-century thought as a coherent, self-enclosed narrative, while also continually conjuring up the shape of a wider philosophical drama extending before and after the story at hand. At one end, this is what explains the close attention that Cassirer devoted in the book to seventeenth-century rationalism, Descartes above all, which, strictly speaking, might be thought to fall outside his purview. At the other, there is Kant, whose thought is consistently presented as marking *both* the "culmination" of the Enlightenment and its cancellation, for the launching of an entirely new phase in the development of philosophy. Cassirer's description of Kant's philosophy as an "edifice which overshadows the Enlightenment even while it represents its final glorification" was perfectly loyal to Kant's own understanding of his relation to the Enlightenment—though it is hardly necessary to add that the guiding spirit behind this narrative was not Kant but Hegel, the original model for this and the rest of Cassirer's "phenomenologies" of form. Given this understanding of Kant, the result of a full-scale presentation of his thought in *The Philosophy of the Enlightenment*, logically enough, could only have been to diminish the Enlightenment, turning it into a mere preamble to Critical Philosophy. Instead, Cassirer chose to reduce Kant to something like a gestural presence in the text, with his place, and that of classical Idealism as a whole, "held" by the series of transitional figures who occupy center stage in the book. Moreover, there was a specific logic in granting Leibniz a certain pride of place among these, in addition to Cassirer's own evident affection for him: rather than being a central figure in the Enlightenment proper, Leibniz serves as the indispensable bridge linking its immediate predecessor, the philosophic culture of rationalism, to its immediate successor, that of classical German Idealism.

It is perhaps not surprising to discover that the Enlightenment was in some sense subordinated to classical Idealism in Cassirer's book, given the depth of his own philosophic commitments to the great themes of the latter tradition. "Needless to say," he wrote in the Preface, "following Kant's achievement and the intellectual revolution accomplished by Kant's *Critique of Pure Reason*, it is no longer possible to return to the questions and answers of the philosophy of the Enlightenment."[30] But neither was there any need for such a "return," since the most original contribution of the Enlightenment to modernity survived the movement itself, finding a still more secure home at the heart of classical Idealism. This was its "activist" conception of philosophic reason, which "attributes to thought not merely an imitative function but the power and the task of shaping life itself." The philosophy of the Enlightenment set out not merely to understand the world, but to use that understanding freely to *remake* it, according to its lights. This is indeed the central, enduring theme of *The Philosophy of the Enlightenment*, and no reader is likely to forget the vividness with which Cassirer presents the idea in the Preface and first chapter of the book. To make such a claim, however, is to point to another paradox, which will return us to the question of Cassirer's politics. For if we ask ourselves what examples Cassirer cites of this kind of philosophic reason in action—what institutions and practices were actually shaped by Enlightened thought—the answer appears to be virtually none. The idea of philosophy as sovereign maker of the world largely remains just that, an idea—it is never brought to earth in concrete instances. It is noticeable that the chapter devoted to politics in

The Philosophy of the Enlightenment, where the notion might have been expected to find its chief illustration, is by far the slenderest in the book; the topic of "enlightened despotism," the zone of philosophical activity *par excellence* in the second half of the eighteenth century, is never broached. Beyond this, probably the largest single lacuna in Cassirer's study is the total disregard of economic theory and practice; neither Smith nor physiocracy make an appearance in the pages of *The Philosophy of the Enlightenment*. The garden later tilled by Peter Gay in *Voltaire's Politics*, and the entire domain of Enlightened political practice, reformist and revolutionary, magisterially cultivated by Franco Venturi, were utterly neglected by Cassirer. If it is appropriate to speak of an "evasion" in the book, it is probably here, in what appears to be the near-total excision of *politics* from an account of the Enlightenment that insists on placing a conception of conscious *agency* at its core.

A full explanation of this anomaly would point us to a larger pattern of omission and occlusion in Cassirer's thought. In a thinker renowned for the encyclopedic breadth of his vision, such gaps as there are come to have, in a sense, a "symptomatic" look to them. There is a very striking contrast, for example, between Hermann Cohen's passionate, life-long engagement with *both* the intellectual traditions of socialism and those of modern Jewish philosophy, and his star pupil's almost complete silence about them. It is unlikely to be accidental that psychoanalysis, too, failed to attract any attention from Cassirer.[31] At all events, the explanations for *both* of the features of *The Philosophy of the Enlightenment* highlighted here—its paradoxical treatment of Kant, simultaneously "in" and "beyond" the Enlightenment, and its apparent repression of the "politics" of the movement—are no doubt to be traced to the same source. At the end of the day, what is most striking about Cassirer's study in its proper historical context, surprisingly enough, is its quality as a *political* intervention of a unique kind. In some ways, Cassirer's liberalism can be seen to have conformed recognizably to a national type, reflecting a wider German concern with the free expression of individual personality, above all in the various domains of culture. At the same time, however, Cassirer's consistent cosmopolitanism—the almost complete lack of any nationalist tincture in this liberalism—marks him out as very unusual indeed in the German context. As we have seen, his reaction to the catastrophe of the Great War was to seek relief in a celebratory recovery of the cultural past of the nation; yet his constant focus throughout *Freiheit und Form* was on those moments when German thought converged with wider European streams—the Reformation, the Enlightenment, and the rights-based ethical liberalism of the present. What seems clear is that he now repeated the gesture in *The Philosophy of the Enlightenment*, on a grander scale, in the face of a still more dire emergency. For by the early thirties, the strain of European liberalism to which Cassirer adhered had reached the very nadir of its historical fortunes. Before its political thought and practice could even begin to stage a recovery from the disaster of the Great War, the inflation of the twenties and then the Depression itself threw its economic institutions and doctrines into utter disarray. Nowhere was the crisis of liberal civilization felt more acutely than in Germany, where the decline of Weimar constitutionalism into Nazi dictatorship proved to be the deepest sounding of its depths.

Cassirer's response to this crisis—obviously personal as well as national—was to seek consolation and inspiration alike in a vivid portrait of European civilization at the moment of its maximum intellectual and cultural unity, in the epoch when the lacerations of early-modern religious conflict first lay securely behind it, and the divisions of later nationalist contention were still well in its future. Cassirer's recovery of the Enlightenment was all the more compelling in that the unity he ascribed to it was neither simple nor facile. The cosmopolitanism he described by no means canceled the differences between national intellectual traditions, which continued to feature prominently in his text. The distinction between Anglo-French *Zivilisation* and German *Kultur*, a token not only of German conservatism but of a good deal of liberal thought as well, was not simply set aside by Cassirer, but surpassed, in something closer to a properly hard-won *Aufhebung*. There was naturally a price to be paid for the resulting "totalization" of the Enlightenment, which, in Cassirer's rendering, became a moment in the career of modern *philosophy* above all. The result, on the one hand, was to make it necessary to set Kant, and German Idealism as a whole, just beyond the precincts of the Enlightenment itself, in order to maintain the full autonomy of the latter.

Whatever else they achieved, Cassirer's efforts in this regard bear the marks of an almost superhuman rhetorical *tact* under the circumstances. On the other hand, the story of the "dramatic action" of the *philosophy* of the Enlightenment also required that a good deal of its actual *politics*, reformist or revolutionary, be set aside as well. In point of fact, it is not quite accurate to speak of a simple repression of a political moment in the text. Instead, what seems to have occurred was a displacement from the political to the *aesthetic* realm—as the other, less divisive domain in which the idea of reason as the active *maker* of the world could be brought to earth. The aesthetic theories of Baumgarten and Kant, the artistic achievements of Lessing and Goethe, were presented, in a sense, as promissory notes for a future politics. If the authority for this move can be traced back to Kant himself, there were contemporary parallels as well. In a famous essay on Walter Benjamin, Fredric Jameson once reminded readers that "nostalgia as a political motivation"—"a nostalgia conscious of itself, a lucid and remorseless dissatisfaction with the present on the grounds of some remembered plenitude"—was not the privilege of Fascism alone, but had its counterparts on the Left.[32] In Cassirer's *Philosophy of the Enlightenment*, we seem to be presented with a similarly "lucid nostalgia" of the Center, from the same epoch—as if encouraging European liberalism, at its darkest hour, to begin to reconstruct its identity by means of a meditation on its happy youth.

Conclusions: Abstraction and Reflection

It would be wrong to suggest that the character of *The Philosophy of the Enlightenment* as a political statement—as one of the masterpieces of Weimar liberalism, a fitting German counterpart to, say, Ruggiero's *Storia del Liberalismo Europeo*—has somehow been overlooked until now. Twenty years after its initial publication, the book could still provoke surprisingly strong responses. One stands out in its harshness, coming from what may be a surprising source. Writing in the *Spectator* in the year after the book's first appearance in English, Alfred Cobban declared without further ado that Cassirer's portrait of the Enlightenment was "profoundly wrong." What the author had produced, in a misguided effort to demonstrate the fundamental unity of European thought, was essentially only a "German history." Among the outrages in *The Philosophy of the Enlightenment* was the fact that the catalytic role that rightfully belonged to Locke had been usurped by Leibniz; and, at the other end of the century, that utilitarianism had disappeared entirely, while the thought of Herder and Kant was presented as the culmination of the Enlightenment. The effect of Cassirer's narrative—obviously unintended by the author, a "good European"—was to add "the Enlightenment to the genealogical tree of the Nazi movement." The English and French reader, Cobban concluded, could be forgiven for declining to see "the founders of German idealism and nationalism" as having contributed very much to the "process of man's progressive self-liberation."[33]

Cassirer had plainly touched a nerve—there is perhaps something refreshing about recalling so strong a reaction to the book, given the combination of veneration and condescension with which *The Philosophy of the Enlightenment* tends to be viewed today. Issues of national pride aside, the example of *Dialectic of Enlightenment* from the Left is there to suggest that Cobban was not entirely wrong to worry, from the Right, about suggestions of a filiation linking the European Enlightenment to European Fascism. At the same time, it also seems clear that what were vices for Cobban were precisely the virtues that recommended *The Philosophy of the Enlightenment* to its post-War audience, especially in the United States. For this was the moment when the brand of liberalism for which Cassirer stood had begun to make its astonishing recovery from the trough of the inter-war years, and was showing the first fruits of this resurgence under American sponsorship. In the epoch of the Schuman Plan and the Treaty of Rome, what could be more appropriate than a portrait of the Enlightenment as, in effect, the joint production of French and German thinkers? In fact, it might be thought that the combination of political will and economic design that lay behind the emergent institutions of the European Community was a perfect illustration of the new kind of historical agency—philosophic reason in action, remaking the world—whose origins Cassirer located in the Enlightenment. Above all, the intellectual reconstruction of liberalism after the War required the careful rehabilitation of the main traditions of German thought and culture. In this regard, one suspects that the lesson of *The*

Philosophy of the Enlightenment for most of its readers in this period, especially those in America, was precisely the opposite of that feared by Cobban—the message that Kant, Lessing, Herder, and Goethe were all "good Europeans" as well, active contributors to the collective, cosmopolitan effort of the Enlightenment.

At the same time, there is an obvious limit to any attempt to explain the reception of Cassirer's book in primarily political terms. In order to arrive at a fuller estimation of the achievements and qualities that have made *The Philosophy of the Enlightenment* an enduring classic, we need to turn to a review whose lavish praise is at least as surprising as Cobban's brusque dismissal. A French translation of *The Philosophy of the Enlightenment* was delayed until 1966, when it was brought out as the inaugural volume in Fayard's *Histoire sans frontières* series, edited by François Furet and Denis Richet. The first major comment came from Michel Foucault, fresh from completing *Les mots et les choses*, writing in the *Quinzaine littéraire* during its first year.[34] What made for the "actuality" of Cassirer's masterpiece, thirty years after its first publication, wrote Foucault, was that we are *all* in some sense "neo-Kantians," living with "the impossibility, for Western thought, of overcoming the gash [*coupure*] opened up by Kant." The supreme merit of *The Philosophy of the Enlightenment* was that it reposed the essential question: "what are the fatalities of reflection and knowledge that made Kant possible and necessitated the constitution of modern thought?" Kant had sought to establish the conditions of possibility of scientific knowledge. In a mimetic gesture that added a profoundly important reflexive dimension, Cassirer set out to establish the conditions of possibility for Kantianism itself, the "enigma" that for two centuries has rendered Western thought "blind to its modernity." For there is nothing less at stake here, Foucault went on, than the identity and autonomy of modernity itself. Two great currents of nostalgic identification have flowed from the birth of the modern epoch at the end of the eighteenth century: a "Hellenism," extending from Hölderlin to Heidegger, and an attachment to the Enlightenment, descending from Marx to Lévi-Strauss. "To be Greek or Enlightened, on the side of tragedy or the Encyclopedia, that of poetry or the well-made language, that of the morning of Being or the noon of Representation, such is the dilemma from which modern thought . . . has yet to escape." Cassirer himself came down on the side of the Enlightenment. But the lesson of his book lay not so much in his political decision, as in the methodological model that accompanied it. For Cassirer's return to the eighteenth century proceeded by means of a "foundational abstraction" that, on the one hand, set aside the appeals to "individual motivation" and "biographical accident" that made for the substance of psychological explanation, and, on the other, deferred consideration of social and economic determinations. The result was to uncover, for the first time, an "autonomous world of discursive thought," whose ordering principles and laws of motion could be grasped in their own terms. What Cassirer had left behind, in his flight from the Nazis, was a manifesto for a new kind of history of thought, still to be accomplished.

There is an attractive irony in the fact that Foucault could hail *The Philosophy of Enlightenment* for showing the way to a new intellectual history, at precisely the moment that spokesmen for the new "social history" of the Enlightenment—whose later practitioners have often looked to Foucault himself for inspiration—were first declaring its model obsolete. In retrospect, it is not at all difficult to see the parallels between Cassirer's "phenomenology" and Foucault's "archeology" of the human sciences, indeed between the project of *The Philosophy of Symbolic Forms* and the whole enterprise of Foucault's thought, at least down to *The Archeology of Knowledge*—convergences all the more striking, given the embattled "humanism" of the one and the strident "antihumanism" of the other. In any case, Foucault was certainly right about one aspect of the lasting appeal of *The Philosophy of the Enlightenment*. We have seen that Cassirer set out to overturn the Romantic verdict on the Enlightenment's "shallowness." His success in establishing its philosophic depth, once and for all, depended on just the manner of "foundational abstraction" described by Foucault—his bracketing of explanations of either a psychological or social kind, in order to focus on a description of the "dramatic action" of the *thought* of the Enlightenment. The result was what remains to this day the most vivid and finely wrought of all general surveys of eighteenth-century philosophy, a major work of historical *literature* as well as scholarship. In fact, Cassirer achieved more than just effective description in *The Philosophy of the Enlightenment*. His roots in the dialectical tradition of classical Idealism made it possible to give the book a narrative thrust that is lacking in Foucault's own handling of "discursive thought," in which, notoriously, narrative explanation of ideas, or their dynamic over time, tends to give way to static description and categorization. This, in turn, probably explains why it has never proven particularly difficult for later historians to restore one "missing" dimension or another to Cassirer's account of the Enlightenment, without dramatically altering its substance. Cassirer's own essay on Rousseau shows how easily the move to biographical evidence and explanation could be made; the different "social histories" of Gay and Darnton reveal something of the same for the restoration of Cassirer's "high Enlightenment" texts to their social and economic context.

But what of the other dimension of *The Philosophy of the Enlightenment* highlighted by Foucault—not its method, but its *parti pris*? It is evident that Foucault respected Cassirer's quiet defense of the Enlightenment, even if the choice was not quite his own. In specifying the two great alternatives facing the modern age—the camps, roughly, of Enlightened rationalism and Romantic reaction—Foucault suggested in an aside that the "monstrosity" of Nietzsche was perhaps to belong to both at the same time; a sentence later, he asserted that if the antithesis still dominated modern thought, it was nevertheless possible to sense it "shaking beneath our feet." The hope of discovering a third path, of eluding a choice between, as it were, Marx and Heidegger, of course animated Foucault for much of his intellectual career. Unlike many of his postmodern successors, however, it is not clear that Foucault was ever satisfied that he found such a path—nor, like other thinkers who followed, was he ever tempted by a retreat to Heidegger. If anything, the itinerary of his later career, with its compulsive returns to the terrain of Kant, suggests that Foucault's final position was rather closer to that of Cassirer than might be expected. As for *The Philosophy of the Enlightenment*, if it is indeed the most compelling of all twentieth-century "defenses" of the Enlightenment, it is surely not by way of any straightforward *identification* with its object of study—in the style, say, of Gay's *The Enlightenment: An Interpretation*. At the outset, Cassirer warned his readers that he intended neither to celebrate nor to criticize the Enlightenment; his motto was instead borrowed from Spinoza—"*non ridere, non lugere, neque detestare, sed intelligere"* ("Smile not, lament not, nor condemn, but understand"). Indeed, much of the power of Cassirer's text derives precisely from its serene, even Olympian "objectivity"—from the sense that one is gazing on the Enlightenment from the "outside," affording a view of it as a whole, as a *totality*, together with a fleeting glimpse of its place within an even larger narrative of struggle and emancipation.

In the end, we are left with Cassirer's own image for grasping our relationship to the eighteenth century from the vantage-point of the twentieth—the notion of the Enlightenment as holding up a "bright clear mirror" to the present. The metaphor is more studied and ambiguous than might appear at first glance. Elsewhere in Cassirer's writing, reflection of this kind could take on a sinister aspect. In the first chapter of *The Myth of the State* he invoked the scene in the "Witch's Kitchen" from the first part of *Faust*, in which Faust, in pursuit of eternal youth, falls prey to a beautiful phantom glimpsed in an enchanted glass—the shadow of his own imagination, scoffs Mephistopheles.[35] The menace in question here was the Romantic retreat to mythical thought, in whose mirror could first be glimpsed the furies later set free by nationalism and fascism. Other thinkers have of course seen a return of repressed elements of mythical thought in the Enlightenment itself, "intertwined" with its rationalism. For his part, Cassirer allowed that a gaze in the mirror of the Enlightenment was likely to be disconcerting: "Much that seems to us today the result of 'progress' will be sure to lose its luster when seen in this mirror; and much that we boast of will look strange and distorted in this perspective." Nevertheless, he went on, "we should be guilty of hasty judgment and dangerous self-deception if we were simply to ascribe these distortions to opaque spots in the mirror, rather than to look elsewhere for their source. The slogan: *Sapere aude*, which Kant called the 'motto of the Enlightenment,' also holds for our own historical relation to that period."[36] More than sixty years later, it is not clear that the enchanted glass of the Enlightenment, with its clear reflections, opacities, and "distortions," has exhausted all of its lessons for us. For those still gazing into this mirror, friends and foes of philosophical modernism alike, *The Philosophy of the Enlightenment* remains an incomparable guide.

MICHAEL MERANZE

Critique and Government: Michel Foucault and the Question 'What Is Enlightenment?'

The figure of Michel Foucault looms large for any contemporary discussion of the legacies of the Enlightenment. As Foucault himself made clear, the question of the Enlightenment and its legacies is an ongoing problem. But not the problem one might expect. Joining Foucault to the question "What's Left of Enlightenment?" does not link chastened critic with triumphant object. Nor does it set exultant "post-modern" against downcast "modern." Instead, the link between Foucault and Enlightenment was a developing question. And that question is concerned, in turn, with the issue of "problematization" and its relationship to enlightenment itself.

During the late 1970s and early 80s, Foucault renewed his reflection on Enlightenment. This reflection focused on two separate objects: on one hand, Immanuel Kant's "What Is Enlightenment?" along with Part II of "Conflict of the Faculties"; on the other, Foucault's own redesigned study of the construction of sexual ethics.[1] For Foucault, to work on enlightenment and on the Enlightenment meant analyzing the conditions of freedom in the contemporary setting and exploring in practical ways the possibilities of transforming the structures and practices of the present. As he articulated it himself, these reflections, in their assumptions and their telos, were crucially concerned with the unstable relationship between "liberty," "maturity," and "capacity." They entailed both a practical ascesis on the self and a historically grounded political project in the world. Foucault's engagement with the Enlightenment was, therefore, simultaneously ethical and political.

I

Foucault maintained that Kant had introduced a new question for thought—that of the present—while leaving an unresolved problem for the future: What is Enlightenment? Kant, Foucault argued, defined enlightenment "in an almost entirely negative way" as "an 'exit,' 'a way out.'" Kant was, again in Foucault's words, "looking for a difference: What difference does today introduce with respect to yesterday?"[2] That difference for Kant was "man's release from his self-incurred tutelage."[3] According to Foucault, Enlightenment for Kant meant transforming your relationship to authority and autonomy. We are still immature when we allow others to guide our reason not from necessity, but from laziness or fear. Enlightenment was an escape, a process through which humanity could achieve its maturity—with maturity defined as the free and continuing use, and obligation, of public reason.

Yet, as Foucault noted, Kant's treatment of Enlightenment was not without its ambiguities. If "Have courage to use your own reason!" was the "motto" of the Enlightenment, this personal demand was only possible within the context of a collective process.[4] The Enlightenment was a moment in the history of European thought. But it was also a responsibility that had to be assumed by individuals—and that could only be actualized through the efforts of individuals. As Foucault put it, Kant's Enlightenment "must be considered both as a process in which men participate collectively and as an act of courage to be accomplished personally."[5] Kant, Foucault suggested, sought to delineate this relationship between collective and individual—or between the Enlightenment and enlightenment.

Kant sought to define the parameters of Enlightenment by distinguishing between the public and private uses of reason. The public use of reason, he argued, must be free, it must be strictly separated from the private use of reason, and private reason must not be free.[6] Kant's wager, at least in 1784, was that an enlightened despotism could secure these conditions and that Enlightenment and humanity would result. According to Kant, this situation displayed:

> a strange and unexpected trend in human affairs in which almost everything, looked at in the large, is paradoxical. A greater degree of civil free-

dom appears advantageous to the freedom of mind of the people, and yet it places inescapable limitations upon it; a lower degree of civil freedom, on the contrary, provides the mind with room for each man to extend himself to his full capacity. As nature has uncovered from under this hard shell the seed for which she most tenderly cares—the propensity and vocation to free thinking—this gradually works back upon the character of the people, who thereby gradually become capable of managing freedom; finally, it affects the principles of government, which finds it to its advantage to treat men, who are now more than machines, in accordance with their dignity.[7]

Here we can locate the theoretical consciousness of what Habermas would later characterize, and others would valorize, as the public sphere. Still, I do not think that many of us would willingly take up Kant's wager on his terms.

But if Kant's reflections pointed to the notion, as he put it, "Argue as much as you will, and about what you will, only obey!" (a familiar enough idea in the university these days), they could, as Foucault took them up, point elsewhere.[8] Kant's efforts to recuperate the constraining capacity of authority in the face of unbridled reason, it is true, suggested the socio-political equivalent of his larger critiques. But Kant's very engagement with his moment, his effort to reflect from inside on the historical movement of thought in his time, offered a glimpse into what Foucault reconceived as a "permanent critique of our historical era."[9]

Kant's "What Is Enlightenment?" thereby named not only the general character of possibilities of thought, but also the specific history in which thinking occurred—while aiming to bring the present to some consciousness of itself. The Kantian definition of enlightenment laid down a continual task and made a continuing demand: that critical thought not only reflect upon but engage with its historical moment. "All this," Foucault insisted, "philosophy as the problematization of a present, and as the questioning by the philosopher of this present to which he belongs and in relation to which he has to situate himself—might well be said to characterize philosophy as the discourse of modernity on modernity."[10] What Kant, and the Enlightenment more generally, bequeathed to thought—and, interestingly, at the same time as the modern academic discipline of philosophy was established—was a notion of the philosophical life as critical thinking on the present. The "critical ontology of ourselves" thus became both philosophical and historical.[11] Philosophy in this sense cut across the disciplines to become a style of thought that took the form of an ongoing task—not merely to interpret the world, but to change it.

The context of this ongoing critique, Foucault argued, lies in the emergence of a form of political rationality that he labeled "governmentality." As Foucault saw it, a veritable explosion of writing and argument over how to govern (oneself, one's family, one's community, a state) occurred in fifteenth- and sixteenth-century Europe, a discourse that was elaborated in the two centuries preceding Kant. The singularity of this rationality lies in its effort to produce a political knowledge that would guide states in an ongoing and exhaustive labor of conducting their "populations" both in individual and collective endeavors. This rationality of "governmentality"—reduced in different ways to practices—meant that the project of governing individuals through their entire lives was freed from its roots in monastic life and extended to the population at large. The spread of the problematic of "governmentality" displaced the nature of political reason and the targets of political power and created a modern political system that combined structures of sovereignty, of discipline, and of government (in the broadest possible sense).

But, and this was an essential point for Foucault, the elaboration of the question "how to govern?" inextricably combined with a second question: "How not to be governed?" Or as Foucault put it:

> Now this governmentalization, which seems to me characteristic enough of these societies of the European West in the sixteenth century, cannot be dissociated from the question "How not to be governed?" I do not mean by this that governmentalization would be opposed, in a kind of inverted contrary affirmation, to "We do not want to be governed, and we do not want to be governed *at all*." What I mean is that in the great anxiety surrounding the way to govern and in the inquiries into modes of governing, one detects a perpetual question, which would be: "How not to be governed *like that*, by that, in the name of these principles, in view of such objectives and by the means of such methods, not like that, not for that, not by them?"[12]

Foucault argued that this questioning of governmentality, this desire not to be governed "like that," is another name for the critical attitude and the motivation for critique. The critical attitude emerged within the matrix of governmentality itself—it took the form of ongoing essays in the exercise of liberty. Kant's answer to the question "What is Enlightenment?," then, takes up its place in the history of governmentality. By demanding the free exercise of public reason while offering to submit to enlightened despotism, and, by taking up the question of autonomy and authority within the context of the limits of reason, Kant's essay marked the inscription of the problem governmentality/critique within the Enlightenment itself. And in its strained relationship to modern political rationality, Kant's intervention signaled a task that continues to haunt the "present."

II

Yet, Foucault contended that we can only take up Kant's challenge with a difference that marks our present. As Foucault put it, "if the Kantian question was that of knowing [*savoir*] what limits knowledge [*connaissance*] must renounce exceeding, it seems to me that the critical question today has to be turned back into a positive one: In what is given to us as universal, necessary, obligatory, what place is occupied by whatever is singular, contingent, and the product of arbitrary constraints? The point, in brief, is to transform the critique conducted in the form of a necessary limitation into a practical critique that takes the form of a possible crossing-over [*franchissement*]."[13] It is, to put it another way, to turn the self-evident into a problem.

This transformation of the self-evident into a problem is what Foucault called the "attitude of modernity." Foucault argued that we break with notions of modernity as moment or process and see it instead as an ethical position—as a way of responding to the challenge Kant laid down in "What Is Enlightenment?" Modernity, he insisted, was less than a condition but more than a project. It was a form of thinking and acting upon both the present and upon the self.

Foucault elaborated his notion of the attitude of modernity through the example of Baudelaire. In his discussion of Baudelaire and the attitude of modernity, Foucault stressed three lessons—that the attitude of modernity involves a "heroic" relationship to the present (one that sought out the essential in the passing moment), an "ironic" relationship to the contemporary (one which seized that essential not to celebrate it but to transform it), and an ascetic relation-ship to the self (one which recognized that work needed not only to be done on the world "out there" but on oneself as well). This com-mitment to transformation—what Foucault oddly calls the ironic rela-tionship to the present—means that irony towards the present is not a movement away from but towards involvement. The ironist of mod-ernity, from Foucault's perspective, does not see everything as mean-ingless nor as a source of merely aesthetic pleasure (and here, he in-sists, the distinction between the modern and the flâneur must be drawn starkly) but as an arena of transformation and experimentation. But this involvement for Foucault, and here was perhaps the wager of his late work, proceeds to society through the self.

The question of the self, then, formed the backdrop of Foucault's late reflection on enlightenment. As is well known, in the late 1970s and early 1980s, Foucault dramatically recast his proposed history of sexuality. What had first been conceived as a study of the modern "experience" of sexuality became an examination—in the ancient world—of a sexual ethics that was not structured around the antin-omy of desire and law. This shift meant exploring both a new histori-cal period and new intellectual terrain as well—that of "techniques" or "arts" of the self. In this effort, Foucault believed that he had un-covered the historical limits of the hermeneutics of the self (and thereby crossed over the parameters of self we have inherited), while at the same time clarifying the ways in which those experiences pre-sented to us as "fundamental" (and here his allusions were fairly clear—to madness, to sexuality, to crime, to knowledge) were them-selves "problematized" in different historical forms. This combina-tion of crossing over and problematizing was precisely what was at stake in his reversal of the Kantian critique.

At the same time, the double movement of crossing over and problematization constituted what Foucault termed "thought." As Foucault put it, "Thought is not what inhabits a certain conduct and gives it its meaning; rather it is what allows one to step back from this way of acting or reacting, to present it to oneself as an object of thought and question it as to its meaning, its conditions, and its goals. Thought is freedom in relation to what one does, the motion by which one detaches oneself from it, establishes it as an object, and re-

flects on it as a problem."[14] Thought is what enables one to problematize what is given, it is the action of marking a difference between
what we are and what we might become.

But here, I think, it is necessary to note a certain ambiguity. As
Foucault makes clear in *The Use of Pleasure* and *The Care of the Self* as
well as numerous lectures and interviews, problematization—and
thereby the work of "thought"—can be found from the ancient world
forward (and not simply in the European world either). Indeed, his
studies of both classical and Christian sexual ethics are designed to reveal the different systems of problematization that they put into play.
Yet if that is the case, then what difference does the Enlightenment
make? Is it simply one moment in a repetitive history of the systems
of thought? Does its significance lie in its merely being the latest
structure of problematization?

The answer to these questions was for Foucault, I think, "no." The
Enlightenment does not, of course, exhaust either thought or problematization. And as Foucault argued, recognition of the Enlightenment must avoid what he called the "blackmail of the Enlightenment." Yet as Foucault's reflections on Kant made clear, the Enlightenment made a decisive transformation in the nature of thought—by
introducing the permanent necessity of problematization itself. Or as
he put it, "the permanent reactivization of an attitude—that is, of a
philosophical ethos that could be described as a permanent critique of
our historical era."[15] It is this permanent necessity of problematization
that makes any sort of "return"—say to the Greeks—impossible, even
if, as it wasn't for Foucault, this return was seen as desirable. According to Foucault, the Enlightenment, which in this case functions as
shorthand for the threshold of modernity, dramatically and irrevoca-
bly marked a break.

Yet, if the Enlightenment remains a decisive event for our thinking, it must itself be subject to critique. That was the point of Foucault's reversal of the Kantian critique from one of necessary limitation to one of possible crossing over and of his studies of madness,
medicine, the human sciences, punishment, and sexuality. But it was
also the point of his late books on the self. For if in the first instance
the target of those books was Christianity, and in the second, psychoanalysis, alongside both lay the question of the Kantian moral law. If

Kant saw freedom in the voluntary acceptance of the inexorable necessity of abstract law, Foucault hoped to imagine a self that gave itself not laws, but rules, and that subjected itself to a personal ascesis, that is, to complex shaping and reshaping.

This critique of the Enlightenment, Foucault insisted, implied "a series of historical inquiries that are as precise as possible," inquiries directed not "retrospectively toward the 'essential kernel of rationality' that can be found in the Enlightenment, which would have to be preserved in any event" but rather "toward the 'contemporary limits of the necessary,' that is, toward what is not or is no longer indispensable for the constitution of ourselves as autonomous subjects."[16] These inquiries would focus on practical systems and would have to be related to practical transformations, efforts focused on relations to things, to others, and to the self. Foucault noted that the "great hope" of the eighteenth-century had been the "simultaneous and proportional growth of individuals with respect to one another"; but that "the relations between the growth of capabilities and the growth of autonomy are not as simple as the eighteenth century may have believed." At stake in the critique of the Enlightenment, he suggested, was the question "how can the growth of capabilities [capacités] be disconnected from the intensification of power relations?"[17] He acknowledged that pursuing these investigations did not mean we would achieve "maturity." But he thought that, in this way, we could take up again the Enlightenment challenge to "work on our limits, that is, a patient labor giving form to our impatience for liberty."[18]

III

But if this linkage of liberty, maturity, and crossing over was, quite literally, Foucault's last word on the subject, it need not be ours. For there is another issue here, another term hovering, as it were, at the margins of Foucault's "What Is Enlightenment?"—solidarity. The term appears in the essay in two different guises. As I indicated above, Foucault, in his reading of Kant, suggests that Enlightenment itself—as phenomenon and process—should be understood as an effort whose singularity is possible only when it occurs in the plural. In this sense, some form of solidarity appears as part of the task of Enlightenment, a process which is both individual responsibility and collective work.

But solidarity also appears negatively, as it were, as an absence that foreshadows death. Early in his essay, almost in passing, Foucault notes that Moses Mendelssohn had replied to the question "What is Enlightenment?" two months before Kant, but that Kant had not seen this reply. Kant himself noted in his own contribution his regret over this fact. As Foucault noted, these twin attempts to account for Enlightenment—one Christian, one Jewish—announced a "common destiny" in Germany. He concluded, in terms that need no explanation, that "we now know to what drama that was to lead."[19] What should we make of this reference to the missed possibilities of solidarity? This allusion is not, I think, some intimation that the Enlightenment led to the Holocaust, nor a suggestion that the Holocaust was inherent in the structure of modern German culture. Instead, it is an acknowledgment of the fragility of solidarities and a call to be attentive to the occasions of their missed opportunities.

It is in line with such attentiveness that I am suggesting that we, today, foreground the issue of solidarity more than Foucault did. It is perhaps not surprising that Foucault did not—given the freighted connotations of the term solidarity that arose from the Durkheimian tradition, Foucault's own work on the dangers of bureaucratic sociality, and his well-documented disappointment in what he saw as the failure of the Mitterrand government to develop a "logic of the left" in the way it related to its citizens. Indeed, it is more than likely that Foucault considered the language of solidarity as a block to conceiving the politics that he was actively involved with during the late 70s and early 80s—vis-à-vis Poland and the question of immigrants, civil rights and the duties of an international citizenship, as well as his reflections on the possibilities of new forms of alliance and affinity.

But, now, at the turn of the century, things look different. We live in a situation where the little social solidarity built into our political system is being torn apart. This process is visible all around us: in the closing of health facilities, the widespread stigmatization of some recipients of governmental assistance, the transfer of fiscal resources from schools to prisons, long-term attacks on labor unions and labor rights, the contraction of social commitments to shared basic rights,

the tightening of social "borders." These are international developments, to be sure, but they have been symbolized in the United
States quite powerfully by California's passage of Propositions 187 and
209.

The challenges posed by this process of retrenchment are linked to
more fundamental properties of the American situation. In his College de France course on "The Birth of Biopolitics," Foucault sought
to "analyze 'liberalism' not as a theory or an ideology—and even less,
certainly, as a way for 'society' to 'represent itself...'—but rather, as a
practice, which is to say, as a 'way of doing things' oriented toward
objectives and regulating itself by means of a sustained reflection.
Liberalism is to be analyzed, then, as a principle and a method of rationalizing the exercise of government, a rationalization that obeys—
and this is its specificity—the internal rule of maximum economy."[20]
Yet even recognizing that Foucault's notion of government was
broader than simply the State, to separate liberalism as a critique of
political rationality from liberalism as ideology or as a form of society
is, at least in the United States, to miss its actual social functioning.
Alongside the structures of the economy, the dominant political id-
iom in the United States has been what Isaiah Berlin termed "negative liberty" which has functioned mostly to throw the individual
back on him- or herself. Given that the classical liberal critique of political power operated by presupposing the necessary separation of the
political from the economic or, in practical terms, the subordination
of society to the market, the result, in social terms, has been all too
predictable. Solidarity has been the language primarily of opposi-
tional and working-class movements—and defeated ones at that. To
put it simply, it is hard, in the America of the early twenty-first century, to be as sanguine about neo-liberalism as Foucault seemed to be
in the France of the early 1980s. Even so, solidarity is a language that
should not be conceded.

This difference in our historical situation points to two final issues.
The first is that reflection on the Enlightenment in the United States
is political in a very direct way. Questions of the Enlightenment are
tied to questions of the American Revolution and the United States'
Constitution—which appear to many as the Enlightenment in Action. When we take up the Revolution and Enlightenment today, we

take up the highly contentious issues of, on the one hand, who has benefited from those events and their legacies, and on the other, the place of religion in the national polity. These questions, moreover, are not imposed from without on the Revolution but emerge from its very heart. It is not meaningless that Tom Paine's three great works of the 1790s were *Rights of Man*, *The Age of Reason*, and *Agrarian Justice*—addressing politics, religion, and society. Paine was, in his way, posing the question "how not to be governed?" Nor is it meaningless that Paine was perhaps the most controversial of the American Revolutionaries. The questions that we pose to the Enlightenment, and that the Enlightenment poses itself, reflect back the American present in highly charged ways.

Nevertheless, I must acknowledge a concern that has been haunting this essay. For who would not be for solidarity, and what difference *does* it make to discuss the Enlightenment in the here and now? Perhaps in the end I am merely a member of the Kantian public sphere arguing as much as I like but eventually obeying in practice the limits, the academic limits, that I might wish to cross over. To these worries and these questions I have little answer. Except that perhaps the last lesson we can learn from Foucault's meditation upon the question "What is Enlightenment?" is that any reflection on the Enlightenment must question its own investment in the Enlightenment and the meaningfulness of its own assumptions and values. Any reflection on liberty and solidarity in relation to maturity would therefore need to problematize these terms in taking them up, to think of them as what Foucault would have called "experiences." For both liberty and solidarity have been thought and practiced in different ways at different points of time and to very different purposes. There are, in other words, liberties and solidarities—liberties and solidarities that must be examined in the historical concreteness of their specific "problematizations." Such reflection may be a new starting point for "thought."

Still, in the end, it is unclear what difference asking these questions will make. But to raise *that* question is, perhaps, merely another way, and in the spirit of Michel Foucault, to ask again the question: "What is Enlightenment?"

A POSTMODERN ENLIGHTENMENT?

LORRAINE DASTON

Enlightenment Fears, Fears of Enlightenment

Introduction

"*Sapere aude*! Have the courage to use your own understanding! is thus the motto of enlightenment."[1] The will to know, *sapere*, has long been a battle cry of enlightenment and the Enlightenment. But why courage? Kant was not being idiosyncratic when he claimed that Enlightenment was a victory over cowardice, over fear. Of all the shadows that menaced the Enlightenment in the eyes of its vanguard, fear cast the darkest and longest. If the *philosophes* attacked ignorance and superstition as root evils, it was because both aroused fear. The Earl of Shaftesbury linked superstition to a pathologically fearful temperament, which reads "Fate, Destiny, or the Anger of Heaven" into every "unusual Sight or Hearing"[2]; the Chevalier de Jaucourt, writing in the *Encyclopédie*, defined superstition as the terror-struck religion that "fears the benevolent Deity, and regards his paternal empire as tyrannical."[3] Even the aesthetic of the sublime, which admired nature as fearful, pointedly excluded the emotion of fear in the beholder.[4]

It was not only that fear paralyzed reason — other passions were just as crippling intellectually. Fear, moreover, compromised autonomy; it was a slavish passion that sunk its victims into that self-imposed tutelage, *Unmündigkeit*, that Kant thought inimical to enlightenment. The excesses of religious enthusiasm, the diseases of the imagination, the despotism of priests and monarchs — all of these spawned and fed upon fear. To be afraid was at once a cognitive and moral predicament: it was to cede both one's reason and one's responsibility to another, to lapse voluntarily into a state of childish (or womanish) minority. Joseph de Maistre took the exact measure of his enlightened enemy when he insisted that fear was the necessary and legitimate principle of all political and religious authority, to be enforced by the executioner who is at once "the horror and the bond of human association."[5] If there was one doctrine shared by figures as otherwise opposed to one another as Montesquieu and Condorcet, as Voltaire and Rousseau, as Hume and Kant, it was that the first and most decisive step toward Enlightenment and away from *Unmündigkeit* was to shake off fear.

Yet ironically, the Enlightenment had its own characteristic fears, besides the fear of fear itself. Still more ironically, the Enlightenment has itself become an object of fear among some latter-day *philosophes*. I want to explore what the Enlightenment was afraid of, and to contrast those fears to what we currently fear about the Enlightenment. For want of time and learning, I shall restrict my inquiry to fears relating to the natural sciences—their methods, their claims, and their authority. More specifically, I wish to focus on two fears which are mirror-image twins of one another: the Enlightenment fear of the fragility of scientific fact, and our contemporary fear of the tyranny of scientific fact. Why did Enlightenment savants fear that facts might be suffocated by the imagination, and why do we fear that the imagination might be suffocated by facts? These obverse-reverse fears about facticity will, I hope, illuminate the grander Enlightenment and post-Enlightenment theme of the relationship between the nature of truth and the truths of nature. What kind of culture believes that truths about nature are the best (or even only) kind of truth? How and why does the nature of truth collapse into truths about nature?

Fragile Facts

Experience we have always had with us, but facts as a way of parsing experience in natural history and natural philosophy are of seventeenth-century coinage. Aristotelian experience had been woven of smooth-textured universals about "what happens always or most of the time"; early modern facts were historical particulars about an observation or experiment performed at a specific time and place by named persons.[6] What made the new-style facts granular was not only their specificity but also their alleged detachment from inference and conjecture.[7] Ideally, at least, "matters of fact" were nuggets of pure experience, strictly segregated from any interpretation or hypothesis that might enlist them as evidence.[8] Some seventeenth-century philosophers were as skeptical as their twentieth-century successors about the bare existence of what we now redundantly call theory-free facts. Descartes, for example, trusted only experiments performed under his own supervision, because those reported by others had made the results "conform to their principles."[9] Even the most vigorous promoters of "matters of fact" acknowledged that these nuggets of pure experience were hard-won. Francis Bacon thought only the strict discipline of method could counteract the inborn tendency of the human understanding to suffuse observation with theory.[10] The 1699 *Histoire* of the Paris Académie Royale des Sciences confessed that the "detached pieces" of knowledge the academicians offered in lieu of coherent theories or systems had been wrenched apart by a "kind of violence."[11] Chiseling out "matters of fact" from the matrix of experience and conjecture in which human perception and understanding automatically lodged them was hard work.

But it was the hard work of smelting and purifying, not that of building and constructing. One of the most striking features of the new-style scientific facts of the seventeenth century is how swiftly and radically they broke with the etymology that connected them to words like "factory" and other sites of doing and making. In Latin and all the major European vernaculars the word "fact" and its cognates derives from the verb "to do" or "to make," and originally referred to a deed or action, especially one remarkable for either valor or malevolence: *facere/factum, faire/fait, fare/fatto, tun/Tatsache*.[12] English still bears traces of this earlier usage in words like "feat" and, especially, in legal phrases like "after the fact." When the word "fact" acquired something like its familiar sense as "a particular truth known by actual observation or authentic testimony, as opposed to what is merely inferred, or to a conjecture or fiction" in the early seventeenth century,[13] it snapped the philological bonds that tied it to words like "factitious" and "manufacture." Conversely, by the mid-eighteenth century, once neutral words like "fabricate" (originally, to form or construct anything requiring skill) or "fabulist" (teller of legends or fables) had acquired an evil odor of forgery and deception in addition to their root senses of construction. For most Enlightenment thinkers, facts *par excellence* were those given by nature, not made by human art. "Facts" and "artifacts" had become antonyms, in defiance of their common etymology.

A full-dress history of facts, both word and thing, would take us far afield from the Enlightenment fears I promised to excavate. I stray into this vast and largely uncharted territory only long enough to point out that facts *have* a history, and that Enlightenment science inherited a view of facts as both difficult to achieve and also diametrically opposed to all that is made or constructed. We are now in a position to understand why Aristotelian and Enlightenment doctrines about how knowledge was gleaned from sensation could be so similar in content and so different in epistemological attitude. Like Aristotle, Locke, d'Alembert, Condillac, and a host of lesser lights of the Enlightenment asserted that sensations imprint the mind as a seal imprints soft wax, that the process of abstraction subtracts sensory features in order to arrive at universals (including those of mathematics), and that all knowledge ultimately derives from sensation or certain mental operations performed upon sensation. But whereas for Aristotle the acquisition of knowledge from sensation was at once automatic and largely unproblematic, Enlightenment sensationalists fretted endlessly about the sources of error in this process. In other words, Aristotelian sensationalism had been a theory of perception and a theory of knowledge; Enlightenment sensationalism was both of these and an epistemology to boot.

Since the early seventeenth century, epistemology has been a pessimistic undertaking, overwhelmingly more attentive to the hindrances rather than to the helps to acquiring knowledge. In keeping with the opposition of natural facts to human artifacts, the errors that most terrified Enlightenment savants in theory and practice were errors of construction, the fear of fashioning a world not reflected in sensation but made up by the imagination. Sensory infirmities worried Enlightenment epistemologists relatively little, prejudices and misconceptions instilled by bad education rather more so, the distortions wrought by strong passions still more, and the unruly creations of the imagination most of all. These latter seemed so pervasive as to make the simplest factual narrative a triumph of vigilance, discipline, and civilization in the minds of some Enlightenment writers. Bernard de Fontenelle thought the inclination to embellish the facts of the matter in retelling so irresistible that "one needs a particular kind of effort and attention in order to say only the exact truth." It took centuries before society advanced to the point of being able to "preserve in memory the facts just as they happened," before which time "the facts kept in [collective] memory were no more than visions and reveries."[14] Condillac suggested that prejudice, passion, and an inflamed imagination skewed the associations among sensations for the putatively sane as well as for the mad. Everyone was to some degree debilitated by "disordered" associations of ideas; mad minds simply formed such erratic associations, confusing "chimeras for realities," more frequently and about more important matters than sound minds did.[15]

The chronic inability to hold fast to fact, to keep the inventive imagination in check, was a midpoint along a continuum to madness, and hence a source of genuine fear, not just philosophical chiding. In Samuel Johnson's allegorical novel *The History of Rasselas Prince of Abissinia,* the philosopher Imlac meets a learned astronomer, "who has spent forty years in unwearied attention to the motions and appearances of the celestial bodies, and has drawn out his soul in endless calculations." Upon further acquaintance, the astronomer proves as virtuous as he is learned, "sublime without haughtiness, courteous without formality, and communicative without ostentation." Unfortunately the astronomer proves to be mad as a hatter. He reveals to Imlac his delusion that he alone can control the world's weather, and therefore the fate of the world's population, for good or ill. Imlac concludes that no one is safe from the imagination: "There is no man whose imagination does not sometimes predominate over his reason, who can regulate his attention wholly by his will, and whose ideas will come and go at his command. . . . All power of fancy over reason is a degree of insanity; . . . By degrees the reign of fancy is confirmed; she grows first imperious, and in time despotick. Then fictions begin to operate as realities, false opinions fasten upon the mind, and life passes in dreams of rapture or anguish."[16]

The predicament of Johnson's astronomer had intellectual, aesthetic, and moral reverberations in the Enlightenment. Intellectual, because by the mid-eighteenth century facts had become not only the alpha but also the omega of science, at least on some philosophical accounts. In his influential *Traité des systêmes* (1749) Condillac argued that explanations were nothing but facts so arranged in "the order in which they each successively explain the others."[17] It was, for example, a "fact" that "an electrical body attracted non-electrical bodies, and repelled those to which it had communicated electricity," and "these facts perfectly explained" a myriad of other electrical phenomena.[18] If facts were fragile achievements, if forty years of painstaking astronomical observation was not enough to safeguard them from deceitful imagination, then the edifice of science quaked from top to bottom. Naturalists also worried about the purity and stability of scientific facts. In his six-volume *Histoires des insectes* (1734–42) René Antoine de Réaumur warned that although "facts were assuredly the solid and true foundations of all parts of physics," including natural history, not all reported facts could be trusted. It would not suffice to suppress hearsay and dubious sources; even sincere, well-trained naturalists could inadvertently adulterate observations with imaginings: "it is not so common a quality as one might imagine, the ability to give one's attention to all the circumstances of a fact that merit observation."[19] An errant imagination was also Georges Cuvier's diagnosis of how Jean-Baptiste Lamarck had gone astray in natural history: for all his scientific gifts, Lamarck was one of those minds which "cannot prevent themselves from mixing true discoveries [*découverts véritables*] with fantastic conceptions . . . they laboriously construct vast edifices on imaginary bases, similar to the enchanted palaces in our old romances [*romans*] which disappear when the talisman upon which their existence depends is broken."[20] No observer was immune to the blandishments of the imagination; hence no natural fact could be trusted implicitly.

Although poetry and the arts were habitually classified as the realm of the imagination by the Encyclopedists and others, even aesthetic theorists feared the creative excesses of that faculty. The artist who loosened the reins of the imagination risked madness as surely as the astronomer who did so. Voltaire sharply distinguished the "active imagination" of the creative artist, poet, or mathematician from the "passive imagination" responsible for fanaticism, enthusiasm, and madness. The passive imagination acts imperiously; its victims are no longer "master" of themselves. The active imagination, in contrast, always partakes of judgment, and "raises all of its edifices with order."[21] Fiction was no servile imitation of nature, but its charge to create a more perfect, "new nature" still kept the imagination on a short leash. What was called the "marvelous," "monstrous," or "fantastic" imagination in the arts risked the "debauchery of genius."[22] Poets and artists were instead directed to obey the cardinal rule of verisimilitude: "A verisimilar fact is a fact possible in the circumstances where one lays the scene. Fictions without verisimilitude, and events prodigious to excess, disgust readers whose judgment is formed."[23] Enlightenment decorum demanded that even fictions be presented as possible facts. Even in the arts the imagination should not invent too inventively.

The reasons for both fear and restraint of the imagination were ultimately moral. To construct a genuinely "new nature" in either science or art was to escape not so much natural as social reality. Imlac attributes the astronomer's madness to solitude, more particularly to the solitude of the intellectual: "To indulge the power of fiction, and send imagination out upon the wing, is often the sport of those who delight too much in silent speculation. When we are alone we are not always busy; the labour of excogitation is too violent to last long; the ardour of enquiry will sometimes give way to idleness or satiety."[24] The melancholy of the scholar was by the eighteenth century an old topos, much written about by early modern physicians and philosophers from Ficino to Burton. But the Enlightenment diagnosis of the scholar's complaint took on new piquancy, for the traditional solitude of the scholar had become linked with a new ideology of autonomy on top of the old ideology of profundity. However wide the chasm between precept and practice—and the eagerness with which Enlightenment intellectuals sought and accepted patronage suggests that the chasm could be very wide indeed—the precept of independence from both the powers of the earth and even from the opinions of fellow *philosophes* was oft and vehemently expressed. This was an ideology of distance, both metaphorical and literal, from all human ties. Adam

Smith praised Newton's alleged indifference to the critical reception of the *Principia*[25]; d'Alembert reckoned foreigners and posterity to be the most impartial, because most remote, judges of merit, and counseled young savants to "Write as if you loved glory, but behave as if you were indifferent."[26] Detachment—from aristocratic favors, from the praise and criticism of one's contemporaries, even from friends and family—preoccupied Enlightenment intellectuals who yearned for independence and impartiality.

But the price of detachment was often solitude, and the price of solitude could be madness. Cut loose from the web of sociability, released from the reciprocal accommodations of sympathy and diversion that "busy" us in conversation, the imagination invents a counter-self and a counter-world. Lovelier and livelier than the real self and world, the fata morgana of the imagination draws the solitaire ever farther from reality, both social and natural. To be mad was no longer, as it was in the seventeenth century, to suffer an excess of black bile, or to be possessed by demons; it was to prefer a personal world of the imagination to the shared world of society. It was, in other words, the ultimate form of independence. Hence the terror of madness precisely among Enlightenment intellectuals who hallowed independence, who fled *Unmündigkeit*. Their incessant warnings against the seductions of the imagination indicate how loose they gauged the grip of reason and reality to be. *Pace* its Romantic critics, the doyens of the Enlightenment did not scorn the imagination; they paid it the respectful compliment of honest fear.

The most famous Enlightenment celebration of solitude, Rousseau's *Rêveries du promeneur solitaire*, fits this pattern precisely. Rousseau retreats from society because he despairs of impartial judgment by his peers and contemporaries. Only posterity, a "better generation" in the future, can reverse the condemnation of the present generation. He therefore lives as if dead to the world: "henceforward I am of no importance among men, and this is unavoidable since I no longer have any real relationship or true companionship with them."[27] From now on he will commune only with plants; he has packed up all his books save Linnaeus' *Systema naturae*. A thirst for independence has driven him to solitude, and solitude has driven him to the delights of "silent speculation." Adrift in a rowboat in the Lake of Brienne,

Rousseau meditates on the wellspring of happiness: "What is the source of happiness in such a state? Nothing external to us, nothing apart from ourselves and our own existence; as long as this state lasts we are self-sufficient like God."[28] This is not the only instance of lonely megalomania in the *Rêveries*. To Rousseau, solitude irresistibly suggests divinity, not only divine virtue but also divine power: "If I had remained free, unknown and isolated, as nature meant me to be, I should have done nothing but good, for my heart does not contain the seeds of any harmful passion. If I had been invisible and powerful like God, I should have been good and beneficent like him . . . . Perhaps in my light-hearted moments I should have had the childish impulse to work the occasional miracle, but being entirely disinterested and obeying only my own natural inclinations, I should have performed scores of merciful or equitable ones for every act of just severity."[29] In this mood of unbounded self-aggrandizement, Rousseau might well have taken over responsibility for world weather from Johnson's deranged astronomer.

It is noteworthy that both Rousseau and Johnson's astronomer devote many of their solitary hours to the careful study of nature, and that constant experience of the strict regularities of nature does not suffice to regulate their delusionary imaginations. Whatever the authority of nature as a justification for this or that social order in Enlightenment thought, its efficacy in enforcing social order was perceived as weak. This was simply a special case of the perceived weakness of facts, including natural facts, in the face of mighty imagination. Enlightenment savants never tired of repeating that theory or "system" must bow down before fact, but the very frequency with which they did so suggested more a chivalrous hope than solid conviction. Unlike T.H. Huxley a century later, Réaumur could not say that Goedart's theory about how insects of one species could sometimes generate insects of another species had been "killed by an ugly fact." Instead, Réaumur had to explain how Goedart could have misinterpreted observations and experiments conducted in good faith but under the sway of a "too strong attachment to a system which fascinated his eyes."[30] Imagination killed facts, not the other way around. Enlightenment facts were as fragile as they were epistemologically precious.

Tyrannical Facts

In the Fourth Walk of the *Rêveries* Rousseau launched a critique on the epistemological claims of facts to be the only kind of truth worthy of the name. In a veiled attack on Fontenelle and other de-bunkers of fables, Rousseau asserted that fables and parables may be factually false, but nonetheless convey weighty moral truths. Fictions may sometimes be "the disguise of truth," not its opposite. In matters where no one's interest is at stake, there is no virtue in "giving a faithful account in trivial conversations of exact times, places and names, without any embroidery or exaggeration." Only some-one who "praises or blames untruthfully is telling a lie . . . even if he is not lying about facts, he is betraying moral truth, which is infinitely superior to factual truth."[31] Facts are only trivially true; deep truths apply only to matters of justice.

This refusal to grant facts a monopoly on truth, which reverberated in the works of many nineteenth-century Romantics, did not imply that facts had grown tyrannical in the sense of Huxley's snarling, ugly fact. Rather, they were seen as presumptuous, as laying claim to a sig-nificance and dignity they did not actually possess. When Baudelaire reviled landscape paintings for their photographic naturalism,[32] when Dickens ridiculed Gradgrind's pedantic obsession with facts,[33] when Nietzsche rejected the aspirations of "scientific" history,[34] they were complaining that facts were inadequate, not inexorable—inadequate to create beauty in art, inadequate to instill virtue in character, inade-quate to give meaning to history. These critical voices were not so much cowed by facts as bored by them.

Our predicament differs from that of both the Enlightenment and its Romantic critics: we are tyrannized by facts. More specifically, we are tyrannized by natural facts. The pitched battles that have been waging for over a century between nature and nurture, most recently in the academic province known as Cultural Studies, testify to this tyranny. Insofar as this weary war has a logic from the side of nurture, it is to reclaim as much territory as possible from nature, to show that a purported natural fact is really a cultural convention, deviously "nat-uralized." A defrocked natural fact forfeits its global inevitability, though not its local validity. It may be a fact about our culture that (to take some topical American examples) that sexuality fashions identity, but not so in ancient Greece; it may be a fact about our culture that there are few women physicists, but not so in Portugal; it may be a fact in our culture that the market governs all, but not so in Amazonia. History and anthropology serve as vast repositories of counterexamples to what is taken for granted in the here-and-now, the implication being that whatever was somewhere, sometime otherwise cannot be natural, cannot be inevitable. Nature tyrannizes; culture, as the current phrase has it, negotiates.

There is much that is interestingly bizarre about the ontology which nature and nurture camps share, however divided they may be on all other issues. Nature is obdurate and enduring; nurture is plastic and mutable. (Both sides seem to have forgotten the solidity of Durkheimian social facts, so real you could stub your toe against them, and the creativity and contingency of biological evolution.) Cultures are by implication imagined piecemeal; otherwise it would make no sense to argue that an exotic practice or belief serve as a model—or at least as a liberating extension of possibility—in our own culture. I take it that very few admirers of an ancient sexual ethic of "souci de soi" wish to reestablish the whole culture of antiquity, kit and caboodle. Rather, they must assume that it is possible to excise surgically one cultural feature they find desirable and leave all the undesirable features (patriarchy, slavery, etc.) safely buried in books. To contemplate such surgery and transplantation is to imagine cultures as aggregates of odd parts rather than as coherent wholes. To make examples drawn from history and anthropology the basis for political action is to deny the integrity and specificity of all cultures, ours and theirs. Yet within our modern metaphysics, it is the crystalline ontology of nature that narrowly restricts possibilities, and the protean ontology of culture that reopens them.

I do not wish to dwell on the oddities of this metaphysics here. Instead, I wish to point out wherein lies its novelty, and to ponder its putative links with the Enlightenment. First, its novelty: The opposition of hard nature *versus* soft nurture which has gripped European and American intellectuals since the middle decades of the nineteenth century is not simply a rephrasing of the ancient opposition between *nomos* and *physis*, or even the eighteenth-century opposition between nature and education. Enlightenment "laws of nature" applied to society were hybrids of the normative and descriptive. Like the physical realm, the moral realm has, as Montesquieu wrote, "its own laws, which are of their own nature invariable, [but] it does not conform to them exactly as the physical world" because of human error and free will.[35] The physiocrat François Quesnay insisted more strongly on the necessity of natural laws, moral as well as physical, but their necessity was more akin to that of a mathematical demonstration than to that of gravitation: "The physical laws which constitute the natural order most advantageous to the human species and which comprise exactly the natural rights of all men, are perpetual, inalterable laws, decidedly the best laws possible. Their evidence imperiously subjugates all human reason and intelligence, with a precision that demonstrates geometrically and arithmetically in each detail, and which leaves no subterfuge for error, imposture, or illicit claims."[36] And even the necessity of the law of gravitation was merely that of the "positive" law "that it has pleased God to give to nature," as human legislatures make and amend human statute law.[37] Hence, it was perfectly possible for the Baron d'Holbach to claim that "nature has formed [women] to exercise the sweetest empire" over the domestic sphere, and then in the next breath to scold women for defying their nature by deserting the hearth for more public pursuits.[38]

Conclusion: Qui est cette dame, la Nature?

Thus the laws of nature posited by the Enlightenment, at least as they touched upon things human, were at once as revered and as fragile as the natural facts of the Enlightenment. Faulty education and downright perversity could and did subvert them. The hard, inexorable nature which makes natural facts seem so tyrannical to us is not the genuine heritage of the Enlightenment. Why, then, is it the mythological heritage? Why does fear of the Enlightenment so often express itself as fear of the tyranny of natural facts, and, more generally, as the tyranny of science? Some critics, for example Theodor Adorno and Max Horkheimer, have gone so far as to make the tyranny of facts the root of all modern tyranny, and thereby to indict the Enlightenment as totalitarian.[39] I do not think it will do to dismiss this fear as a simple historical misunderstanding. It *is* a historical misunderstanding, but no simple one. There is nothing arbitrary about mythologies, even if there is much that is false. So I repeat, why is fear of the Enlightenment a fear of the tyranny of natural facts?

The short answer is, I think, that Enlightenment social and political theorists did indeed create a new cult of nature. Not that the authority of nature had not been invoked before to back up social norms, especially sexual norms—medieval and Renaissance texts call upon nature for support with some frequency. But nature had rarely, if ever, been invoked on its own. On the contrary, its authority derived from God's authority, and quite literally so: God was the author of nature, as Aquinas put it. Moreover, medieval appeals to the dictates of nature were overwhelmingly conservative defenses of the social status quo. What was genuinely new about the Enlightenment cult of nature was, first, that it elevated nature to supreme authority—insofar as God still appeared, it was, as in the American Declaration of Independence, as "Nature's God"—and second, that it enlisted nature in the cause of critique and reform of the social status quo. Examples are too numerous to list—only recall that human rights began life as "natural rights." When de Maistre snarled, "Who is this lady, Nature?," he pinpointed with characteristic clarity what conservatives of all stripes loathed about the Enlightenment. Nature had usurped the authority of God, and nature was, still worse, a radical.

Sometime in the middle decades of the nineteenth century nature became a conservative again, the dictator of what must be against what might be. Hence the biological turn of nineteenth-century conservatism, most terribly in doctrines of racism, and the symmetric unmasking strategies of nineteenth-century radicalism, which resisted "naturalization." What both sides tacitly agreed upon was that nature was indeed inexorable and—*pace* the Enlightenment—amoral, indifferent to human concerns. What they fought over, and still are fighting over, is what does and does not fall into the category of the natural. We have inherited this war, and we therefore understand nature's authority as tyrannical rather than reasonable. But we still hold nature to be an authority; moreover, we still covertly grant nature moral as well as physical authority. Reproaches like "unnatural mother" are not only still intelligible; they are still devastating. This is the truth at the heart of the mythology of the Enlightenment: we may have lost all sense of nature's fragility, but we still acknowledge, however tacitly, nature's moral authority—indeed, her tyranny. The Enlightenment may have disenchanted nature by denying her a soul, but it then promptly reenchanted her by granting her a scepter.

We will stop fearing the Enlightenment when, in true Enlightenment fashion, we disenchant nature anew. That which is natural is neither inevitable, nor desirable. The natural is not even the opposite of the cultural. We desperately need a new metaphysics that will allow us to believe, not just mouth, this credo of disenchantment. It is one of the oddest oddities of current intellectual life that nature, once the battering ram of social criticism (think of Condorcet), and history, once the bulwark of tradition (think of Burke), have exchanged political valences. History now purportedly subverts the status quo with counterexamples; nature purportedly shores it up with stubborn facts. We need a politics which can argue honestly as politics—without nature, without history. This, too, would be an exit from self-imposed tutelage, from Kant's "selbst verschuldeten Unmündigkeit," to external authority, even if it was the authority the Enlightenment loved best.

DENA GOODMAN

Difference: An Enlightenment Concept

"The dismantling of the universal is widely considered one of the founding gestures of twentieth-century thought," Naomi Schor has written. While giving wide chronological berth to universalism's nefarious implications—from the Spanish inquisition to the "genocidal massacres of our own blood-soaked century"—Schor plants universalism itself firmly in the Enlightenment, and then draws a straight line from it to the Holocaust. "Following Max Horkheimer and Theodor Adorno," she explains, "the Enlightenment leads to Auschwitz; after Auschwitz, the Enlightenment is a bankrupt, discredited, blighted dialectic."[1] In this chapter I would like to address the demonization of the Enlightenment by postmodern critics like Naomi Schor by questioning the simple identification between Enlightenment and universalism on which it is based.

Schor, herself, it must be said, maintains her distance from this simplistic identification of universalism with the Enlightenment— but only to point out that *universalism* has a long history, going back to the Greeks, and that the Enlightenment is but one "very crucial" episode in this history. She thus frees universalism from the Enlightenment, but the Enlightenment remains nevertheless a synecdoche for universalism: an episode in its history that can conveniently be made to stand for it.

I would like to challenge the identification of universalism with Enlightenment—not to deny that universalism was a central theme in Enlightenment thought, but to assert that difference was an equally important theme. I will argue that difference, too, is an Enlightenment concept, and that any understanding of the Enlightenment must account for the discourse of difference as well as and in relation to that of universalism. Moreover, I would suggest that contemporary discourse is seriously impoverished when the discursive possibilities opened up by the Enlightenment are reduced to universalism. One arena in which this conceptual poverty is most obvious and troubling is feminism.

In fact, Schor's article is a contribution to the current debate among feminists concerning whether feminism should abandon its traditional faith in the universal discourse of equality and rights that constitutes the Enlightenment legacy and should instead join forces with postmodernism in combating the universal and its false promises.[2] As feminist theorists have increasingly chosen the postmodern position, a cry of protest has arisen from those (historians in particular) who see no alternative but to embrace the universal even more tightly: "The Declaration of the Rights of Man and Citizen in August 1789 put rights on the agenda, and they have stayed there in one form or another ever since," declares Lynn Hunt. "To dismiss this as the origins of totalitarianism or a con job to deprive women of their rights is to willfully overlook a bigger and ultimately more important story, that of the challenge posed to the old order by new conceptions of individual rights."[3]

If we look more closely at the Enlightenment legacy for feminism, however, we find that it contributes as much to the discourse of difference as it does to universalistic individualism. Consider, for example, article III of Olympe de Gouges's *Déclaration des droits de la femme* (1791): "The Principle of all sovereignty rests essentially with the nation, which is nothing but the union of woman and man; no body and no individual can exercise any authority which does not come expressly from it."[4] Jeanne Deroin's Saint-Simonism, which stressed the complementarity of men and women in the construction of a whole "social individual," is equally indebted to an Enlightenment discourse of difference. As Joan Scott writes, the premise of Deroin's argument for rights was the complementarity of men and women based on their difference, and the incompleteness of one without the other.[5] Modern feminism reflects not one but two dominant strains in Enlightenment thought: a universalistic discourse of individualism and a discourse of difference founded on gender complementarity and natural sociability.

Yet Scott, like Schor and Hunt, takes universalism to be the Enlightenment's only legacy and thus the sole discursive basis of modern feminism. She argues that "women's ambiguous status as objects and subjects" emerged directly from the universalistic discourse of the Revolutionary Declaration of the Rights of Man and Citizen. The recognition of women "as civil agents and their exclusion from politics," she asserts, in turn "engendered feminism."[6] It was the Declaration's universalism alone, and not the more complex Enlightenment legacy of universalism and difference, which established the discursive parameters within which feminist writers from Olympe de Gouges on maintained that women had both the same (universal) political rights as men and (different) special needs which demanded protection. Because Scott sees only universalistic individualism coming out of the Enlightenment, she argues that, for feminists, the Enlightenment has "only paradoxes to offer."[7]

Feminism does have roots in the Enlightenment, but the Enlightenment cannot be reduced to a universalistic discourse of individualism. In the eighteenth century, individualism was not a simple assertion of autonomy, but was framed within theories of natural sociability and gender complementarity, as well as by practices of voluntary association which shaped eighteenth-century culture.[8] The individual was not simply cut loose from all ties to brave it alone in the world, as romantics would later represent him; rather individuality and sociability went hand in hand, just as it was individuality that made the public more than just a mass and publicity that allowed individuality to be enacted and experienced.[9] Moreover, to the degree that the individual was gendered masculine, he operated within a world in which both sexes played significant and acknowledged roles. Indeed, the masculine discourse of universalism was at least in part a reaction against the discourse of difference in which women as women had a significant place. These two competing discourses define a range of discursive and political possibilities which together may be said to constitute an Enlightenment legacy richer than that imagined by either postmodernists or feminists.[10] In locating the Enlightenment discourse of difference, I aim to expand not only our understanding of the eighteenth century, but the discursive and political possibilities available to us today.

The Enlightenment discourse of difference was articulated in the cultural spaces of urban sociability in which the practices of civility were cultivated. Difference, it should be noted, has always been at the bottom of the need for civility. In the seventeenth century, French men and women came to aristocratic salons to learn how to act nobly, which is to say, how to distinguish themselves from others through the practice of civility. In the salon, one set of differences, based on birth, was devalued and replaced with another, based on comportment, manners, and a shared discourse. To be civil was to act nobly, and thus to be noble. Nobles were people who shared a set of manners and a discourse, defined by rules of comportment which regulated how they were to relate to one another as persons who were admittedly different, in a society defined by ranks and orders. "The *honnête homme* was the man of whatever social origin who appropriated to himself noble *civilité*," writes Carolyn Lougee. "The ideology of the salons rested on this substitution of behavior for birth."[11]

If civility was primarily a sign of aristocratic status in the seventeenth century, it was also a means to avoid or overcome potential conflict. The noble warrior may have been "civilized" into a gentleman through the practices of the salon, but the warrior ethos was only transformed, not eliminated. Civility controlled differences within the group, even as it distinguished the group from those excluded from it. At the same time that the rules by which civility was maintained defined a society which excluded many as it included some, within that exclusive group, the same rules allowed differences to be both fostered and controlled. Civility became the key to a new culture that acknowledged difference because it enabled meaningful and fruitful interactions among people defined by it.[12]

In the eighteenth century, when the elite who engaged in public discourse expanded well beyond the limits of the Parisian nobility, aristocratic civility gave way to the broader and more egalitarian notion and practice of politeness. "*Civility*," the chevalier de Jaucourt wrote in the *Encyclopédie*, "does not say as much as *politeness*, and makes up but a portion of it."[13] As *le monde* became more diverse and suffused with Enlightenment values, the aristocratic civility which recognized rank and status as legitimate differences came to be seen as superficial, even hypocritical. True politeness was more than mere civility and the very opposite of flattery; it smoothed away from discourse all rudeness, bombast "and other defects contrary to common sense and civil society, and reclothed it with gentleness, modesty, and the justice sought by the mind, and which society needs in order to be peaceful and agreeable."[14]

In the eighteenth century, civil conversation took on a new social function as well, but one equally concerned with organizing social and discursive relations among people defined by difference: it enabled men of letters to cooperate in the project of Enlightenment despite the differences of *opinion* continually brought to the fore by their critical method. It also allowed men of letters to exchange ideas as equals despite their very different social origins and economic situations: the marquis de Condorcet, the noble bastard d'Alembert, the master cutler's son, Diderot, the peasant-born Marmontel. As Jean-Baptiste Suard wrote in 1784:

> In a nation where a continuous communication reigns between the two sexes, between persons of all estates, and between minds of all sorts . . . it is necessary to set some limits to the movements of the mind as well as those of the body and to observe the feelings of those to whom we speak in order to temper the sentiments or thoughts that would shock their beliefs or injure their pride.[15]

As the philosophes extended their invitation to join in the project of Enlightenment to all readers, the Enlightenment became a new kind of society in which politeness was crucial: a society in which differences did not disappear but, rather, became all the more visible and audible in their proximity to others. Because civil conversation allowed those men and women who embraced it to interact with one another despite cultural differences, either real or assumed, it set them apart from those who believed difference to be natural, immutable, and unbridgeable; it became a practice of Enlightenment.[16]

Politeness was one of the conditions of the common quest for knowledge and understanding, for seeking truth and spreading enlightenment. Progress depended on politeness because the pursuit of knowledge depended on it, and the pursuit of knowledge was not a solitary activity, but a sociable one. Rather than an occasion to demonstrate status, conversation was a medium of Enlightenment. Commerce, conversation, Enlightenment itself, were all created out of a culture of interaction and exchange among groups and individuals whose differences made such relations meaningful rather than tautological, but which also necessitated rules, structures, and institutions to make them work.

The philosophes soon looked to salon conversation not only to structure the work of Enlightenment, but as the model for civil society itself. As Daniel Gordon has written, the philosophes "tended to idealize 'civil society' as a vast gathering of free and polite individuals—a kind of universal salon."[17] In the writings of the philosophes, a harmonious civil society was both a challenge to the absolute state and an alternative to the "stormy liberty" they saw operating across the English Channel.[18] For the philosophe, according to one contributor to the *Encyclopédie,* "civil society is, so to speak, a divinity on earth."[19]

More concretely, civil society was put forward as the ground upon which any legitimate political and economic structure (including the monarchy) must be built. The abbé Morellet, for example, grounded social and political order neither in the will of the monarch (as absolutists such as Hobbes did); nor in laws and civic virtue (as republicans such as Rousseau did); but in the "aggregate of private exchanges" which constituted civil society.[20] This meant organizing a diverse people into a harmonious whole through the invention of political institutions, and in particular through the invention of "public opinion" as a source of political authority and legitimacy that, like the salonnière and the rules by which she governed her guests, stood apart from and above them.[21]

The wheels of commerce had to be greased to run smoothly; the guiding metaphor of the salon was the harmonious orchestration of strings or instruments.[22] Suzanne Necker, herself a prominent eighteenth-century salonnière, saw politeness precisely in terms of organizing a society of people who were not only different, but who enjoyed differential power in relation to each other. In her view, politeness redressed the balance of power between strong and weak, men and women, adults and children. "Politeness," she wrote, "conforms to the principle of equality that is so often spoken of; it is the rampart of those who cannot defend themselves, and that as well on which their praise and their merit are based."[23]

As Necker's remark suggests, gender difference and the question of the role and status of women are embedded in the history of civility. In salons like hers, men and women learned to interact in a way that acknowledged gender difference without sexualizing it. In the microcosm of the salon they created a model society in which women were the civilizing force that enlightened historians from Voltaire on claimed them to be: the benign force that brings out what is noble in men and suppresses not only their brutality, but their hostility toward each other, thus making them both civil and civilized.[24] Gender difference played a major role not only in the maintenance of civility, but in the definition of civilization and Enlightenment.

Both "weak" and "strong" versions of the civilizing force of women were operative in the age of the salons, from the 1630s to the revolution of 1789: the weak version can be found in the idea that civil conversation, and thus society and civilization, depended simply on the bringing together of men and women. The stronger set of claims emphasized the specific talents, characteristics, and virtues of women that were necessary to society and civilization and which produced a civil conversation. Voltaire's claim in the preface to his tragedy *Zaire* (1736) that "the continual commerce between the two sexes, so lively and so polite, has introduced a politeness quite unknown elsewhere," represents the first position; Claude-Charles Guyonne de Vertron's claim in *La Nouvelle Pandore* (1698) that "the virtue of women reestablishes what the vice of men ha[s] corrupted," represents the second.[25] In addition, what women are thought to do to produce civilization or civility, or to civilize men, varied over time. In the seventeenth century, when civility was the mark of nobility, women were prized as models of civility and teachers of civil conversation. Nicolas Faret, for example, the author of *L'Honnête homme ou l'art de plaire à la cour* (1630), advised his (male) readers "to go into town and observe those among the ladies of quality who are esteemed as the most *honnête* women, and at whose homes the most beautiful assemblies are held." Faret led the way in holding up female conversation as a model of civility, "the most difficult and the most delicate."[26]

The salons that flourished during the reign of Louis XIV became the basis of *le monde*—an autonomous society, beyond the reach of king and court. In these salons, in which aristocratic men and women conversed together, gender difference was itself the subject, the *topos* of conversation. The *querelle des femmes*, revived at various points throughout Western history, became in the second half of the seventeenth century the matrix of salon discourse. As Carolyn Lougee has shown, the woman question now "intersected with crucial controversies over social organization and was interwoven with the major issues of social transformation which concerned seventeenth-century Frenchmen"; it was, she writes, "a controversy central to its own age."[27] Recently Joan DeJean has argued similarly that the *fin-de-siècle* war known as the *querelle des anciens et des moderns* was in fact a battle in the *querelle des femmes* and "a struggle between conflicting visions of French society."[28]

In the eighteenth century, however, as the salon became a model for civil society, and a civil society in which men of letters were, by their own definition, centrally important, the salonnière was no longer revered as a model of civil conversation to be imitated by men and women alike, and the topos of gender difference was marginalized if not eliminated from salon discourse.[29] Instead, the salonnière came to be valued for traits that men either could not or need not imitate because they were gender specific, traits that were understood in terms not simply of gender difference, but of gender complementarity. Moreover, these traits were ascribed to women's nature. As, under the scrutiny of critical reason, all differences between men came to be viewed by the enlightened as culturally derived—a function of class to be overcome by education, or of power to be overcome by political reform—gender difference alone survived as natural and immutable, to be nurtured rather than transcended.[30]

By the 1770s, when the great salonnières of the Enlightenment had made their mark, women were no longer admired for their own conversational skills, but for their ability to orchestrate, to govern, the conversation of men. Male salon-goers were able to identify specific attributes of women that made them especially capable of fulfilling the particular role assigned to them. As Antoine-Léonard Thomas wrote in his *éloge* of Madame Geoffrin:

These sorts of societies ... require a certain power to temper them. It seems
that this power is no better held than in the hands of a woman. She has a
natural right that no one disputes and that, in order to be felt, has only to be
shown. Madame Geoffrin used this advantage. [In her salon], the reunion
of all ranks, like that of all types of minds, prevented any one tone from
dominating.[31]

Of Julie de Lespinasse, the Comte de Guibert wrote similarly: "Her
great art was to show to advantage the minds of others, and she enjoyed doing that more than revealing her own."[32]

While men did not stop writing about the beneficial effects on society as a whole of commerce between men and women, they increasingly emphasized the governing role of women in a society composed of men. Thus in 1777, Jacques-Henri Meister mourned the loss
of two Enlightenment salonnières in political terms: "The disorder
and anarchy that have reigned in this party since the death of Mlle de
Lespinasse and the paralysis of Mme Geoffrin prove how much the
wisdom of their government had averted evils, how much it had dis-
sipated storms, and above all how much it had rescued it from ridicule."[33] It was this governing role that disturbed Rousseau and caused
him to put forward (in *Emile* and *La Nouvelle Héloïse*) an alternative
role for women as wives and mothers which would prove to be as ap-
pealing to women as to men.

Gender difference became institutionalized in the different roles
played by men and women in the model society of the salon. The
definition of the salonnière—the articulation of her attributes, her
functions, and her contribution to the Republic of Letters and the
project of Enlightenment through her work in the salon—signaled
the opening of a sort of career for elite women that gave them the opportunity to have utility and thus real value within the society of their
day. At the same time, however, it defined in gendered terms different and complementary roles for men and women within that society
and thus limited the ambitions of women to a role defined for them
by men. In so doing, it displaced the "Woman Question" from the
center of discussions about the shape and meaning of society and civilization as these two were being redefined and, in a sense, answered it
by framing the discussion itself in gendered terms. At the same time
that women became more visible in their dominant role as salonnières, the question of gender virtually disappeared from the dis-

course of society. The status of women was recognized in the dominant theory of history as a gauge of civilization—most notably by Diderot, who demanded that women be seen as "so many thermometers of the least vicissitudes of morals and customs"—but their role was firmly established as the civilizers of men rather than as contributors to the cultural progress from which they benefited.[34]

The shift from a salon discourse focused on the Woman Question to one framed in gendered terms by the different roles and responsibilities of men and women in it marked a marginalizing of women from the actual discussion of society and its future precisely as that discussion became more political and more public, as Erica Harth has suggested.[35] In the writing of Jean-Jacques Rousseau, women were displaced from the space of discussion altogether—they were, in effect, sent out of the room in which any serious discussion took place. We can thus situate Rousseau's influential discourse on women and gender in a development that begins with a practice of civil conversation in which men and women participate, to one in which unruly men are governed by rules enforced by women, to one from which women are excluded. Gendered difference moves from the basis of civility to the instrument of civility to the boundary of civility. With the exclusion of women from it, moreover, the conversation in which men engage is no longer civil and no longer acknowledges difference.

The association of women with civility made them vulnerable to the critique of civilization itself, mounted by Rousseau but shared to some degree, as Sylvana Tomaselli has shown, even by Diderot in his contributions to Raynal's *Histoire des deux Indes*.[36] For Rousseau, difference may be the reason for civility; it may be the means of achieving it, but civil society—and thus the difference that marks it—is rejected as the foundation of political association. In Rousseau's world, the exclusion of women allows men to get along through the articulation of a general will that is by definition, their will alone. The polity is not built on a society marked by difference; it is the unitary expression of a group of men who have no need for either society or any other form of community because they are themselves defined by their equality, not by their differences. This is Jürgen Habermas's point when he writes that "Rousseau projected the unbourgeois idea of an intrusively political society in which the autonomous private sphere, that is, civil society, emancipated from the state, had no place."[37] Keith Baker makes a related point in arguing that when the National Assembly adopted a Rousseauian "discourse of the political, grounded on the theory of a unitary will," in the fall of 1789, it rejected " a discourse of the social, grounded on the notion of the differential distribution of reason, functions, and interests in modern civil society."[38] Accepting a Rousseauian discourse meant rejecting a discourse of modernity, in which social progress went hand in hand with social difference and differentiation; it meant rejecting the very notions of civilization and society associated with women as being outside the political community of citizen-men.[39]

Rousseau's individuals were not only equal, they were by nature free. Rousseau criticized civility not only because he saw a simpler solution to the problem of difference in the removal of women from the political scene, but because he saw civility as a curb on natural freedom. After all, civil conversation is governed conversation. It should thus not be surprising that since the French Revolution, the value of civility has been seriously problematized, compromised in fact, by the threat that traditional government has been seen to pose to natural liberty.[40] Before the Revolution, civility was criticized for the artificiality it tended to produce, for its attention to form and appearance. (The substitution of politeness for "mere" civility was an attempt to rescue civility from this critique.) In that discourse, civility was unnatural because it was artificial and superficial, not because it was unfree. Essence and sincerity were at stake, not liberty.[41] Before the Revolution, only Rousseau really worried about freedom being sacrificed at the altar of civility; his contemporaries were more concerned about the destructive and deceptive potential of language for human society than they were with its role in representing individual identity and thus personal freedom. Indeed, as Roger Chartier points out, the value of civility in the view of Rousseau's contemporaries was its role in "the tightening of men's interdependence."[42]

The real divide between Rousseau and the philosophes put (natural) masculine freedom on one side, and civil (governed) society on the other. As Ernst Cassirer recognized long ago, Rousseau's "radical opposition" to the Enlightenment was grounded on a rejection of the conviction that "all political and social enterprise must stand on the same foundation."[43] In Rousseau's view, a just political order must be founded on the freedom of individual men, not on the differentiated society in which women played a conspicuous role. The governing role of women was a red flag for Rousseau not only because it put men under the rule of women, but because it compromised masculine freedom and thus violated nature. In the name of freedom, nature, and masculinity, Rousseau not only tore out the social foundations of the state, he created a new role for women outside both the polity and political discourse—a valued role as wife and mother that would compensate for the loss of society's value and the significant role of women in assuring mutual respect in it.

Because, of course, difference—gender difference—does not just wither away with society. Rather, in Rousseau's powerful vision it is relocated in the family. Rousseau's critique of civilization opened up a space of true happiness for modern men and women only in a domestic sphere seen as a haven from the depraved modern, urban world created and dominated by competitive, acquisitive, rational men. Women who sought to imitate men by cultivating their reason, or who made a name for themselves in society (writers and salonnières, in short) were not only ridiculous, but foolish, since in defying their nature they ran away from the happiness that they alone could enjoy. Why should women want to imitate men or be jealous of their freedom, when reason and the freedom based on it were merely poor substitutes for the happiness based on instinct and natural virtue available to them alone?[44]

Rousseau took the theory of gender complementarity at the heart of a society-based notion of civilization and used it as the basis of two separate spheres: the moral sphere of the family, whose soul was the natural virtue of woman; and the public sphere of the commercial economy and the state, in which men were driven by rational calculation and self-interest.[45] The polity would now be composed of equal men rather than of differentiated men and women; it would be governed not by someone defined as different, but by a general will defined as the unity of all relevant (that is, male) wills. In *Du Contrat social* (1762) Rousseau laid out the democratic political principles by which the public sphere of men ought to be governed; in *La Nouvelle Héloïse* (1761) he imagined the private sphere of a patriarchal family in which gender complementarity was again inscribed: where the husband ruled with the guidance of reason, but the wife was the emotional and moral center around which the family was built. Society and civility were eliminated from both the moral and the political universe.

In drawing the line between masculinity and freedom, on the one hand, and mixed-gender civility and civilization, on the other, Rousseau redefined gender roles and re-opened the woman question. Difference—gender difference—was at the heart of civilization and was the basis of civility. At the same time, it defined the boundary between the political and the not-political. If we follow the philosophes—Voltaire, Morellet, d'Alembert, Diderot, and others—we see difference as the ground upon which all of society's structures, institutions, rules of interaction are built, and we thus accept it within political discourse; if we follow Rousseau, we use gender difference as a dividing line between the political and the familial, and as a basis, therefore, of definition and exclusion—as the basis for a unitary and exclusively masculine political identity. But in either case, civilization (civility, civil society) is associated with women. The open question is the relationship of the political and the social, of polity and civility. Where one stands on the "woman question" depends on where difference lies.[46]

The masculine republican tradition that goes back to Rousseau has certainly endured, but so has a commitment to a notion of civilized society based on mixed-gender sociability—as evidenced by the despairing cry voiced by the writer Drieu la Rochelle in 1927: "This civilization no longer has clothes, no longer has churches, no longer has palaces, no longer has paintings, no longer has books, no longer has sexes," he wrote.[47] In his final complaint, Drieu was reiterating the association of civilization with gender difference. As Mary Louise Roberts writes: "The blurring of the boundary between 'male' and 'female'—a civilization without sexes—served as a primary referent for the ruin of civilization itself."[48] That association has its origins in the discourse of the Old Regime and has survived, but as the social complement of Rousseauian masculine individualism, rather than as a competing political discourse. Still defined as the social, civilization has now become simply a nostalgic way of reinserting the missing third term in the Rousseauian dualism—between the family and the polity—without, however, displacing either or calling them into question.

It is this understanding of society and civilization which underlies Mona Ozouf's recent championing of a French feminism that is uniquely and eminently civil. In her "Essay on French Singularity," Ozouf turns to the tradition of mixed-gender sociability that originated in the salons of Old Regime Paris for her understanding of the unique character of French feminism. She sees the "complexity" of the Old Regime as the basis of Frenchwomen's true freedom because, she explains, "in a world of differences, sexual difference was only one among many others, negligible in relation to differences of estate."[49] The salon serves as her example of how those marked by a variety of differences came together in the eighteenth century by accepting a common code of behavior. Indeed, Ozouf gives and endorses a classic account of the civilizing role of women in the Old Regime. "In short," she writes, "feminine arts civilized men, and from one end of the social ladder to the other."[50]

What makes French feminism unique (and admirable), according to Ozouf, is the way in which it is built on an aristocratic tradition of commerce between the sexes and a democratic tradition that in principle sets no limits on equality, even if in practice it is slow to realize its potential. "The result is a particular society, where the demand for equality among individuals remains fundamental, but can be combined with an emphasis on differences which are always subordinate."[51]

In support of Ozouf's thesis, Elisabeth Badinter has inscribed gender difference into the heart of a narrative of French history whereby men and women each stand for a different set of values; the triumph of the feminine in the seventeenth and eighteenth centuries (with a significant but temporary setback in the 1790s) defines both modern French history and civilization itself as functions of the feminine value of civility. The triumph of feminine civility, however, maintains gender difference in the form of gallantry while eliminating all forms of contestation. The victory of the feminine is the victory not of women over men, but of the social over the political.[52]

Badinter and Ozouf may be right in saying that the French have remained more civil than others, but civility's triumph has been limited to a social realm divorced from the political; that is, it is limited by the priority of a political model grounded in liberty and equality which sets the boundaries of society and civility. Despite the great nostalgia for the Old Regime and for the salon culture central to it evinced by both Ozouf and Badinter, they are in fact inscribing that nostalgia within a Rousseauian vision of a masculine polity based on an equality of sameness, and a feminine society in which civility harmonizes differences. Not only is feminism depoliticized, as Michelle Perrot has pointed out,[53] but the association of women with society and men with politics remains unchallenged.

Ozouf does not provide a satisfactory response to the postmodern feminist critique of the Enlightenment because she does not call into question the individualistic and exclusionary basis of the modern political order. Rather, she endorses that order and reinforces two ideas that mitigate against both the feminist campaign for equality and a much-called for civility in political discourse: a belief, first, in the civilizing role of women—in the natural role of women to discipline and thus to civilize naturally free and unruly men; and second, a resistance to the government of the tongue in the realm of politics. A serious feminist response to the postmodern critique would not simply idealize women, salons, and civility; it would reassert the Enlightenment commitment to a society defined by difference as the basis of an inclusionary political order and institutions.

For the most important and original insight of the philosophes for feminism is not that women civilize men; it is that difference underlies the social and makes both society and the state necessary and meaningful and valuable. Politics operates in this constructed social field and builds its institutions on it, rather than developing abstractly from a social contract among abstract, autonomous individuals.[54] The structures of society and politics, in this view, are not simply necessary evils, encroachments on natural freedom and equality, but human constructions built to organize human differences and make them useful—not to minimize, eliminate, or deny them.

However, as long as society and civility are associated with women, and politics, natural truth-telling, and truth-seeking language are associated with men, men will resist both women and civility because not just truth and honesty are stake, but masculinity itself. Rugged individualism will never allow itself to be civilized in these terms.[55] Civility, however, is not a compromise with truth, honesty, and nature, just as society is not a refuge from the hurly-burly of politics: it is a necessary condition of (political) discourse. It is a necessary condition of all relations rooted in discourse, which means all social and political relations including those whose aim is truth or knowledge.

The Enlightenment discourse in which difference is central is not simply an alternative to that other Enlightenment discourse—the one in which universal reason plays the crucial role. It must serve as the discursive context for universalism by means of which we can place the reasoning individual back in a social world marked by differences. At the same time, the universal discourse of reason can continue to play the critical role it has played since Descartes launched it in the seventeenth century: it can de-naturalize those differences and de-essentialize them. Not, however, in order to dismiss them, but in order to organize them usefully and fairly for the greater good of society and the happiness of individuals. Viewed in this way, the Enlightenment concept of difference can be helpful in laying the groundwork for both the multicultural community called for by feminists, and the new civility in the public sphere demanded by cultural critics from both the left and the right.

In a 1992 article on "The Campaign Against Political Correctness," Joan Scott suggested that the university become an "alternative" and "a place from which to search for a different understanding of what a community might be." In other words, that it play the role in our culture that the salon played in Old Regime France. The humanities in particular, she writes, "offer the best possibility of thinking about difference and community in new ways." Just as the seventeenth-century followers of Descartes placed difference at the center of salon conversation, of conversation about society, so must we in the university do the same today. In what I hope can now be seen as the discourse of Enlightenment, Scott concludes that "communities cannot be based on conformity, but on an acceptance and acknowledgment of difference."[56]

Rules of civility, she might have added, are what make such communities possible in the modern world. Thus, it would seem, the current linking of a breakdown of American society with a "civility crisis." However, the cultural commentators who have made such a linkage do not acknowledge the significance of difference as a real basis for community and thus the need for civility; nor do they question the individualism that makes civility suspect in the modern world. Deborah Tannen, for example, who wants us to question "the assumption that it's *always* best to address problems and issues by fighting over them," is careful to deny that she is a proponent of civility because, she explains, "'civility' suggests a superficial, pinky-in-the-air veneer of politeness spread thin over human relations like a layer of marmalade over toast. This book is about a pervasive warlike atmosphere that makes us approach public dialogue . . . as if it were a fight."[57] Because she sees civility as superficial and agonism as essential to society, Tannen looks elsewhere for a solution to the crisis she finds in social and political discourse. Like agonism, individualism is simply a fact of life. All we can do, therefore, is look for ways to "blunt the most dangerous blades of the argument culture."[58]

Unlike Tannen, Stephen L. Carter embraces the notion of civility. It is, he asserts, one of the elements of good character. For Carter, civility is not superficial, not merely "good manners"; rather, it is a moral principle, an "attitude of respect, even love, for our fellow citizens." It is, he declares, "morally better to be civil than to be uncivil." Carter calls civility a "precondition of democratic dialogue" and posits as a moral imperative that it "requires us not to mask our differences but to resolve them respectfully." Civility "adds value to the better society we are struggling together through our differences to build."[59]

Carter, however, locates civility not in the social practices of a secular society erected in the wake of the Reformation, but in the Christianity it sought to replace. He makes of civility a new universal, a restatement of Christian love appropriate for modern, secular society. "The key to reconstructing civility," he argues,

> is for all of us to learn anew the virtue of acting with love toward our neighbors. Love of neighbor has long been a tenet of Judaism and Christianity, and a revival of civility in America will require a revival of all that

is best in religion as a force in our public life. Only religion possesses the majesty, the power, and the sacred language to teach all of us, the religious and the secular, the genuine appreciation for each other on which a successful civility must rest.[60]

As a universal—like reason or Christian love—civility here denies the value of difference in transcending it. For Carter, the value of civility does not lie in its recognition of the differences that underlie society and its ability to manage them, but in its ability to act as a counterweight to individualism. "We cannot return to a world in which individual identity was subsumed within a larger and often brutal whole," he concedes. "What we can do is try, within the limits of democracy, to construct a civility that will lead future generations to admire what we tried to do for civilization rather than condemn us for our barbarism."[61] If Rousseau posited a retreat to the family as a moral refuge from an individualistic polity, Carter calls for a new civility to moralize that polity. "Civility," he writes, "is principally an ethic for strangers. In a democracy, especially a large one, we are most of us strangers to each other. ... Civility supposes an obligation to a larger if anonymous group of fellow citizens."[62] In the end, this latest call for civility does not entail a displacement of the individual or his natural freedom from the foundations of democracy. An appeal to Christian love will not solve the problem of a society that does not acknowledge or accept difference as fundamental.

We do need civility, but not as a refuge from the "rough and tumble" masculine ways of politics or as a new morality designed to transcend or soften it. As long as civility continues to be opposed to individualism, critics will blast the former for opposing the masculine values associated with the latter. Thus Randall Kennedy writes against the new "civilitarians" such as Tannen and Carter:

> The civility movement is deeply at odds with what an invigorated liberalism requires: intellectual clarity, an insistence upon grappling with the substance of controversies; and a willingness to fight loudly, openly, militantly, even rudely for policies and values that will increase freedom, equality, and happiness in America and around the world.[63]

Civility must be seen not as coming from outside a political discourse among people whose right to speak is based on their individual reason, but as the very constitution of a society defined by difference.

Until the differences from which disagreements arise are acknowledged as the basis of society, the reason for its existence, civility will not be recognized as the means to harmonize them. Nor will the necessity and legitimacy of people willing to enforce the rules of civility be recognized—people who are willing to stand outside the conversation, its passions, egos, and interests—as salonnières did by virtue of their gender—in order to do the necessary and legitimate work of governance.

We need salonnières as much as we need civility, but we don't need to assign the role of salonnière to women. Unlike the men and women of the eighteenth century, we can analyze and understand the function of the salonnière as we understand the function of civility: in relation to difference, but not as grounded in nature. The full legacy of the Enlightenment helps us to grapple with difference as reasonable men and women. It allows us to see not only that differences are socially constructed, but that society is itself constructed out of differences and government developed to manage them. Standing on a differentiated society, the political sphere need not exclude women on the grounds of their difference from men, just as it need not submerge all men in an artificial equality based on a constructed sameness. Rather than grounding a choice between universalism and difference, the complex legacy of the Enlightenment allows us to refuse that choice as well as its derivatives: between universalistic feminism and difference feminism, between political rights and social power, and between politics and civility. The Enlightenment does this by opening the possibility of redefining the political such that difference, society, and civility are all essential to it.

LAWRENCE E. KLEIN

Enlightenment as Conversation

Notwithstanding Jean-François Lyotard's identification of the post-modern with "incredulity toward metanarratives," postmodernism has its own grand narrative. Anxious about its definition in time as in so much else, postmodernism has been accompanied by a passion to historicize, to define a history of modernity against which critique can then be launched. There has been a proliferation of grand narratives, theoretical histories, teleologically driven, developmental stories organized around some concept of modernity, in which "a series of elisions tend to prescribe a definite route here."[1] The Enlightenment is invariably a station on this itinerary. In those stories, there was *an* (i.e. *one*) Enlightenment, it had a series of doctrinal commitments, these commitments have dominated not only the philosophy but the cultures of the developed West, and the dominance of these doctrinal commitments is responsible for many of our predicaments. The grand narrative of postmodernism is cast in a range of figures, among which personification is prominent: the narrative concerns genealogies and lineages, ancestors and their legacies.

Although the postmodern narrative identifies several related candidates as the Enlightenment's legacy, this essay responds to scientism and the corresponding claim that Enlightenment intellectuals, inspired by Descartes, first assumed the posture of the distanced observer seeking mastery over what he sees. In the first instance, this mastery is intellectual, though, by an easy extension, it is political. The posture is marked by the distance between observer and observed, who are separated by a kind of ontological gap; a hierarchical relation that privileges the intellectual and political authority of the observer; and the disembodied or decontextualized position of the observer, which gives rise to the claim to provide objective knowledge of universal validity. This scientistic posture is the signal comportment of the Enlightenment in postmodernism's grand narrative, as well as the signal legacy of the Enlightenment targeted by the postmodern critique.

This characterization can make for a nice fit between the very term "Enlightenment" and its presiding epistemology. According to Ludmilla Jordanova and Peter Hulme, light took on "a new vitality" as "a central metaphor for knowledge" in this period: "there was a whole epistemology behind the use of images of 'light' in the eighteenth century, one that was boosted by the belief that all knowledge came from the senses and that vision was queen among the senses, with observation at the heart of the acquisition of solid knowledge. Enlightenment was less a state than a process of simultaneous unveiling and observation."[2]

However, as Lorraine Daston has recently reminded us, it was highly important to eighteenth-century writers that their "light" not be confused with the sort of private illumination that had come in their time to be associated with the pathology known as enthusiasm. She writes that "the peculiar light of the enlightened" in the eighteenth century was "a sociable light. It was not the inner light of mystical vision, but rather the outer light of letters, lectures, treatises, memoirs, novels, journals, and conversations." We understand what she means, but the metaphors are awkward. When she continues, "whereas enthusiasm caught fire from a blinding, undeniable intuition that admitted neither elaboration nor rebuttal, enlightenment was kindled by argument, explanation, demonstration, and discussion with a network of interlocutors," we feel more precisely the jarring effects of a significant mixing of metaphor: metaphors of light and sight have shifted into metaphors of sound and speech.[3]

The same shift is undertaken, rather more strategically, by James Schmidt, who notes that "the Enlightenment's critics are in agreement . . . that there is something sinister about the light it casts."[4] He contends, however, that light has come to be over-estimated as a trope of Enlightenment because theorists have failed to attend to what eighteenth-century writers themselves said. As a signal piece of evidence, he points out that Kant's answer to the question, "What is enlightenment?," "did not invoke those images of light that have cast such a shadow over recent criticisms of the Enlightenment. He instead talked about speech. For him, enlightenment demanded not a world in which everything stood naked to the light but rather a world in which it was possible to speak without fear."[5]

Following Daston and Schmidt, this essay approaches the Enlightenment as a moment in the history of human communication. It draws on historical research that locates the medium of the Enlightenment not in light and vision but in sound and speech. In this Enlightenment, engaged conversers rather than detached observers are in the foreground. In this Enlightenment, science does not run rampant but instead submits to the disciplines of sociability.

One reason to consider the Enlightenment as a conversational episode is simply to make clear that the intellectual cultures of the eighteenth century had many concerns besides observation and such related themes as taxonomy, abstraction, objectivity, and discipline: more than that was going on in the eighteenth century. In turn, the diversity of the Enlightenment undermines the simplistic grand narrative which postmodern writers have so often felt they required: scientism was not the only legacy of the Enlightenment, if we insist on seeing our relation to the past in that metaphor. However, my goal is not to suggest an alternate narrative of modernity to the grand narrative of postmodernity. Indeed, as I will suggest at the end of this essay, we can put postmodern insight to better historical use by abandoning grand narrative altogether. Finally, an account of the conversational Enlightenment helps to undermine the much-vaunted opposition between Enlightenment and postmodernity that shapes the grand narrative. In searching for an alternative to the alleged legacy of the Enlightenment, postmodern writers have themselves often put a high value on conversation: condemning the Enlightenment, they identify remedies for its legacy in modes most favored in the Enlightenment itself—the irony that is the heart of this essay.

⌐

According to Dick Hebdige, "the spirit of postmodernism" requires "the renunciation of the claims to mastery and 'dominant specularity.'"[6] In renouncing Enlightenment scientism, some critics have identified an alternative cognitive comportment in conversation or dialogue. In the words of David Simpson, conversation has risen to prominence among "tools of storytelling as we now do it, if we are liberal intellectuals laying claim to the novelty of a postmodern commitment."[7] A scene of embodied humans interacting in particular spaces seems a desirable substitute for the disembodied eyeball peering into the microscope. *Conversation* offers a better way than *observation* for thinking about cognition and knowledge: conversation replaces distance with engagement, elitism and authority with participation, solitude with sociability, hierarchy and elitism with equality, and the illusion of a privileged cognitive station with a frank admission of the situated perspective of all knowledge claims.

The postmodern commitment has at least two main uses for conversation, as the basis for all claims to knowledge and as a model for acquiring it. The first use is illustrated in the writings of Richard Rorty. For Rorty, conversation is an alternative to the scientism—adumbrated as early as Plato, put in place by Descartes and Locke, adopted as the cognitive program of the Enlightenment, and finally, passed on to modern Western culture.[8] This scientism has always sought to establish knowledge on the basis of a correspondence to an external reality; it involves a search for a knowledge that stands outside the contingencies of language, history and culture. Among other things, it is responsible for the bifurcation of the cognitive world into scientific and non-scientific kinds of knowledge. Rorty's pragmatism rejects "the common presupposition that there is an invidious distinction to be drawn between kinds of truth. For the pragmatist, true sentences are not true because they correspond to reality"; likewise, the undeniable effectiveness of modern science is not a function of the correspondence of its statements to reality.[9] Rorty does not deny that there is such a reality: "To say that the world is out there, that it is not our creation, is to say, with common sense, that most things in space and time are the effects of causes which do not include human mental states." But he insists that truth should not be considered a mirror of that reality since what we call truth must be articulated in sentences, "sentences are elements of human languages," and "human languages are human creations."[10] In short, humans and their cognitions are entirely embedded in language. This "ubiquity of language" means that we never encounter reality "except under a chosen description."[11] There are no starting points or ending points outside language. Thus, knowledge is not a matter of confrontation between knower and reality but rather a matter of conversation, arising in the conversational relations of inquirers.[12] As Rorty notes, "there are no constraints on inquiry save conversational ones—no wholesale constraints derived from the nature of the objects, or of the mind, or of language, but only those retail constraints provided by the remarks of our fellow-inquirers."[13]

To think of knowledge as grounded in conversation rather than in correspondence is, for Rorty, a new way of describing our knowledge, a new way to cast the metaphors through which we articulate our purchase on the world.[14] To that extent, Rorty's redescription leaves scientific knowledge as it is: evolutionary biology, plate tectonics, quantum physics should be no less persuasive to us if, with Rorty, we forfeit their correspondence to external reality. However, Rorty's refiguration of knowledge does affect the discipline of philosophy since it requires the abandonment of epistemology, the project that has defined philosophy since the seventeenth century, and its dream of grounding knowledge on commensurability, "the assumption that all contributions to a given discourse are . . . . able to be brought under a set of rules which will tell us how rational agreement can be reached . . . ."[15] Whatever new role is found for philosophy—or whatever takes its place, since Rorty also talks of the need for a post-philosophical culture[16]—it will be at the hub of conversations. In a telling metaphor, with specific relevance for this essay, Rorty suggests that the philosopher might run *the salon* "where hermetic thinkers are charmed out of their self-enclosed practices."[17]

But philosophy is not the only field of knowledge in which the postmodern attraction to conversation implies reinventing the discipline. In anthropology, for instance, conversation has been advanced not just as the ground of knowledge but as a kind of method with implications for the nature of anthropological insight.[18] James Clifford has been in the fore in calling for the rejection of the scientistic model. The anthropologist is to abandon the pretensions to detachment and objectivity in the participant observation model and assume the shape of a fully equipped and located human being; moreover, the object of inquiry must be regarded as a fully equipped and located being. The relations between these two are necessarily dialogic. According to Clifford, "it is more than ever crucial for different peoples to form complex concrete images of one another, as well as of the relationships of knowledge and power that connect them; but no sovereign scientific method or ethical stance can guarantee the truth of such images. They are constituted . . . in specific historical relations of dominance and dialogue."[19] The nature of the knowledge produced is quite different, then, under conversational conditions: "It becomes necessary to conceive of ethnography not as the experience and interpretation of a circumscribed 'other' reality, but rather as a constructive negotiation involving at least two, and usually more, conscious, politically significant subjects."[20]

For Rorty, the scientistic posture leads to false claims about the nature of our knowledge; for Clifford, it leads to false knowledge claims *tout court* with morally and politically odious implications. Both assertions of the importance of conversation and dialogue are rooted in a powerful sense of the ubiquity of language: our knowledge is always embedded in language, language is inherently discursive, and our discourse is always particular, located and contingent.

In what follows I do not take issue with the attractiveness of conversation and dialogue as models of intellectual and political community. The point, rather, is that in the eighteenth century plenty of people used conversation to organize not only their perceptions of the world but also their practical engagements with it. A fundamentally rhetorical, that is, linguistic, view of the world, with a concomitant sensitivity to historical and cultural context, was a central feature of the Enlightenment.[21]

～

While the postmodern critique of the Enlightenment supposes that, in the words of Dorinda Outram, science and technology "supplied the central cultural structure of the Enlightenment,"[22] recent work on the period suggests that conversation and sociability were of preeminent significance. According to Dena Goodman, "the central dis-cursive practices of the Enlightenment Republic of Letters were po-lite conversation and letter writing, and its defining social institution was the Parisian salon."[23] Goodman's contention betokens the direc-tion that Enlightenment studies have taken in recent years. The En-lightenment is defined now not by a set of doctrines but by a set of communicative practices, along with such concepts as conversation, politeness and sociability, which contemporaries used to comprehend their distinctive practices.[24]

Of course, the eighteenth century did not invent ideas about con-versation, but rather built on traditions of early modern and medieval provenance (which, in turn, were informed by ancient writings). In-deed, the conversational turn in Enlightenment studies has involved a rethinking of Enlightenment origins. The Enlightenment has often been interpreted as continuing and popularizing the scientific achievements of the seventeenth century. The *philosophes* have been seen as translating the work of "the trio of English 'pioneers,' Bacon, Newton and Locke," to a wider and more practical field or of adopt-ing, in a similar way, "the *way of thinking* introduced by Descartes."[25] However, from the standpoint of communicative practice, the En-lightenment was developing and elaborating other strands of early modern culture, namely, the traditions of conversation, politeness and sociability that were important in elite European society, at princely courts and elsewhere, from the Renaissance on.[26]

Particularly important for the Enlightenment were seventeenth-century French ideas about the sociability appropriate for *honnêtes hommes*, developed by such writers as Guez de Balzac, the chevalier de Méré and the sieur de Saint-Évremond. These writers were looking, in the midst of a court culture, for forms of sociability in which an aris-tocratic dignity, independent of the royal court, could be asserted. The key features of their conversational ideal were equality, reciproc-ity and a certain ease and informality. This is the territory explored persuasively by Daniel Gordon, for whom "the whole preoccupation with the art of conversation in the late seventeenth century, in fact, constitutes the key element in the gradual transformation of aristo-cratic thought into Enlightenment philosophy. . . . [O]n the basis of the metanorms of exchange developed in seventeenth-century theories of conversation, eighteenth-century thinkers imagined other, not necessarily verbal, activities as forms of civility."[27]

Though both Dena Goodman and Daniel Gordon are students of France, a consequence of their rethinking of Enlightenment origins and character is to reposition England in the narrative of Enlightenment. Although seventeenth-century English luminaries from Bacon to Newton have long been recognized as inspirational for the Enlightenment, England was also usually considered to have been immune to the Enlightenment.[28] However, in relation to the conversational Enlightenment, England is a most central locale, not only because in the early eighteenth century English writers gave an influential rearticulation to the ideal, but because from the early eighteenth century England pioneered an elaborated world of conversational opportunity.

The impulse in England to assert the importance of conversation grew out of local political and ideological needs. In the wake of the 1688 Revolution, English Whigs constructed a cultural ideology organized around notions of conversation and politeness in order to legitimate the new political and cultural order which emerged then and survived into the nineteenth century.[29] In the decades after the Glorious Revolution, this ideology lost its partisan color and came to shape social, intellectual and cultural patterns throughout Britain in ways that were more and more generalized. Polite conversability became a great self-image of the age, a blueprint for many aspects of middling and upper-class culture. At the same time, it became influential throughout Europe, being appropriated and adapted to varieties of circumstances.

The Enlightenment was inspired by Bacon, Newton and Locke, but it also relied on the conversational idioms reinvented by the Whig cultural ideologists.[30] Anthony Ashley Cooper, the third earl of Shaftesbury, is a particularly interesting figure to examine. Not only was he a tutelary spirit of the conversational Enlightenment, but his example defies, in highly significant ways, generalizations about the Enlightenment in the postmodern critique. I offer him here as an Enlightenment opponent of scientism, a figure who refused to accept that science should set philosophy's agenda. As Hans-Georg Gadamer has indicated, Shaftesbury should be located among long-standing rhetorical, historicist and culturalist strands of discourse that were highly active in the eighteenth century.[31]

～

Nothing could be farther from the scientistic character ascribed by the postmodern critique to the Enlightenment than Shaftesbury's apothegmatic statement: "To philosophize, in a just signification, is but to carry good breeding a step higher." [32] He enunciated here his patently moral, aesthetic and political goals for philosophy, namely, to enhance the virtue, taste, and citizenship of gentlemen. Shaping the subjectivity of gentlemen was precisely the task, in Shaftesbury's view, that modern philosophy, embodied in the likes of Descartes, Hobbes and Locke, had begun to abandon.

However, the apothegm also indicated the close connection between philosophy and conversation since the heart of good breeding was the art of conversation. Shaftesbury's project of enlightenment was nothing less than the recovery of conversation. "If the best of our modern conversations," he wrote,

> are apt to run chiefly upon trifles, if rational discourses (especially those of a deeper speculation) have lost their credit and are in disgrace because of their formality, there is reason for more allowance in the way of humour and gaiety. An easier method of treating these subjects will make them more agreeable and familiar. To dispute about them will be the same as about other matters. They need not spoil good company or take from the ease or pleasure of a polite conversation.[33]

Building on ancient traditions of rhetoric as well as more recent expositions of conversation, Shaftesbury sought a *rapprochement* between philosophy and the world that would create, with philosophical worldliness, a new model of public discourse. Thus, he was an exemplar of the process, discussed by Daniel Gordon, through which face-to-face conversation was transmuted into a norm for society as a whole, and he was, as Jürgen Habermas envisioned it, a philosopher of the public sphere. Shaftesbury's project of enlightenment was an effort not to extend the accomplishment of seventeenth-century philosophy but to remedy the disintegrating effect of its having abandoned the world.

Shaftesbury showed how polite conversation could elicit values of social, cultural and ultimately political import. He indicated the parameters of this discursive practice by reflecting on a recent "free" conversation:

> It was, I must own, a very diverting [conversation], and perhaps not the less so for ending as abruptly as it did, and in such a sort of confusion as almost brought to nothing whatever had been advanced in the discourse before . . . . A great many fine schemes, it is true, were destroyed; many grave reasonings, overturned; but, this being done without offence to the parties concerned and with improvement to the good humour of the company, it set the appetite the keener to such conversations. And I am persuaded that, had Reason herself been to judge of her own interest, she would have thought she received more advantage in the main from that easy and familiar way than from the usual stiff adherence to a particular opinion.[34]

This conversation was serious without being solemn. In fact, it was diverting in the senses both that it was agreeable and that it was full of diversity. Its lack of order did not impede its intellectual value.[35] Indeed, this conversation—critical, open-ended, amiable—served the interests of reason by undermining unfounded opinion, by covering many topics and by encouraging further discussion. What Shaftesbury meant by "reason" here and elsewhere is unclear. Certainly, he stood on the trajectory from scholastic notions of right reason toward notions of empirical and discursive reason.[36] But reason may not have signified much more here than reasonableness, a pragmatic standard that arose by agreement among those present in the conversation. In any case, it is impossible to see Shaftesbury's use of "reason" as conforming to a model of Enlightenment reason as disembodied and decontextualized. Reason, for Shaftesbury, was a collaborative project conveyed by conversation.

Conversation was also anti-authoritarian. It implied activity among the participants. If, as Shaftesbury said, reason was a habit actuated in the practice of conversation, conversers were agents: they resisted the passivity of mere listening.[37] Attached to their activity was also a kind of equality. If not equally endowed with reason or wit, participants in conversation were equal in their capacity to deploy what they had of them.

Conversation also managed to be aligned both with liberty and discipline. An important reason that such a conversation was pleasurable was that it was free: it involved "a freedom of raillery, a liberty in decent language to question everything, and an allowance of unravelling or refuting any argument without offence to the arguer."[38] The freedom that conduced to pleasure here was freedom to question and even to ridicule. Such discursive or intellectual freedom was not a legal entitlement or a politically sanctioned domain of latitude but, rather, the precondition of rational interchange, a convention for the operation of conversation. This was an endorsement of freedom that had nothing to do with rights—it is important to remember, in light of post-modern complaints about the language of rights, that there are many ways to persuade us that freedom is a value, and the language of rights is only one. At the same time, politeness depended on self-restraint, a willingness to make concessions to others, whether they deserve it or not. In the paradigm of politeness, liberty and discipline were hardly antagonistic but rather were folded in upon one another as values. Postmodernism in the Foucauldian vein has given discipline such a bad name that one must be explicit about its obvious necessity for collaborative human action.

For Shaftesbury, then, polite conversation was, in Habermas's expression, an ideal speech situation: the very nature of a polite conversation implied a normative framework for human relations since its conventions implied the values of freedom, equality, activity, pleasure, and restraint. Unpacking Shaftesbury's conversational ideal illustrates cultural tendencies that hardly accord with the identification of the eighteenth century with triumphant scientism. Indeed, his model of intellectual sociability offers many of the virtues of conversation to which postmodernists are attracted.

Shaftesbury's conversational ideal was also significant, in the discourse of philosophy, as an intervention that aimed precisely to limit and reverse the influence of science and scientifically inspired philosophy. In the philosophical dialogue, "The Moralists," a character complained that philosophy "is no longer active in the world" because "we have immured her, poor lady, in colleges and cells and have set her servilely to such works as those in the mines. Empirics and pedantic sophists are her chief pupils. The school syllogism and the elixir are the choicest of her products."[39] Academics and virtuosi represented the chief menaces to any significant, that is, worldly, philosophy: they were responsible for the gap which Shaftesbury's project of enlightenment was meant to bridge. While one of these menaces was, fairly predictably, the Church, the other was none other than modern philosophy as it had taken shape in the seventeenth century under the impress of natural investigations and as it was embodied in Descartes, Hobbes and Locke.[40] As Shaftesbury's figurative language indicated, philosophy had abandoned the world. The empiric in his cell was not just the scientist but also the modern philosopher; epistemology, the modern philosophical project, was on the same level as alchemy. Shaftesbury sneered at the analysis of ideas in Locke's *Essay on Human Understanding* and made slighting references to "clear ideas" and the Cartesian cogito. Bored by the new learning of the seventeenth century, Shaftesbury rejected one of its important outcomes, the reorientation of philosophical reflection around questions of knowledge. Thus, Shaftesbury attacked the privileges claimed by science and by epistemology, offering an Enlightenment protest against scientism.

Moreover, Shaftesbury was sensitive to precisely the abstractive universalism for which postmodernists have criticized the Enlightenment. He took seriously neither the attempt by Descartes to fathom the world by withdrawing from it nor the attempts by Hobbes and Locke, in keeping with the natural law tradition, to imagine humans outside of culture and history as the basis for theorizing the character of society and politics. Shaftesbury's enlightenment project stood against that sort of abstractive universalism and advanced instead an attempt to historicize human moral experience and ground it in conversation.[41]

Thus, in the name of polite philosophy, Shaftesbury's enlightenment project rejected the writers who were later canonized as the guiding spirits of "the Enlightenment." By pointing out the continuity between philosophy and politeness, Shaftesbury was prescribing ethical, aesthetic, and civic contents for philosophy. He was also proposing the ideal of the gentleman as philosopher. This ideal required a new site for philosophy, the conversation of gentlemen, and a new form to philosophic activity that was fundamentally dialogic. Thus, Shaftesburian politeness produced a new map of cultural space, in which cultural sites with their protocols of admission and operation were redefined and reevaluated.

Shaftesbury was certainly influential, through Hutcheson to the

Enlightenment in Scotland and through Diderot to the Enlightenment in France. However, he was also representative: his re-appraisal
of discursive and cultural spaces was part of wider patterns of cultural
transformation in contemporary Britain and Europe. It was hardly accidental that Shaftesbury's contemporary, Joseph Addison, defined
the *Spectator*'s aims as relocating philosophy and, so, remapping the
cultural world, bringing "Philosophy out of Closets and Libraries,
Schools and Colleges, to dwell in Clubs and Assemblies, at Tea-
Tables, and Coffee-Houses."[42] As in Shaftesbury, philosophy here was
being transferred from what were represented as solitary or cloistered
environments to worldly and sociable ones. First English-speakers
and then Europeans of many nations imitated the Whig periodicals of
Addison and Steele: they produced their own moral weeklies on the
model of the *Spectator*; but, more tellingly, they sought to reproduce
in their own lives the moralized clubbability represented in the works
of Addison and Steele.[43]

Conversation, politeness, and sociability had remarkable success in-
filtrating a wide range of discussion in the European eighteenth century. Among many writers, the conversational ideal was extensively
reiterated. Conversation was lauded as a concrete activity, and such
praise did much to enhance the elaboration of actual sites of conversation. However, conversation was also a figure of the entire civilizing
process, central to so much Enlightenment thinking. Writers dwelled
on the meanings of natural human sociability. However, the endorsement of sociability was more than a simple counter to theories of ego-
ism, expressed by Thomas Hobbes or Bernard Mandeville. It implied
an understanding of the social and cultural development of the human
individual and species through communication and interaction. Self
and society were refined and advanced through the process of conversation, understood in a generously metaphorical way.[44] Such socially and
culturally produced selves were far from aloof Cartesian subjectivities.

Even more remarkable was the way that the conversational ideal
came to shape experience. The ideal was a set of representations that
assumed a lived reality. It directed the actual elaboration of sites of
edifying sociability; the aims of conversation were repeatedly for-
malized in collective projects from local clubs to encyclopedic inven-
tories of human experience. Indeed, this sort of association has be-

come in recent interpretations an indicator, when not a defining attribute, of Enlightenment.

The forms and sites of such association were myriad. The coffeehouse provided one convenient locale because it provided an accessible, inexpensive, and fairly democratic place not just for drinking beverages but also for consuming printed material and discussing all it suggested. Coffeehouses also provided a place for lectures, scientific demonstrations, concerts, exhibits and auctions. Not all coffeehouses were polite, nor were all activities at any coffeehouse polite, but coffeehouses could be characterized as places for decorous conversation which refined the taste and polite capacities of those present.[45]

At the other end of the institutional spectrum was the salon, an occasion for conversation that met regularly at the home of a high-born woman who, as *salonnière*, exercised an ordering and disciplining function. From the seventeenth century, salons were sites for a redefinition of the French nobility according to the value of politeness. In the eighteenth century, the French tradition of *politesse* merged with Addisonian and Shaftesburian ideas, making salons occasions for a rich, bracing, and edifying conversation that defined the Enlightenment in France.[46]

Between the coffeehouse and the salon were the many kinds of associations and societies that scholars have been identifying all over Europe: language societies, learned academies, Masonic lodges, reading circles, literary and all manner of other clubs. There was great variety here, but many of these shared basic features: they sought to combine sociability and edification in orderly conversation among people from different orders of society.[47]

Thus, the Enlightenment was a conversable world not just in theory but in cultural practice. This is what Lorraine Daston, cited earlier, means by the "sociable light" of the eighteenth century. Sociability did not mean amicability, but even antagonism was subjected to rules: "views were developed, propounded, and criticized within reactive contexts—in conversations, correspondences, disputes, and above all, reviews." The intellectual life of the Enlightenment was "a great echo chamber" of reverberating opinion, whose rhythms followed "the movements of conversation," even when they worked "across time and space."[48]

ᗡ

In such a culture, conversation came to be a model for many intellectual practices, including natural science. While Shaftesbury and Addison both regarded natural science as peripheral to polite culture, recent research suggests that scientific activity in the eighteenth century prospered as a facet of this conversable culture. In the words of the editors of the recent *The Sciences in Enlightened Europe*, "the polite culture of taste and conversation is the relevant context for much Enlightenment science, not the world of professionalization or institutional formation."[49] The polite character of eighteenth-century natural science is worth emphasizing here because science and decontextualized scientific modes of reasoning are central targets in the postmodern critique of the Enlightenment legacy. But historians of science have shown that even eighteenth-century science was embedded in the culture of conversation and as such was hardly fit to leave scientism as its legacy.

From the 1970s, the notion of polite science was introduced into the historiography to account for the social conditions of scientific production in the eighteenth century.[50] The expression "polite science" was pointedly used to distinguish it from what came later and suggested the ways in which eighteenth-century science was ineligible as the progenitor of modern science. The politeness of science was partly a matter of the personnel of scientific investigation: eighteenth-century science was dominated by a gentlemanly cohort who practiced or sponsored scientific investigation as one feature of a more general conversable amateur culture. The idea of polite science also helped to specify the settings and goals of scientific investigation—exactly the range of conversable settings, discussed above, that we now take as indicative of the presence of Enlightenment in the eighteenth century. To an extent, politeness could even be used to characterize the content of scientific work: a science framed by a natural theology, which expressed also the cultural ideology of a gentlemanly oligarchy.[51] One can even make the case that the effort to detach reason from context, science from its surroundings, and to arrogate it to a troop of experts, was an anti-Enlightenment project by nineteenth-century figures who, for their own very good reasons, wanted to unfasten science from the well integrated role it had in the general culture of the eighteenth century.[52]

~

By emphasizing the conversational theme, I risk being cast as a defender of the Enlightenment; nevertheless, this essay does not seek to defend the Enlightenment by balancing the negatives in the postmodern critique with a cozier characterization or by constructing an alternative and more hopeful genealogy for modernity.[53] If anything, this essay is a defense of historical thinking against the unhistorical propensity to offer treatments of the Enlightenment in the tone of either accusation or defense. The forensic tone arises, of course, because, in relation to the contested category of the Modern, the Enlightenment is assigned a privileged status as founder, ancestor, and legacy-leaver.

However, historians should have a rather large investment in forswearing this kit of metaphors. That is because the engagement of professional history with the past is defined by a commitment to the notion of context—understanding things, developments, people, writings, whatever, with respect to other things, developments, people, writings, that are contemporary. The violation of this commitment provides us with our Scarlet Letter, that grave sin called Anachronism. The metaphorical array including genealogy and legacy is an invitation to anachronism because it interprets aspects of the past by reference to what they are alleged to have led to.

Some arguments against this approach are found in that war-horse of the modern professional historical consciousness, *The Whig Interpretation of History* by Herbert Butterfield. Butterfield's target in this classic book was a kind of historical genealogist: the Whig historian who wants to know "to whom do we owe our liberty?" In *The Whig Interpretation of History*, Butterfield's best examples came from the historiography of the Reformation, which, in Butterfield's time and for long afterward, was depicted as a turning point on the road to modernity, with Martin Luther as a hero of individualism, liberty, and even tolerance, while the Church at Rome was characterized as a retrogressive villain.

Butterfield made two salient rebuttals to this approach to history. One was an insistence on the local nature of past struggles: "The issue between Protestants and Catholics in the sixteenth century was an issue of their world and not of our world, and we are being definitely unhistorical, we are forgetting that Protestantism and Catholicism have both had a long history since 1517, if we argue from a rash analogy that the one was fighting for something like our modern world while the other was trying to prevent its coming."[54] It follows, according to Butterfield, that one should regard Protestant and Catholics as "distant and strange people." This is exactly the opposite assumption of the genealogist who is looking for familiars in the past.

The second and more important point on which Butterfield insisted is the reductionism of a genealogical approach that tends to abstract individuals, or ideas, or themes from a larger historical process. He writes, "It is not by a line but by a labyrinthine piece of network that one would have to make the diagram of the course by which religious liberty has come down to us, for this liberty comes by devious tracks and is born of strange conjunctures, it represents purposes marred perhaps more than purposes achieved, and it owes more than we can tell to many agencies that had little to do with either religion or liberty. We cannot tell to whom we must be grateful for this religious liberty and there is no logic in being grateful to anybody or anything except to the whole past which produced the whole present. . . ."[55] History, he concluded, is not the study of origins; rather it is the analysis of "all the mediations by which the past was turned into our present."[56]

Like the Reformation, the Enlightenment was not one project but rather an array of projects. Modernity was central to many of these projects, but this modernity was an eighteenth-century one. The labors of these people were local in a setting of immense complexity. If one wants "legacies," one has to recognize that the "legacies" of their projects are multiple, if not infinite, and, at the same, these "legacies" are strictly untraceable.

The fact is that many insights associated with postmodern theory support the kind of historical consciousness advertised in Butterfield's famous book. These insights have redeployed and sharpened valuable tools of analysis for understanding the complexity of human life, past and present. With the encouragement of postmodern concerns and emphases, historical study is recasting its accounts.[57] The developments that one finds in most areas of historical investigation include:

foregrounding multiplicity and contestation instead of unity and unanimity; attending to developments at the margins as well as those at the center, and, beyond that, rethinking the figure of "center/margin" and its application; evaluating the claims of historical actors with greater skepticism, especially the suspiciously high-minded claims of Art, Science, Philosophy, and Truth; shedding "the economic," "the social," and other claimants to be the ultimate ground of historical explanation; and finally, insisting that the terrain for historical investigation is practice (a.k.a. culture), the point at which such categories as "structure," "event," "experience," "performance," and "meaning" collide.

Finally, and most relevant to the Enlightenment, postmodernism has encouraged greater diffidence about the long-term patterns. Indeed, the skepticism about grand narratives, associated with Jean-François Lyotard, has helped to sanction a rethinking of stories that had assumed a commonplace character. By insisting that people come to terms with the concept of the "postmodern," postmodernism has problematized "the modern" and the polarities, such as archaic/modern, which have given shape to much historical storytelling. Resonances between past and present which were usually drowned out by the din of "the modern" and "modernization" have become audible again. It has become possible to discuss the history of the last three centuries without assigning tried and true roles to the Industrial Revolution, the French Revolution, the rising middle class, the declining aristocracy, and so forth. "Watershed," "turning point," and "point of origin" are being cast out of the metaphorical kit in favor of new metaphors.

The irony is that, while the concept of the postmodern can be used to free the imagination to rethink the narratives of recent centuries, it can also be used to provide a grand narrative with a vengeance, a story that violates many of the insights that are properly associated with the postmodern. Instead of being a story about diversity, it is a story about unanimity. Instead of being a story about contestation, it is a story about a strict hegemony. Instead of suggesting that practice has to be examined as the site of cultural power, it assumes that what canonical writers write suffices for characterizing an entire culture. Instead of allowing for discordance in kinds of change over time, indeed for a multiplicity of narratives, it assumes a synchronicity of change across the aspects of society.

In the interests of a complex vision of the eighteenth century, I have discussed the conversational ideal and its impact. However, this essay is not intended as a contribution to an alternative genealogy to that of the postmodern critique of scientism. This is not a sketch towards a history of the rise of modern conversation or modern politeness or modern publicity or modern science. Is antiquarianism the alternative to genealogy? I think not. The features discussed are sufficiently different from those in our society that they are genuinely foreign. At the same time, they seem to be recognizable: they have a resonance with some of the predicaments in which we find ourselves. Resonance seems a more persuasive metaphor than genealogy for comprehending our relation to this past. As Quentin Skinner has pointed out, history helps us assess the present not just by showing the origins of current ideas and practices but also by indicating abandoned ideas and practices—the many routes not taken.[58] Anyone (whether postmodernist or not) who senses that conversation and dialogue may contribute to the prospect of social, political, and cultural renewal may gain something from reflecting on the Enlightenment as an age of conversation, which provides historical testimony to both the limits and possibilities of a conversational model.

NOTES

Notes

Hollinger: The Enlightenment and Cultural Conflict

For helpful comments on versions of this paper presented at several workshops and conferences, I wish to thank Keith Baker, David Bates, Malachai Hacohen, Steven Lukes, Peter Reill, and Bernard Yack.

1. See, for example, Ernest Gellner, *Postmodernism, Reason and Religion* (London: Routledge, 1992).

2. John Gray, *Enlightenment's Wake: Politics and Culture at the Close of the Modern Age* (London: Routledge, 1995).

3. Conor Cruise O'Brien, *On the Eve of the Millennium: The Future of Democracy through an Age of Unreason* (New York: Free Press, 1996); Stephen Toulmin, *Cosmopolis: The Hidden Agenda of Modernity* (New York: Free Press, 1990); Alasdair McIntyre, *After Virtue: A Study in Moral Theory* (Notre Dame, Ind.: University of Notre Dame Press, 1981); Gray, *Enlightenment's Wake*.

4. For an example of deep suspicion of the Enlightenment expressed within the context of the multiculturalist debates, see Robin Kelley, *Yo' Mama's Disfunktional!: Fighting the Culture Wars in Urban America* (Boston: Beacon Press, 1997).

5. Lionel Trilling, "On the Teaching of Modern Literature," published first in 1961 and later reprinted in Trilling, *Beyond Culture: Essays on Literature and Learning* (New York: Viking, 1965), 3–30

6. H. Stuart Hughes, *Consciousness and Society: The Reconstruction of European Social Thought, 1890–1930* (New York: Knopf, 1958).

7. For an interpretation of the process by which the modern canon was created and maintained, see David A. Hollinger, "The Canon and Its Keepers: Modernism and Mid-Twentieth Century American Intellectuals," in Hollinger, *In the American Province: Studies in the History and Historiography of Ideas* (Bloomington: Indiana University Press, 1985), 74–91.

8. Carl Schorske, *Fin-de-Siècle Vienna: Politics and Culture* (New York: Knopf, 1980).

9. Richard Ellmann and Charles Fiedelson, Jr., *The Modern Tradition: Backgrounds of Modern Literature* (New York: Oxford University Press, 1965).

10. Robert B. Pippin, "Nietzsche and the Origins of the Idea of Modernism," *Inquiry* 26 (1983): 151; Robert B. Pippin, *Modernism as a Philosophical Problem: On the Dissatisfactions of European High Culture* (Cambridge, Mass.: Blackwell, 1991), 4, 20.

11. For an example of the genre, see Steven Best and Douglas Kellner, eds., *Postmodern Theory: Critical Interrogations* (New York: Guilford Press, 1991).

12. Much of this paragraph, and parts of the previous two, are adapted from my "Postscript 1993," in *Modernist Impulses in the Human Sciences 1870–1930,* ed. Dorothy Ross (Baltimore: Johns Hopkins University Press, 1994), 46–53, which updates an essay of 1987, "The Knower and the Artificer," reprinted in the volume edited by Ross.

13. One of the few books on the modernist-postmodernist divide to gasp this is Andreas Huyssen, *After the Great Divide: Modernism, Mass Culture, Postmodernism* (Bloomington: Indiana University Press, 1986), esp. 188–91.

14. François Lyotard, *The Postmodern Condition: A Report on Knowledge*, trans. Geoff Bennington and Brian Massumi (Minneapolis: University of Minnesota Press, 1984).

15. Richard Rorty, "Postmodern Bourgeois Liberalism," *Journal of Philosophy* 80 (1983): 583–89.

16. Frederic Jameson, "Postmodernism, or the Cultural Logic of Late Capitalism," *New Left Review* 146 (1984): 53–92.

17. The most brilliant of these virtuoso performances was David Harvey, *The Condition of Postmodernity: An Enquiry into the Origins of Cultural Change* (Cambridge, Mass.: Blackwell, 1989).

18. Theodor Adorno and Max Horkheimer, *Dialectic of Enlightenment*, trans. John Cumming (New York: Herder and Herder, 1972).

19. Gellner, *Postmodernism, Reason and Religion*, 80.

20. Kwame Anthony Appiah, "Cosmopolitan Patriots," *Critical Inquiry* 23 (spring 1997): 617–39.

21. Ian Hacking, *Representing and Intervening: Introductory Topics in the Philosophy of Science* (New York: Cambridge University Press, 1983).

22. Michael Ignatieff, *Blood and Belonging: Journeys into the New Nationalism* (New York: Farrar, Straus, and Giroux, 1994).

23. Lawrence Birken, *Hitler as Philosophe: Remnants of the Enlightenment in National Socialism* (Westport, Conn.: Praeger, 1995); I allude to Joseph W. Bendersky's review in *American Historical Review* 101 (Dec. 1996): 1570–71.

24. Goeffrey Galt Harpham, "So…What *Is* Enlightenment? An Inquisition into Modernity," *Critical Inquiry* 20 (spring 1994): 524–56.

Rorty: The Enlightenment and 'Postmodernism'

1. Carl Becker, *The Heavenly City of the Eighteenth-Century Philosophers* (New Haven: Yale University Press, 1991), 64–65. The phrase in quotation marks about our natural faculties is from Locke.

2. John Gray, *Enlightenment's Wake: Politics and Culture at the Close of the Modern Age* (London: Routledge, 1995), 170.

3. The text of Gray's book omits "than," but it seems to be required if the sense of the sentence is what I take it to be.

4. Slavoj Zizek, *Looking Awry: An Introduction to Jacques Lacan through Popular Culture* (Cambridge, Mass.: MIT Press, 1991), 157, 156.

Knudsen: The Historicist Enlightenment

1. The literature on German Enlightenment historiography has become enormous. Among the recent works I have found most valuable are Andreas Kraus, *Vernunft und Geschichte* (Freiburg: Herder, 1963); Karl Hammer and Jürgen Voss, eds., *Historische Forschung im 18. Jahrhundert* (Bonn: Rohrscheid, 1976) [hereafter *Historische Forschung*]; Notker Hammerstein, *Jus und Historie* (Göttingen: Vandenhoeck and Ruprecht, 1972); Joachim Streisand, *Geschichtliches Denken von der deutschen Frühaufklärung bis zur Klassik*, 2nd ed. (Berlin: Akademie Verlag, 1967); Peter Hanns Reill, *The German Enlightenment and the Rise of Historicism* (Berkeley: University of California Press, 1975); the essays by Manfred Riedel, Wolf Lepenies, and Eckart Pankoke in Reinhart Koselleck, ed., *Studien zum Beginn der modernen Welt* (Stuttgart: Klett-Cotta, 1977), 300–374; and Reinhart Koselleck, *Vergangene Zukunft* (Frankfurt: Suhrkamp, 1979). A revaluation of much of this literature is contained in a volume edited by Peter Hanns Reill, Hans Erich Bödeker, Georg G. Iggers, and myself: *Aufklärung und Geschichte: Studien zur deutschen Geschichtswissenschaft im 18. Jahrhundert* (Göttingen: Vandenhoeck and Ruprecht, 1986) [hereafter *Aufklärung und Geschichte*]. Regarding the relations of the Enlightenment and historicism, see the orthodox portrait in Helen P. Liebel, "The Enlightenment and the Rise of Historicism in Germany," *Eighteenth-Century Studies* 4/4 (1971): 359–85; also Georg G. Iggers, *The German Conception of History* (Middletown, Conn.: Wesleyan University Press, 1968), 3–43; Iggers, "Historicism," *Dictionary of the History of Ideas*, 4 vols. (New York: Scribner, 1973), 2:456–64. Maurice Mandelbaum has long argued for a broader, depoliticized notion of historicism; see his most recent statement in *History, Man and Reason* (Baltimore: Johns Hopkins University Press, 1971), 41–138, as well as the thoughtful essay by Thomas Nipperdey, "Historismus und Historismuskritik heute," in his *Gesellschaft, Kultur, Theorie* (Göttingen: Vandenhoeck and Ruprecht, 1976), 59–73.

2. See Reill, *German Enlightenment*, chs. 4–5; Notker Hammerstein, "Reichshistorie," in *Aufklärung und Geschichte*, 82–104.

3. See, for instance, Otto Dann, "Das historische Interesse in der deutschen Gesellschaft des 18. Jahrhunderts," in *Historische Forschung*, 405–6.

4. There is a line of classical and idealist thought assimilated by the mainstream German Enlightenment through the works of Bolingbroke, Shaftesbury, and Montesquieu; see, for example, Rudolf Vierhaus, "Montesquieu in Deutschland: zur Geschichte seiner Wirkung als politischer Schriftsteller im 18. Jahrhundert," in Vierhaus, *Deutschland im 18. Jahrhundert: Politische Verfassung, Soziales Gefüge, Geistige Bewegungen* (Göttingen: Vandenhoeck and Ruprecht, 1987), 9–32. See also the general comments in Isaac Kramnick, *Bolingbroke and His Circle* (Cambridge, Mass.: Harvard University Press, 1968), 144, 294; Isaac Kramnick, "Republican Revisionism Revised," *American Historical Review* 87 (1982): 629–44. It is not always easy to sort out neoplatonic and Aristotelian patterns of thought in the context of later eighteenth-century historical writing. The use made of these traditions was different among philosophers than among historians.

5. For Herder, see Emil Adler, *Herder und die deutsche Aufklärung* (Vienna: Europa Verlag, 1968), 136–46. Hans Aarsleff has shown persuasively Herder's dependence on Condillac and cast doubt on Isaiah Berlin's interpretation. See Aarsleff's discussion and his exchange with Berlin, "Vico and Berlin," *London Review of Books* 3, no. 20 (1981): 6–8; 4, no. 10 (1982): 4–5; see also Aarsleff, *From Locke to Saussure: Essays on the Study of Language and Intellectual History* (Minneapolis: University of Minnesota Press, 1987), esp. 117, 150–59 195–98, 218–20. For Berlin's views, see "Herder and the Enlightenment," in his *Vico and Herder* (New York: Viking, 1976), 143–216; also "The Counter-Enlightenment," in *Against the Current: Essays in the History of Ideas*, ed. Henry Hardy (New York: Viking, 1980). On Möser, see Knudsen, *Justus Möser and the German Enlightenment* (Cambridge: Cambridge University Press, 1986).

6. Wilhelm Dilthey, "Das achtzehnte Jahrhundert und die geschichtliche Welt," in *Gesammelte Schriften*, 4th ed. (Stuttgart: B. G. Teubner, 1969), 3: 210–68; Friedrich Meinecke, *Die Entstehüng des Historismus*, ed. and intro. Carl Hinrichs (Munich: Oldenbourg, 1959); Heinrich Ritter von Srbik, *Geist und Geschichte vom deutschen Humanismus bis zur Gegenwart*, 2 vols. (Munich: Oldenbourg, 1950), 1: 84–166. Ulrich Muhlack's recent defense of the traditional historicist position is a thought-provoking account: *Geschichtswissenschaft im Humanismus und in der Aufklärung: Die Vorgeschichte des Historismus* (Munich: Oldenbourg, 1991).

7. Josef Engel, "Die deutschen Universitäten und die Geschichtswissenschaft," *Historische Zeitschrift* 189 (1959): 260–65; Konrad Jarausch, "The Institutionalization of History in Eighteenth Century Germany," in *Aufklärung und Geschichte*, 25–48.

8. Hans Georg Gadamer, *Wahrheit und Methode: Grundzüge einer philosophischen Hermeneutik* (Tübingen: J. C. B. Mohr [Paul Siebeck], 1965), 1–39,

153–62; Hans Frei, *The Eclipse of Biblical Narrative* (New Haven: Yale University Press, 1974). For classicism, see Ulrich Mulack, "Historie und Philologie," and Anthony Grafton, "'Man muß aus der Gegenwart heraufsteigen': History, Tradition, and Traditions of Historical Thought in F. A. Wolf," both in *Aufklärung und Geschichte*, 49–82, 416–29.

9. Michael Ermarth, "Hermeneutics and History," in *Aufklärung und Geschichte*, 193–224.

10. Ermarth, "Hermeneutics and History"; Reill, *German Enlightenment*, 105–12. See also the older study by Hans Müller, *Johann Martin Chladenius* (Berlin: Vaduz, 1917). Muhlack vigorously disputes this view, stressing instead the differentials in historical method; see *Geschichtswissenschaft*, 400–405.

11. Otto Dann, "Das historische Interesse," 392–95; Ingeborg Salzbrunn, "Studien zur deutschen historischen Zeitschriftenwesen von der Göttinger Aufklärung bis zur Herausgabe der Historischen Zeitschrift" (Ph.D. diss., Münster, 1959), intro.; Marlies Prüsener, "Lesegesellschaften im 18. Jahrhundert," *Archiv für Geschichte des Buchwesens* 13 (1973): 427–31, 495–504.

12. Hans Thieme, "Die Zeit des späteren Naturrechts: Eine privatrechtsgeschichtliche Studie," *Zeitschrift für Rechtsgeschichte* 56 (1936): 202–36; Diethelm Klippel, *Politische Freiheit und Freiheitsrechte im deutschen Naturrecht des 18. Jahrhunderts* (Paderborn: Schoningh, 1976); Jürgen Schlumbohm, *Freiheit: die bürgerliche Emanizapationsbewegung in Deutschland im Spiegel ihres Leitwortes* (Düsseldorf: Padagögische Verlag Schwann, 1975), 84–88.

13. Knudsen, *Justus Möser*, chs. 4, 6.

14. Rudolf Vierhaus, "Geschichtsschreibung als Literatur im 18. Jahrhundert," in *Historische Forschung*, 416–31; Bödeker, "Reisebeschreibung im historischen Diskurs der Aufklärung," in *Aufklärung und Geschichte*, 276–98.

15. Friedrich Nicolai, *Beschreibung der königlichen Residenzstädte Berlin und Potsdam*, 3 vols., 3rd ed. (Berlin, 1786); on Nicolai as a historian, see Horst Moller, *Aufklärung in Preußen: der Verleger, Publizist und Geschichtsschreiber Friedrich Nicolai* (Berlin: Colloquium Verlag, 1974), 322–517.

16. Knudsen, "Friedrich Nicolai's 'wirkliche Welt': On Common Sense in the German Enlightenment," in *Mentalitäten und Lebensverhältnisse*, ed. by colleagues and students (Göttingen: Vandenhoeck and Ruprecht, 1982), 90–91.

17. Johann Gottlob Fichte, *Friedrich Nicolais Leben und sonderbare Meinungen*, in vol. 8 of his *Sämmtliche Werke* (Berlin, 1846), 5.

18. Ursula A. J. Becher, "August Ludwig von Schlözer—Analyse eines historischen Diskurses," in *Auflärung und Geschichte*, 345.

19. Quoted in Marcus Paul Bullock, *Romanticism and Marxism: The Philosophical Development of Literary Theory and Literary History in Walter Benjamin* (New York: P. Lang, 1987), 6.

20. Rudolf Vierhaus, "Historiography between Science and Art," in *Leo-*

pold von Ranke and the Shaping of the Historical Discipline, ed. Georg G. Iggers and James M. Powell (Syracuse, N.Y.: Syracuse University Press, 1990), 61–69.

21. Bernd Faulenbach, *Ideologie des deutschen Weges: Die deutsche Geschichte in der Historiographie zwischen Kaiserreich und Nationalsozialismus* (Munich: Oldenbourg, 1980), 130–41.

22. Bruno Bauer, *Geschichte der Politik, Kultur und Aufklärung des 18. Jahrhunderts* (Charlottenburg, 1843); Georg Gervinus, *Einleitung in die Geschichte des 19. Jahrhunderts* (Leipzig, 1853); Karl Biedermann, *Deutschland im achtzehnten Jahrhundert*, 4 vols. (Leipzig, 1867–70); Hermann Hettner, *Geschichte der deutschen Literatur im achtzenten Jahrhundert*, 3 vols. (Leipzig, 1867–80); Franz Mehring, *Die Lessing Legende* (Berlin, 1893).

23. See James Schmidt, ed., *What Is Enlightenment? Eighteenth Century Answers and Twentieth Century Questions* (Berkeley and Los Angeles: University of California Press, 1996).

24. Wolfgang J. Mommsen, "Ranke and the Neo-Rankean School in Imperial Germany," in *Ranke and the Shaping of the Historical Discipline*, 125–40; Georg Iggers, *The German Conception of History*, 90–124.

25. Helmuth Kiesel, "Aufklärung und neuer Irrationalismus in der Weimarer Republik," in *Aufklärung und Gegenaufklärung in der europäischen Literatur, Philosophie und Politik von der Antike bis zur Gegenwart*, ed. Jochen Schmidt (Darmstadt: Wissenschaftliche Buchgesellschaft, 1989), 497–521.

26. Jonathan Knudsen, "Friedrich Meinecke," in *Paths of Continuity: Central European Historiography from the 1930s to the 1950s*, ed. Hartmut Lehmann and James Van Horn Melton (Cambridge: Cambridge University Press, 1994), 49–71.

27. Jörn Rüsen, "Meineckes Entstehung des Historismus: Eine kritische Betrachtung," in *Friedrich Meinecke heute*, ed. Michael Erbe (Berlin: Colloquium Verlag, 1981), 89. See also the sharp criticism of René König, *Soziologie in Deutschland: Begründer, Verächter, Verfächter* (Munich: Hanser, 1987), 272–74.

28. *Historische Zeitschrift* 139 (1929): 599. See also Hans Schleier, *Die bürgerliche Geschichtsschreibung der Weimarer Republik* (Berlin: Akademie Verlag, 1975), 299–300.

29. *Historische Zeitschrift* 149 (1934): 582–86. See also Iggers, *The German Conception of History*, 217.

30. Meinecke, *Die Deutsche Katastrophe: Betrachtungen und Erinnerungen* (Wiesbaden and Zurich: Brockhaus, 1946).

31. Auerbach, *Mimesis: The Representation of Reality in Western Literature*, trans. Willard Trask (Princeton: Princeton University Press, 1953), 392.

32. *Gesammelte Aufsätze zur romanischen Philologie* (Bern, 1967).

33. Heinz Dieter Kittsteiner, "Walter Benjamin's Historicism," *New German Critique* 39 (1986), 179–215.

Sluga: Heidegger and the Critique of Reason

1. Martin Heidegger, "The Word of Nietzsche: 'God is Dead,'" in *The Question Concerning Technology*, trans. William Lovitt (New York: Harper and Row, 1977), 112.

2. Michael Zimmerman, *Heidegger's Confrontation with Modernity: Technology, Politics, Art* (Bloomington: Indiana University Press, 1990), 218. The following references are to the same text.

3. Zimmerman quotes this phrase from Jeffrey Herf, *Reactionary Modernism: Technology, Culture, and Politics in Weimar and the Third Reich* (New York: Cambridge University Press, 1984), 12.

4. This may, in part, be due to a recent tendency to overanalyze the significance of Heidegger's 1929 debate with Ernst Cassirer in Davos. In recent accounts of the event Cassirer, the later author of a book on the Enlightenment, is cast as the defender of an enlightened Neo-Kantianism while Heidegger is assigned the role of the anti-Enlightenment agitator.

5. See Hildegard Feick, *Index zu Heideggers "Sein und Zeit,"* 4th ed. (Tübingen: Niemeyer, 1991), 122–31. Heidegger's most extensive remarks about the Enlightenment occur in one of his earliest lecture courses, eight years before *Being and Time*, and even then his words are motivated by other concerns. The context is a critical examination of the nineteenth-century concept of culture. According to Heidegger that concept embodies two contradictory elements: a profound historical consciousness, on the one hand, and a belief in itself as an unusually valuable achievement, on the other. In order to explain this peculiar conjunction Heidegger reaches back to the Enlightenment origins of this notion of culture and traces its transformation since then. He writes that "Culture — *les nations les plus éclairées* — are for Bayle, Bossuet, Montesquieu the nations of culture rather than the peoples of nature"; see Heidegger, *Phänomenologie und transzendentale Wertphilosophie*, summer semester 1919, in *Gesamtausgabe* (Frankfurt: Klostermann, 1987), 56/57: 132. The notion of Enlightenment is thus, on Heidegger's account, not a historical one but refers to culture or civilization in general. But eventually the term came to signify the distinctive culture of the eighteenth century and thus "the concept of the Enlightenment turns into a methodological category for the purpose of a historiographical and chronological characterization." But the Enlightenment, understood in this way, had a peculiar relation to history. "That was due to the then absolute domination of a mathematized natural science and of rational thinking in general. The triumphs of pure thought let them seek the ideal of spirit in general to which all experience of mankind was supposed to converge. The Enlightenment saw itself as the fulfillment of history on its way out of barbarism, superstition, deception, and chaos" (ibid.). The Enlightenment conception of history "resolved all historical processes into conceptual connections, causes, and intentions, conceptually transparent purposes" (133). Even Kant understood history in the Enlight-

enment sense; culture meant for him "formation and completion of rational determinations, rules, and purposes of mankind" (ibid.). Only with Herder there emerged, according to Heidegger, "a decisive clarification of historical consciousness," a recognition "of the autonomous, individual value of every nation, of every age, of every historical phenomenon in general" (ibid.). The distinctive feature of the Enlightenment is thus, in Heidegger's early account, its as yet undeveloped historical consciousness, its one-directional and purpose conception of historical processes, and its adherence to an absolute and, hence, unhistorical notion of reason.

6. Heidegger, *Nietzsche*, trans. Joan Stambaugh, David Farrell Krell, and Frank A. Capuzzi, ed. David Farrell Krell (San Francisco: Harper, 1991) 4: 99. Here as elsewhere I have altered translations where that seemed important or useful.

7. Ibid., 3: 50.

8. Ibid. It is evident that Heidegger did not mean his critique of reason to issue in an irrationalist world view.

9. Heidegger, *"Das Denken beginnt erst dann, wenn wir erfahren haben, daß die seit Jahrhunderten verhherlichte Vernunft die hartnäckigste Widersacherin des Denkens ist,"* in *Holzwege* (Frankfurt: Klostermann, 1952), 247.

10. Geoffrey Warnock, "Reason," in *The Encyclopedia of Philosophy*, ed. Paul Edwards (New York: Macmillan, 1967), 7: 83.

11. See Jacob and Wilhelm Grimm, *Deutsches Wörterbuch*, vol. 12 (Leipzig: S. Hirzel, 1893), cols. 913, 927ff. *"Dem Vernehmen nach"* means "according to hearsay."

12. Heidegger, *The Principle of Reason*, trans. Reginald Lilly, 120 (Bloomington: Indiana University Press, 1996).

13. Heidegger, *Nietzsche*, 3: 218.

14. Ludwig Wittgenstein, *On Certainty*, trans. D. Paul and G. E. M. Anscombe, ed. G. E. M. Anscombe and G. H. V. Wright (New York: Harper, 1969), sections 97 and 99.

15. Nietzsche, *The Gay Science*, trans. Walter Kaufmann (New York: Vintage Books, 1974), section 125. The following numbers refer to sections in this text.

16. Foucault, *Madness and Civilization*, 289.

17. Nietzsche, *The Will to Power*, trans. Walter Kaufmann and R. J. Hollingdale (New York: Vintage Books, 1986), section 407.

18. Heidegger, "The Word of Nietzsche," 64. The following page references are to the same text.

19. Quoted in Hans Sluga, *Heidegger's Crisis* (Cambridge, Mass.: Harvard University Press, 1993), 214.

20. Heidegger, *Introduction to Metaphysics*, trans. Ralph Manheim (New Haven: Yale University Press, 1995), 199. The value-theorists, it should be added, were also given to think of the world in terms of the notion of organic unity, a concept Nietzsche dismisses as one of the shadows of God.

21. Heidegger, "The Word of Nietzsche," 62. The following page references are once more to that text.

22. Heidegger, *The Principle of Reason*, 104. The following page references are to the same text. In these lectures Heidegger makes much of the fact that the Latin *ratio* is rendered in German as both *Grund* and *Vernunft*. Thus, Leibniz's *principium rationis* becomes in German *Der Satz vom Grund*.

23. Heidegger, "The Word of Nietzsche," 55 and 57.

24. Heidegger, *The Principle of Reason*, 113.

25. Wittgenstein, *On Certainty*, section 559. The following references are to sections of the same text.

26. Nietzsche, *The Will to Power*, section 693.

27. "The Word of Nietzsche," 81. The following references are once again to pages of this text.

28. Heidegger, *Discourse on Thinking*, trans. John H. Andersen and E. Hans Freund (New York: Harper, 1966), 53. The following reference is to the same text.

29. Max Horkheimer and Theodor Adorno, *Die Dailektik der Aufklärung* (Amsterdam: Querido, 1947), 13.

30. Heidegger, *The Principle of Reason*, 129.

Wright: "A Bright Clear Mirror"

1. For Gay's declaration of independence from Cassirer, see Peter Gay, "The Social History of Ideas: Ernst Cassirer and After," in *The Critical Spirit: Essays in Honor of Herbert Marcuse*, ed. Kurt H. Wolff and Barrington More, Jr. (Boston: Beacon Press, 1967), 106–20.

2. See above all Darnton's double review (first published in 1971) of Gay's *Enlightenment* and the famous collection *Livre et société*—the first seen as descended from Cassirer, the second from Mornet: Robert Darnton, "The Social History of Ideas," in *The Kiss of Lamourette: Reflections in Cultural History* (New York: Norton, 1990), 219–52.

3. Dena Goodman, *The Republic of Letters: A Cultural History of the French Enlightenment* (Princeton: Princeton University Press, 1994), 63.

4. The chief sources in print for biographical information on Cassirer are Dimitry Gawronsky, "Ernst Cassirer: His Life and His Work," in *The Philosophy of Ernst Cassirer*, ed. Paul Arthur Schlipp, vol. 6 of *The Library of Living Philosophers* (New York: Tudor Publishing, 1949), 1–37; and Toni Cassirer's memoir, *Mein Leben mit Ernst Cassirer: Erinnerungen von Toni Cassirer* (Hildesheim: Gerstenberg Verlag, 1981). For the shape of Cassirer's intellectual career, see David Lipton, *Ernst Cassirer: The Dilemma of a Liberal Intellectual in Germany, 1914–1933* (Toronto: Toronto University Press, 1978); Walter Eggers and Sigrid Mayer, *Ernst Cassirer: An Annotated Bibliography* (New York: Garland Publishing, 1988), i–xxiv; and especially Heinz Paetzold, *Ernst Cassirer—Von Marburg nach New York: Eine philosophische Biographie* (Darm-

stadt: Wissenschaftliche Buchgesellschaft, 1995). The latter has also published a fascinating set of comparative reflections on aspects of Cassirer's thought: Heinz Paetzold, *Die Realität der symbolischen Formen: Die Kulturphilosophie Ernst Cassirers im Kontext* (Darmstadt: Wissenschaftliche Buchgesellschaft, 1994).

5. Yale published an English translation in 1981: Ernst Cassirer, *Kant's Life and Thought*, trans. James Haden, intro. Stephan Körner (New Haven: Yale University Press, 1981).

6. See Toni Cassirer, *Mein Leben mit Ernst Cassirer*, 118–19.

7. For Troeltsch's review, see the *Theologische Literaturzeitung* 18–19 (1917): 368–71.

8. Ernst Cassirer, *Wesen und Wirkung des Symbolbegriffs* (Darmstadt: Wissenschaftliche Buchgesellschaft, 1969), 175.

9. Ernst Cassirer, *Philosophie der symbolischen Formen*, vol. 3, *Phänomenologie der Erkenntnis* (Darmstadt: Wissenschaftliche Buchgesellschaft, 1964), 235; *The Philosophy of Symbolic Forms*, vol. 3, *The Phenomenology of Knowledge*, trans. Ralph Mannheim (New Haven: Yale University Press, 1957), 202.

10. *Phänomenologie der Erkenntnis*, 117–18; *The Phenomenology of Knowledge*, 100.

11. Ernst Cassirer, *Philosophie der symbolischen Formen*, vol. 1, *Die Sprache* (Darmstadt: Wissenschaftliche Buchgesellschaft, 1964), 15; *The Philosophy of Symbolic Forms*, vol. 1, *Language*, trans. Ralph Mannheim (New Haven: Yale University Press, 1955), 83.

12. Ernst Cassirer, *Philosophie der symbolischen Formen*, vol. 2, *Das Mythische Denken* (Darmstadt: Wissenschaftliche Buchgesellschaft, 1964), ix–x.

13. *Phänomenologie der Erkenntnis*, vi; *The Phenomenology of Knowledge*, xiv.

14. John Michael Krois, *Cassirer: Symbolic Forms and History* (New Haven: Yale University Press, 1987), 79. For a lucid account of Cassirer's relation to Hegel and Kant, see Donald Phillip Verene, "Kant, Hegel, and Cassirer: The Origins of the Philosophy of Symbolic Forms," *Journal of the History of Ideas* 30 (1969): 33–46.

15. For Heidegger's review of *Mythical Thought*, see *Deutsche Literaturzeitung für Kritik der Internationalen Wissenschaft* 21 (1928): 1000–1012.

16. See "A Discussion between Ernst Cassirer and Martin Heidegger," trans. Francis Slade, in *The Existentialist Tradition: Selected Writings*, ed. Nino Langiulli (Garden City, N.J.: Anchor, 1971), 192–203. For a succinct and authoritative analysis, see Pierre Aubenque, "Le Débat de 1929 entre Cassirer et Heidegger," in *Ernst Cassirer: De Marburg à New York: L'Intinéraire philosophique*, ed. Jean Seidengart (Paris: Editions de Cerf, 1990), 81–96.

17. Ernst Cassirer, "Kant and the Problem of Metaphysics: Remarks on Martin Heidegger's Interpretation of Kant," in *Kant: Disputed Questions*, ed. Moltke S. Gram (Chicago: Quadrangle Books, 1967), 155. The review was first published in *Kant-Studien* 36 (1931): 1–26.

18. *Die Philosophie der Aufklärung* (Tübingen: J. C. B. Mohr, 1932), vii; *The*

Philosophy of the Enlightenment, trans. Fritz C. A. Koelln and James P. Pettegrove (Princeton: Princeton University Press, 1951), v [hereafter *PA* and *PE,* respectively].

19. *PA,* xii; *PE,* viii.
20. *PA,* xvi; *PE,* xi–xii.
21. *PA,* 47; *PE,* 36.
22. *PA,* 177; *PE,* 133.
23. *PA,* 312; *PE,* 233.
24. *PA,* 367; *PE,* 274.
25. *PA,* 399; *PE,* 298.
26. *PA,* 372; *PE,* 278.
27. *PA,* 482; *PE,* 360.
28. *PA,* xiv; *PE,* x.
29. Lipton, *Ernst Cassirer: The Dilemma of a Liberal Intellectual in Germany,* 166.
30. *PA,* xv; *PE,* xi.
31. On this subject, see Gay's anecdotal remarks, in "The Social History of Ideas," 118, note 13.
32. Fredric Jameson, "Walter Benjamin; Or, Nostalgia," *Marxism and Form: Twentieth-Century Dialectical Theories of Literature* (Princeton: Princeton University Press, 1971), 82.
33. Alfred Cobban, "The Enlightenment and Germany," *Spectator,* 26 Sept. 1952, 406–7.
34. Michel Foucault, "Une histoire restée muette," *Quinzaine littéraire* 8 (1966): 3–4.
35. See Cassirer, *The Myth of the State* (New Haven: Yale University Press, 1946), 5.
36. *PA,* xvi; *PE,* xi.

Meranze: Critique and Government

An earlier version of this essay appeared as "Michel Foucault, the Enlightenment, and the Contexts of Critique," in the *American Journal of Semiotics* 12, nos. 1–4 (1995; delayed publication in 1998), special issue on semiotics and history, guest-edited by William Pencak, 311–22. I would like to thank Keith Baker, Michael Bernstein, Helen Deutsch, Page duBois, William Pencak, Paul Rabinow, Peter Reill, and Steven Rosswurm for their assistance.

1. Michel Foucault, "What Is Enlightenment?" in Michel Foucault, *Ethics: Subjectivity and Truth,* vol. 1 of *The Essential Works of Foucault,* ed. Paul Rabinow (New York: New Press, 1997), 303–19; Foucault, "The Art of Telling the Truth," in *Foucault: Politics, Philosophy, Culture,* ed. Lawrence Kritzman (New York: Routledge, 1988), 86–95; Foucault, "Introduction," in Georges Canguilhem, *The Normal and the Pathological* (New York: Zone Books, 1989), 7–24; Foucault, *The Use of Pleasure,* vol. 2 of *The History of Sexu-*

ality (New York: Pantheon Books, 1985); Foucault, *The Care of the Self*, vol. 3 of *The History of Sexuality* (New York, Pantheon Books, 1986).

2. Foucault, "What Is Enlightenment?" 305.

3. Immanuel Kant, "What Is Enlightenment?" in Kant, *On History*, ed. Lewis White Beck (Indianapolis, Ind.: Bobbs-Merrill, 1963), 3.

4. Ibid.; Foucault, "What Is Enlightenment?" 306.

5. Ibid.

6. Kant, "What Is Enlightenment?" 4–7; Foucault, "What Is Enlightenment?" 307–8.

7. Kant, "What Is Enlightenment?" 10.

8. Ibid.

9. Foucault, "What Is Enlightenment?" 312.

10. Foucault, "The Art of Telling the Truth," 88.

11. Foucault, "What Is Enlightenment?" 316.

12. Michel Foucault, "What Is Critique?" in *What Is Enlightenment? Eighteenth-Century Answers and Twentieth-Century Questions*, ed. James Schmidt (Berkeley and Los Angeles: University of California Press, 1996), 384.

13. Foucault, "What Is Enlightenment?" 315.

14. Michel Foucault, "Polemics, Politics, and Problematizations: An Interview with Michel Foucault," in Foucault, *Essential Works*, 1: 117.

15. Foucault, "What Is Enlightenment?" 312.

16. Ibid., 313.

17. Ibid., 317.

18. Ibid., 319.

19. Ibid., 304.

20. Michel Foucault, "The Birth of Biopolitics," in Foucault, *Essential Works*, 1: 73–74.

Daston: Enlightenment Fears, Fears of Enlightenment

1. Immanuel Kant, "Was ist Aufklärung? [1784]," in *Immanuel Kant: Politische Schriften*, ed. Otto Heinrich von der Gablentz (Köln/Opladen: Westdeutscher Verlag, 1965), 1; the translation used is by James Schmidt, in James Schmidt, ed. *What Is Enlightenment? Eighteenth-Century Answers and Twentieth-Century Questions* (Berkeley and Los Angeles: University of California Press), 1996.

2. Anthony Ashley Cooper, Third Earl of Shaftesbury, *A Letter Concerning Enthusiasm, to my Lord****** (London, 1708), 349.

3. Chevalier de Jaucourt, "Superstitieux," in *Encyclopédie, ou Dictionnaire raisonné des sciences, des arts et des métiers*, 17 vols., ed. Jean d'Alembert and Denis Diderot (Paris/Neuchâtel, 1751–80), 15: 669.

4. As Kant notes, "Wer sich fürchtet, kann über das Erhabene der Natur nicht urteilen, so wenig als der, welcher durch Neigung und Appetit ein-

genommen ist, über das Schöne"; see *Kritik der Urteilskraft* [1790], ed. Karl Vorländer (Hamburg: Felix Meiner, 1990), 106 [Bk. II. 28].

5. Joseph de Maistre, *Les Soirées de Saint-Petersbourg*, in *Œuvres complètes*, 7 vols. (Lyon: Librairie Générale Catholique et Classique, 1884), 4: 33.

6. For an account of the transformation of scientific experience in the seventeenth century, see Peter Dear, *Discipline and Experience: The Mathematical Way in the Scientific Revolution* (Chicago and London: University of Chicago Press, 1995).

7. On the ideology of "matters of fact" and the problem of assent in late seventeenth-century natural philosophy, see Steven Shapin and Simon Schaffer, *Leviathan and the Air Pump: Hobbes, Boyle, and the Experimental Life* (Princeton: Princeton University Press, 1985), 22–26, 39–40, 76–79, et passim.

8. On the fact/evidence distinction in the early modern context, see Lorraine Daston, "Marvelous Facts and Miraculous Evidence in Early Modern Europe," *Critical Inquiry* 18 (1991): 93–124.

9. René Descartes, *Discours de la méthode* [1637], Part VI.

10. Francis Bacon, *Novum organum* [1620], I: 46.

11. *Histoire de l'Académie Royale des Sciences: Année 1699*, 2nd ed. (Paris, 1718), Préface.

12. See relevant entries in the *Oxford English Dictionary*, *Grimms Wörterbuch*, and *Dictionnaire historique de la langue française*.

13. "Fact," *OED*: The first usage in this sense is dated 1632, albeit with Latin antecedents. The parallel evolution of the French 'fait' occurs somewhat later, with complications; see Lorraine Daston, "Strange Facts, Plain Facts, and the Texture of Scientific Experience in the Enlightenment," in *Proof and Persuasion: Essays on Authority, Objectivity, and Evidence*, ed. Elizabeth Lunbeck and Suzanne March (Belgium: Brepols, 1996), 42–59.

14. Bernard de Fontenelle, *De l'origine des fables* [1724], ed. J.-R. Carré (Paris: Librairie Félix Alcan, 1932), 14, 33.

15. Etienne Bonnot de Condillac, *Essai sur l'origine des connaissances humaines* [1749], in *Œuvres*, 23 vols. (Paris, An VI/1798), 1: 67.

16. Samuel Johnson, *The History of Rasselas, Prince of Abissinia* [1759], ed. J. P. Hardy (Oxford: Oxford University Press, 1968), 98–99, 104–5.

17. Condillac, *Traité des systêmes* [1749], in *Œuvres*, 1: 123.

18. Ibid., 203.

19. René Antoine Ferchault de Réaumur, *Mémoires pour servir à l'histoire des insectes*, 6 vols. (Paris: Imprimerie Royale, 1734–42), 2: xxxiv.

20. Georges Cuvier, *Recueil des éloges historiques lus dans les séances publiques de l'Institut de France* (Paris: Firmin Didot Frères, Fils, 1861), 3: 180.

21. Voltaire, "Imagination," in *Encyclopédie*, 8: 560–63.

22. Jean François Marmontel, "Fiction," in *Encyclopédie*, 6: 679–83.

23. Jaucourt, "Vraisemblance," in *Encyclopédie*, 17: 484.

24. Johnson, *Rasselas*, 105.

25. Adam Smith, *The Theory of Moral Sentiments* [1759], ed. D. D. Raphael and A. L. Macfie (Oxford: Oxford University Press, 1976), 124.

26. Jean d'Alembert, "Essai sur la société des gens de lettres et des grands, sur la réputation, sur les mécènes et les récompenses littéraires," in *Mélanges de littérature, d'histoire et de philosophie*, new ed. (Amsterdam, 1759), 352–53.

27. Jean-Jacques Rousseau, *Reveries of the Solitary Walker* [1782], trans. Peter France (London: Penguin, 1979), 30, 33.

28. Ibid., 89.

29. Ibid., 101–2.

30. Réaumur, *Histoire*, 2: xxxv.

31. Rousseau, *Reveries*, 69–71.

32. Charles Baudelaire, *Salon de 1859*, in *Curiosités esthétiques: L'Art romantique et autres œuvres critiques*, ed. Henri Lemaître (Paris: Éditions Garnier, 1962), 317–19.

33. Charles Dickens, *Hard Times* [1854], ed. John Craig (Harmondsworth: Penguin, 1969), 47–52.

34. Friederich Nietzsche, "Vom Nutzen und Nachteil der Historie für das Leben [1874]," in *Unzeitgemässe Betrachtungen* [1873–76], ed. Peter Pütz (München: Goldmann, 1992), 111–14.

35. Charles de Secondat de Montesquieu, *De l'esprit des lois* [1748], ed. G. Truc, 2 vols. (Paris: Garnier, 1961), 1: 6.

36. François Quesnay, "Despotisme de la Chine [1767]," in *Œuvres économiques et philosophiques de Quesnay*, ed. Auguste Oncken (Paris, 1888), 645.

37. "Raison," *Encyclopédie*, 13: 773–74.

38. Paul Henry Thiry d'Holbach, *Système social: Ou principes naturels de la morale et de la politique avec un examen de l'influence du gouvernement sur les moeurs*, 3 vols. (London, 1773), 3: 135.

39. Max Horkheimer and Theodor W. Adorno, *Dialektik der Aufklärung: Philosophische Fragmente* [1947] (Frankfurt am Main: Fischer, 1988), 12–35.

Goodman: Difference: An Enlightenment Concept

I am particularly grateful to Pierre Saint-Amand for pushing me to write an earlier version of this article for a symposium at Brown University in 1996, and Benoît Melançon for allowing me to refine my argument in an address to the Canadian Society for Eighteenth-Century Studies in 1999. Martin Staum also offered insightful comments at a conference at the University of Calgary. Several colleagues offered thoughtful, detailed critiques of talks and drafts along the way. I am happy to acknowledge especially Madeleine Dobie, Daniel Gordon, Randa Graves, Sarah Maza, Heather McPherson, and Philip Stewart.

1. Naomi Schor, "French Feminism Is a Universalism," *Differences: A Journal of Feminist Cultural Studies* (1995): 15.

2. See Linda J. Nicholson, ed., *Feminism/Postmodernism* (New York: Routledge, 1990), esp. Jane Flax, "Postmodernism and Gender Relations in Feminist Theory," 39–62, and Christine Di Stefano, "Dilemmas of Difference: Feminism, Modernity, and Postmodernism," 63–82. The feminist debate is reviewed and extended in Robin May Schott, "The Gender of Enlightenment," in Schott, ed., *Feminist Interpretations of Immanuel Kant* (University Park: Penn State University Press, 1997), 319–37.

3. Lynn Hunt, "Forgetting and Remembering: The French Revolution Then and Now," *American Historical Review* 100 (Oct. 1995): 1132.

4. Olympe de Gouges, "The Declaration of the Rights of Woman," in *Women in Revolutionary Paris 1789–1795*, ed. Darline Gay Levy, Harriet Branson Applewhite, and Mary Durham Johnson (Urbana: University of Illinois Press, 1975), 90.

5. Joan Wallach Scott, *Only Paradoxes to Offer: French Feminism and the Rights of Man* (Cambridge, Mass.: Harvard University Press, 1996), 74–75.

6. Ibid., 20.

7. I discuss Scott's argument at length in "More than Paradoxes to Offer: Feminist Theory as Critical Practice," *History and Theory* 36 (Oct. 1997): 392–405.

8. See Daniel Gordon, *Citizens without Sovereignty: Equality and Sociability in French Thought, 1670–1789* (Princeton: Princeton University Press, 1994); Dena Goodman, *The Republic of Letters: A Cultural History of the French Enlightenment* (Ithaca: Cornell University Press, 1994); Londa Schiebinger, *The Mind Has No Sex? Women in the Origins of Modern Science* (Cambridge, Mass.: Harvard University Press, 1989), chap. 8; Lieselotte Steinbrügge, *The Moral Sex: Woman's Nature in the French Enlightenment*, trans. Pamela E. Selwyn (Oxford: Oxford University Press, 1995).

9. Both Jürgen Habermas and Lynn Hunt have shown the importance of the family for the development of the individual in the eighteenth century. "In the intimate sphere of the conjugal family privatized individuals viewed themselves as independent even from the private sphere of their economic activity—as persons capable of entering into 'purely human' relations with one another," writes Habermas in *The Structural Transformation of the Public Sphere: An Inquiry into a Category of Bourgeois Society*, trans. Thomas Burger with the assistance of Frederick Lawrence (Cambridge, Mass.: MIT Press, 1989), 48. Hunt concludes similarly: "The history of the family romance in French revolutionary politics shows that the individual was always imagined as embedded in family relationships and that these relationships were always potentially unstable." *The Family Romance of the French Revolution* (Berkeley: University of California Press, 1992), 202.

10. Pauline Johnson has a different approach but a similar aim in "Feminism and the Enlightenment," *Radical Philosophy* 63 (Spring 1993): 3–12. I am

sympathetic to Johnson's argument that postmodern feminists have a tendency to consider Enlightenment rationalism a form of dogmatism rather than to recognize in it the critical practices in which they themselves engage in the endeavor to unmask it and the "unfinished cultural project" in which they are thus participating. "Feminism's current critique of Enlightenment formulations appears as another vital episode in the unfolding of the Enlightenment project itself," she writes. "Feminism's discovery of the prejudices built into the various articulations of this project is nothing more than an extension and clarification of the meaning of the Enlightenment" (4). Here I am making a rather different argument, from a different perspective, but one that might complement rather than challenge Johnson's.

11. Carolyn C. Lougee, *"Le Paradis des Femmes": Women, Salons, and Social Stratification in Seventeenth-Century France* (Princeton: Princeton University Press, 1976), 52; Jacques Revel, "The Uses of Civility," in *A History of Private Life*, ed. Roger Chartier, vol. 3, *Passions of the Renaissance*, trans. Arthur Goldhammer (Cambridge, Mass.: Harvard University Press, 1989), 190–94. Both Lougee and Revel make a crucial distinction between the reciprocity of salon civility and the hierarchical civility of the court, but Revel argues that with the triumph of Louis XIV and Versailles, the salon model "had no future." This dubious proposition is contested most notably by Gordon in *Citizens without Sovereignty*. See especially his discussion of the theory of Norbert Elias (88–94).

12. Elizabeth C. Goldsmith, *Exclusive Conversations: The Art of Interaction in Seventeenth-Century France* (Philadelphia: University of Pennsylvania Press, 1988), 1–15.

13. Louis de Jaucourt, "Civilité, Politesse, Affabilité," in *Encyclopédie, ou Dictionnaire raisonné des sciences, des arts et des métiers*, 35 vols. (Paris: Briasson, 1751–65), 3: 497. Abbé Nicolas Trublet wrote similarly: "The polite man is necessarily civil, but the man who is simply civil is still not polite, will not at all pass for polite around those who know, and can never be called polite, if this term is taken in the full breadth of its significance. Politeness supposes civility, but it adds to it. The former concerns principally the matter of things, the latter how to say and do them." "De la politesse" (1735), in Marc Fumaroli, ed., *L'Art de la conversation* (Paris: Garnier, 1997), 248. Roger Chartier discusses Jaucourt's article and others in "From Texts to Manners, a Concept and Its Books: *Civilité* between Aristocratic Distinction and Popular Appropriation," in *The Cultural Uses of Print in Early Modern France*, trans. Lydia G. Cochrane (Princeton: Princeton University Press, 1987). His argument, however, is rather different from the one I am making here.

14. "Politesse," in *Encyclopédie*, 12: 916.

15. Quoted in Gordon, *Citizens without Sovereignty*, 144.

16. The prevalence of the belief in natural and immutable difference is suggested by the responses to the Academy of Dijon's 1754 essay competition

on the question: What is the origin of inequality among men; and is it authorized by natural law? Jean-Jacques Rousseau famously answered the second part of the question in the negative, but the vast majority of the known entrants took the other side. See Roger Tisserand, *Les concurrents de J.J. Rousseau à l'Académie de Dijon pour le prix de 1754* (Paris: Boivin et cie, 1936).

17. Daniel Gordon, "Beyond the Social History of Ideas: Morellet and the Enlightenment," in *André Morellet (1727–1819) in the Republic of Letters and the French Revolution*, ed. Jeffrey Merrick and Dorothy Medlin (New York: Peter Lang, 1995), 50.

18. See Keith Michael Baker, *Inventing the French Revolution: Essays on French Political Culture in the Eighteenth Century* (Cambridge: Cambridge University Press, 1990), 178–85.

19. "Philosophe," in *Encyclopédie*, quoted in Gordon, "Beyond the Social History of Ideas," 49.

20. Gordon, "Beyond the Social History of Ideas," 47–48.

21. On public opinion, see Baker, *Inventing the French Revolution*, chap. 8; on the salonnière, see Goodman, *Republic of Letters*, chap. 3.

22. See, e.g., Marmontel's praise of Julie de Lespinasse: "She found [her guests] here and there in the world, but [they] were so well matched that, when they were [with her], they found themselves in harmony like the strings of an instrument played by an able hand." Jean-François Marmontel, *Mémoires,* ed. John Renwick (Clermont-Ferrand: G. De Bussac, 1972), 1: 220.

23. [Suzanne Curchod Necker], *Nouveaux mélanges extraits des manuscrits de Mme Necker,* ed. Jacques Necker (Paris: C. Pougens, 1801), 2: 291.

24. Sylvana Tomaselli, "The Enlightenment Debate on Women," *History Workshop Journal* 20 (1985): 101–24.

25. Quoted in Gary Kates, *Monsieur d'Eon Is a Woman: A Tale of Political Intrigue and Sexual Masquerade* (New York: Basic Books, 1995), 154.

26. Quoted in Goldsmith, *Exclusive Conversations,* 20.

27. Lougee, *Paradis des Femmes,* 209.

28. Joan DeJean, "The (Literary) World at War, or, What Can Happen When Women Go Public," in *Going Public: Women and Publishing in Early Modern France,* ed. Elizabeth C. Goldsmith and Dena Goodman (Ithaca: Cornell University Press, 1995), 116, 127.

29. Kates, *Monsieur d'Eon Is a Woman,* 157. This is also Erica Harth's point in "The Salon Woman Goes Public... Or Does She?" in Goldsmith and Goodman, *Going Public,* esp. 192–93. Harth goes further in arguing that this shift was responsible for suppressing women's public writing.

30. On the reinforcing and naturalizing of gender difference in the *Ency-clopédie*, for example, see Steinbrügge, *The Moral Sex,* chap. 2. I would also point to Diderot's discussion of slavery in Bk. 11 of Abbé Guillaume-Thomas-François Raynal, *Histoire philosophique and politique du commerce et des établis-*

sements des Européens dans les deux Indes (3rd ed., 1780), for a good example of the minimizing of differences among men and the emphasis on women's different nature.

31. Antoine-Léonard Thomas, "A la mémoire de Madame Geoffrin," in *Eloges de Madame Geoffrin, contemporaine de Madame Du Deffand*, ed. André Morellet (Paris: H. Nicolle, 1812), 89.

32. Jacques-Antoine-Hippolyte, comte de Guibert, "Eloge d'Eliza," in *Lettres de Mlle de Lespinasse*, ed. Eugène Asse (Paris, n.d.), 360.

33. Friedrich-Melchior Grimm et al., *Correspondance littéraire, philosophique, et critique*, ed. Maurice Tourneux (Paris: Garnier, 1877–82), July 1777.

34. Denis Diderot, "Sur les femmes," in *Qu'est-ce qu'une femme?* ed. Elisabeth Badinter (Paris: P.O.L., 1989), 179; see also Antoine-Léonard Thomas, "Essai sur le caractère, les moeurs et l'esprit des femmes dans les différents siècles," in Badinter, 51–54; and Montesquieu, *De l'esprit des lois*, Bk. XIX, chap. 15: "Everything is closely related: the despotism of the prince is naturally conjoined to the servitude of women; just as the liberty of women is tied to the spirit of the monarchy." On this theme in Enlightenment historiography, see Tomaselli, "Enlightenment Debate on Women."

35. Harth, "Salon Woman Goes Public," 192.

36. Tomaselli, "Enlightenment Debate on Women," 114–18.

37. Habermas, *Structural Transformation*, 97.

38. Baker, *Inventing the French Revolution*, 305. Lynn Hunt makes the same distinction in her discussion of the Marquis de Sade's *La Philosophie dans le boudoir* (1795): "Sodomy, like incest and the community of women, are ways of effacing the system of signs that constituted French society in the eighteenth century (and perhaps any society)," she explains. "By advocating them, Sade in effect demonstrates the contradictions between the ideal of fraternity, taken to its logical extreme, and the idea of society." Hunt, *Family Romance*, 146.

39. Baker, *Inventing the French Revolution*, 240–41.

40. John Keane is one of the most interesting of recent political theorists struggling with the seeming contradiction between freedom and civility. A chapter on "Uncivil Society" in his book *Civil Society, Old Images, New Visions* (Stanford: Stanford University Press, 1998) opens: "The emerging consensus that civil society is a realm of freedom correctly highlights its basic value as a condition of democracy" (114). By assuming both that natural freedom is the foundation of civil society, and that freedom and civility are necessarily in conflict, Keane can only suggest ways in which *incivility* can be eliminated from civil society. He does not ask how freedom can be achieved through a civil society organized by institutions of civility, but rather, "Can anything be done to prevent or to reduce incivility, particularly when it threatens whole populations?" (154).

41. Chartier, "From Texts to Manners," 84–87.

42. Ibid., 99.

43. Ernst Cassirer, *The Philosophy of the Enlightenment*, trans. Fritz C. A. Koelln and James P. Pettegrove (Boston: Beacon Press, 1955), 269.

44. On this point, see Steinbrügge, *Moral Sex*, chap. 5.

45. Much has been written on the theory of separate spheres and Rousseau's significance in its articulation for the modern world. An important and early formulation is Genevieve Lloyd, *The Man of Reason: "Male" and "Female" in Western Philosophy* (1984), 2d ed. (Minneapolis: University of Minnesota Press, 1993), 75–79.

46. Kates makes a similar point in *Monsieur d'Eon Is a Woman*, 169.

47. Quoted in Mary Louise Roberts, *Civilization without Sexes: Reconstructing Gender in Postwar France* (Chicago: University of Chicago Press, 1994), 2.

48. Roberts, *Civilization without Sexes*, 4.

49. Mona Ozouf, "Essay on French Singularity," in *Women's Words*, trans. Jane Marie Todd (Chicago: University of Chicago Press, 1997), 229.

50. Ibid., 231.

51. Ibid., 281–82.

52. Elisabeth Badinter, "L'Exception française," *Débat*, no. 87 (Nov.–Dec. 1995): 123.

53. Michelle Perrot, "Une Histoire sans affrontements," *Débat*, no. 87 (Nov.–Dec. 1995): 132–34.

54. Such a vision accords with Keith Baker's assertion that "society" emerged in the seventeenth century when the ontological link was broken between "the Creator and the created," and thus became itself the "ontological horizon of human life." Cut adrift, humanity conceived as society developed a new theology, a new epistemology, a new politics. "In political terms," Baker explains, society emerged "as a middle ground between civil war and absolute rule ..., an autonomous domain of individualism without anarchy, order without arbitrary power." Keith Michael Baker, "A Foucauldian French Revolution?" in *Foucault and the Writing of History*, ed. Jan Goldstein (Oxford and Cambridge, Mass.: Blackwell, 1994), 195–96. See also his "Enlightenment and the Institution of Society: Notes for a Conceptual History," in *Main Trends in Cultural History*, ed. W. F. B. Melching and W. R. E. Velema (Amsterdam and Atlanta, Ga.: Rodopi, 1994). Daniel Gordon, however, sees sociability as the basis of "a nonpolitical *polis* where citizens without sovereignty could be free" (*Citizens without Sovereignty*, 6). I find this conclusion extreme in that it does not see beyond the opposition between politics and society any better than Rousseau does. I see no reason why political institutions cannot be built on the ground of society, why society must be opposed to either democracy (Rousseau) or absolutism (philosophes).

55. One might draw this same conclusion from reading Paul Cohen, *Freedom's Moment: An Essay on the French Idea of Liberty from Rousseau to Foucault* (Chicago: University of Chicago Press, 1997). Cohen argues that the "French idea of freedom" is defined by a tradition of "consecrated heretics" who span

the political spectrum. He concludes that this *singularité française* is decidedly masculine. "The heretics appear to cast freedom itself in a fundamentally masculine mold," he writes (182).

56. Joan Wallach Scott, "The Campaign against Political Correctness: What's Really at Stake," *Radical History Review* 54 (1992): 76–77.

57. Deborah Tannen, *The Argument Culture: Moving from Debate to Dialogue* (New York: Random House, 1998), 3, 26.

58. Ibid., 290.

59. Stephen L. Carter, *Civility: Manners, Morals, and the Etiquette of Democracy* (New York: Basic Books, 1998), xii–xiii, 25, 132.

60. Ibid., 18.

61. Ibid., 278–79.

62. Ibid., 279–80.

63. Randall Kennedy, "The Case against 'Civility,'" *American Prospect* (Nov.–Dec. 1998): 84.

Klein: Enlightenment as Conversation

1. Dick Hebdige, *Hiding in the Light: On Images and Things* (London and New York: Routledge, 1988), 202. For Lyotard, see *The Postmodern Condition*, trans. Geoff Bennington and Brian Massumi (Minneapolis: University of Minnesota Press, 1984), xxiv. On diverging postmodern approaches to history, Pauline Marie Rosenau, *Post-Modernism and the Social Sciences* (Princeton: Princeton University Press, 1992), 62–76.

2. Peter Hulme and Ludmilla Jordanova, eds., *The Enlightenment and Its Shadows* (London and New York: Routledge, 1990), 3–4.

3. Lorraine Daston, "Afterword: The Ethos of Enlightenment," in *The Sciences in Enlightened Europe*, ed. William Clark, Jan Golinski, and Simon Schaffer (Chicago and London: University of Chicago Press, 1999), 497. For essays emphasizing the vexed attitude of Enlightenment to enthusiasm, see Lawrence E. Klein and Anthony J. LaVopa, eds., *Enthusiasm and Enlightenment in Europe, 1650–1850* (San Marino, Calif.: Huntington Library Press, 1998).

4. James Schmidt, "Introduction," in James Schmidt, ed., *What Is Enlightenment? Eighteenth-Century Answers and Twentieth-Century Questions* (Berkeley and Los Angeles: University of California Press, 1996), 27.

5. Ibid., 29.

6. Hebdige, *Hiding in the Light*, 183.

7. David Simpson, *The Academic Postmodern and the Rule of Literature* (Chicago and London: University of Chicago Press, 1995), 41. For the communicative ambitions within postmodernism, see Margaret Rose, *The Post-Modern and the Post Industrial: A Critical Analysis* (Cambridge: Cambridge University Press, 1991), 44, 46, 49, 57, 61, 102–3, 112, 155. Of course, other strands of the postmodern point toward "a sublime, asocial now" and "a with-

drawal from the immediately given ground of sociality": see Hebdige, *Hiding in the Light*, 200–202. Moreover, intellectuals of a postmodern persuasion have no monopoly on conversation and dialogue as metaphors of renewal.

8. For Rorty's own "grand narrative," see David L. Hall, *Richard Rorty* (Albany, N.Y.: State University of New York Press, 1994), 11–64.

9. Richard Rorty, *Consequences of Pragmatism* (Minneapolis: University of Minnesota Press, 1982), xvi–xvii.

10. Richard Rorty, *Contingency, Irony, and Solidarity* (Cambridge: Cambridge University Press, 1989), 5.

11. Rorty, *Consequences of Pragmatism*, xxxix.

12. Richard Rorty, *Philosophy and the Mirror of Nature* (Princeton: Princeton University Press, 1980), 163.

13. Rorty, *Consequences of Pragmatism*, 165. A parallel orientation appears in Stanley Fish, *Is There a Text in This Class? The Authority of Interpretive Communities* (Cambridge, Mass.: Harvard University Press, 1980), 1–17.

14. Seeing "intellectual history … as the history of metaphor" (16) is a principal burden of the essay, "The Contingency of Language," in Rorty, *Contingency, Irony, and Solidarity*, 3–22.

15. Rorty, *Philosophy and the Mirror of Nature*, 316.

16. Rorty, *Consequences of Pragmatism*, xxxix.

17. Rorty, *Philosophy and the Mirror of Nature*, 317.

18. For related initiatives in history, literature, and sociology, see respectively: Dominick LaCapra, *Rethinking Intellectual History: Texts, Contexts, Language* (Ithaca and London: Cornell University Press, 1983), 16–69, 23–71; Stephen Greenblatt, *Shakespearean Negotiations: The Circulation of Social Energy in Renaissance England* (Berkeley and Los Angeles: University of California Press, 1988); and Paul Atkinson, *The Ethnographic Imagination* (London and New York: Routledge, 1990), 179–80.

19. James Clifford, *The Predicament of Culture* (Cambridge, Mass.: Harvard University Press, 1988), 23. See also Nigel Rapport, "Edifying Anthropology: Culture as Conversation, Representation as Conversation," in *After Writing Culture*, ed. Allison James, Jenny Hockey, and Andrew Dawson (London and New York: Routledge, 1997), 177–93.

20. Clifford, *Predicament of Culture*, 41.

21. In suggesting that historical investigation challenges theoretical history or the grand narrative of postmodernism, I do not pretend that historical investigation operates outside the influence of theory. Enlightenment studies have evolved in recent decades in dialogue with theoretical debates. While the influences of Theodor Adorno and Max Horkheimer and of Michel Foucault have inspired research emphasizing eighteenth-century obsessions with observation, taxonomy, abstraction, objectivity, and discipline, Hans-Georg Gadamer, Norbert Elias, Pierre Bourdieu, and Jürgen Habermas (each with his own grand narrative) have inspired historical accounts of a conversational Enlightenment.

22. Dorinda Outram, "The Enlightenment Our Contemporary," in Clark, Golinski, and Schaffer, eds., *The Sciences in Enlightened Europe*, 39.

23. Dena Goodman, *The Republic of Letters: A Cultural History of the French Enlightenment* (Ithaca and London: Cornell University Press, 1994), 3.

24. For a recent summary of this evolution in Enlightenment studies, see Clark, Golinski, and Schaffer, eds., *The Sciences in Enlightened Europe*, 5–29.

25. Hulme and Jordanova, eds., *The Enlightenment and Its Shadows*, 2, 3.

26. Peter Burke, "The Art of Conversation in Early Modern Europe," in *The Art of Conversation* (Ithaca: Cornell University Press, 1993), 89–122, and references cited there.

27. Daniel Gordon, *Citizens without Sovereignty: Equality and Sociability in French Thought, 1670–1789* (Princeton: Princeton University Press, 1994), 127–28. See also Peter France, *Politeness and Its Discontents* (Cambridge: Cambridge University Press, 1992), 53–73, and the essays in *Yale French Studies* 92 (1997), edited by Elena Russo and devoted to "Exploring the Conversible World: Text and Sociability from the Classical Age to the Enlightenment."

28. Roy Porter, "The Enlightenment in England," in *The Enlightenment in National Perspective*, ed. Roy Porter and Mikuláš Teich (Cambridge: Cambridge University Press, 1981), 1–5.

29. Lawrence E. Klein, *Shaftesbury and the Culture of Politeness* (Cambridge: Cambridge University Press, 1994); John Burrow, *Whigs and Liberals: Continuity and Change in English Political Thought* (Oxford: Clarendon Press, 1988).

30. According to Dena Goodman, "When men of letters entered the Parisian salon in the eighteenth century, ... they saw themselves as French Shaftesburys, Addisons, and Steeles and helped transform Parisian salons into centers of this new style of conversation"; see *The Republic of Letters*, 125.

31. Hans-Georg Gadamer, *Truth and Method* (London: Sheed and Ward, 1975), 10–39.

32. Anthony Ashley Cooper, Third Earl of Shaftesbury, *Characteristics of Men, Manners, Opinions, Times*, ed. Lawrence E. Klein (Cambridge: Cambridge University Press, 1999), 407.

33. Ibid., 37.

34. Ibid., 33.

35. "Vicissitude is a mighty law of discourse and mightily longed for by mankind": Ibid., 34.

36. Robert Voitle, "The Reason of the English Enlightenment," *Studies on Voltaire and the Eighteenth Century* 27 (1963): 1735–74.

37. "*Am I always only to be a listener?* is as natural a case of complaint in divinity, in morals, and in philosophy, as it was of old the satirist's in poetry." Conversational engagements were agonistic ("A free conference is a close fight"): Shaftesbury, *Characteristics*, 34.

38. Ibid., 33.

39. Ibid., 232.

40. The following discussion is drawn from Klein, *Shaftesbury and the Progress of Politeness*, 51–69.

41. Ibid., 28–29, 67–68.

42. *Spectator* 10 (12 Mar. 1711) in Donald F. Bond, ed., *The Spectator* (Oxford: Clarendon Press, 1965), I: 44.

43. For France, see Peter France, "The Sociable Essayist: Addison and Marivaux," in *Politeness and Its Discontents*, 74–96. For Germany, see Pamela Currie, "Moral Weeklies and the Reading Public in Germany, 1711–1750," *Oxford German Studies* 3 (1968): 69–86. For Italy, see Rebecca Messbarger, "Reforming the Female Class: *Il Caffè*'s 'Defense of Women,'" *Eighteenth-Century Studies* 32 (1998–99): 355–69.

44. For France, see Gordon, *Citizens without Sovereignty*, 61–85, and articles in *Yale French Studies* 92 (1997). For Germany, see Hans Erich Bödecker, "Aufklärung als Kommunikationsprocess," *Aufklärung* 2 (1987): 89–111. For Britain, see Scott Black, "Social and Literary Form in the *Spectator*," *Eighteenth-Century Studies* 33 (1999–2000): 21–42; Marina Frasca-Spada, "The Science and Conversation of Human Nature," in Clark, Golinski, and Schaffer, eds., *The Sciences in Enlightened Europe*, 218–45; John Mullan, *Sentiment and Sociability: The Language of Feeling in the Eighteenth Century* (Oxford: Clarendon Press, 1988); J. G. A. Pocock, *Virtue, Commerce and History* (Cambridge: Cambridge University Press, 1985), 48–50, 234–39, 246–53; and articles in a special number of *Eighteenth-Century Life* 15 n.s., nos. 1, 2 (1991) on "Sociability and Society in Eighteenth-Century Scotland."

45. Hans Erich Bödecker, "Das Kaffeehaus als Institution aufklärerischer Gesellligkeit," in *Sociabilité et société bourgeoise en France, en Allemagne et en Suisse, 1750–1850*, ed. Etienne François (Paris: Editions Recherche sur les civilisations, 1987); Brian William Cowan, "The Social Life of Coffee: Commercial Culture and Metropolitan Society in Early Modern London" (Ph.D. dissertation, Princeton University, 2000); Ulla Heise, *Coffee and Coffeehouses*, trans. Paul Roper (West Chester, Penn.: Schiffer 1987); Lawrence E. Klein, "Coffeehouse Civility, 1660–1714: An Aspect of Post-Courtly Culture in England," *Huntington Library Quarterly* 59 (1996): 30–51; Steven Pincus, "'Coffee Politicians Does Create': Coffeehouses and Restoration Political Culture," *Journal of Modern History* 67 (1995): 807–32.

46. Goodman, *The Republic of Letters*, esp. 73–135.

47. In general, see Dorinda Outram, *The Enlightenment* (Cambridge: Cambridge University Press, 1995), 14–30; and evidence throughout the national surveys in Porter and Teich, eds., *The Enlightenment in National Perspective*. Also, Günter Birtsch, "The Berlin Wednesday Society," in Schmidt, *What Is Enlightenment?* 215–52; Dino Carpanetto and Giuseppe Ricuperati, *Italy in the Age of Reason, 1685–1789*, trans. Caroline Higgitt (London and New York: Longman, 1987); Margaret Jacob, *Living the Enlightenment: Freemasonry and Politics in Eighteenth-Century Europe* (New York and Oxford: Oxford University Press, 1991); Ulrich Im Hof, *The Enlightenment*, trans. Wil-

liam E. Yuill (Oxford: Basil Blackwell, 1994); Richard van Dülmen, *The Society of the Enlightenment: The Rise of the Middle Class and Enlightenment Culture*, trans. Anthony Williams (Oxford: Polity Press, 1992).

48. Lorraine Daston, "Afterword: The Ethos of Enlightenment," in Clark, Golinski, and Schaffer, eds., *The Sciences in Enlightened Europe*, 497–98.

49. Clark, Golinski, and Schaffer, eds., *The Sciences in Enlightened Europe*, 172.

50. Arnold Thackray, "Natural Knowledge in Cultural Context: The Manchester Model," *American Historical Review* 79 (1974): 672–709; Roy Porter, "Gentlemen and Geology: The Emergence of a Scientific Career, 1660–1902," *Historical Journal* 21 (1978): 809–36, esp. 811–25; Roy Porter, "Science, Provincial Culture and Public Opinion in Enlightenment England," *British Journal for Eighteenth-Century Studies* 3 (1980): 20–46.

51. John Gascoigne, *Joseph Banks and the English Enlightenment: Useful Knowledge and Polite Culture* (Cambridge: Cambridge University Press, 1994); Steven Shapin, *A Social History of Truth: Civility and Science in Seventeenth-Century England* (Chicago: University of Chicago Press, 1994); Alice Walters, "Conversation Pieces: Science and Politeness in Eighteenth-Century England," *History of Science* 35 (1997): 121–54. For France, see Geoffrey V. Sutton, *Science for a Polite Society: Gender, Culture, and the Demonstration of Enlightenment* (Boulder, Colo.: Westview Press, 1995).

52. Adrian Desmond's *The Politics of Evolution: Morphology, Medicine, and Reform in Radical London* (Chicago and London: University of Chicago Press, 1989) is a superb account of this process.

53. This is the strategy of Stephen Toulmin, *Cosmopolis: The Hidden Agenda of Modernity* (Chicago: University of Chicago Press, 1990), which organizes its grand narrative as a "dual trajectory of Modernity" (172) emerging out of, on the one hand, Renaissance humanism and, on the other, seventeenth-century exact science.

54. Herbert Butterfield, *The Whig Interpretation of History* (New York: W. W. Norton, 1965), 36–37.

55. Ibid., 45.

56. Ibid., 47.

57. Though primarily a critic of postmodern and poststructural opinions that challenge the discipline of history, Richard J. Evans also remarks on the contributions to historical thinking and research of "postmodernism in its more moderate guises," in *In Defense of History* (New York: W. W. Norton, 1999), 216.

58. Quentin Skinner, *Liberty before Liberalism* (Cambridge: Cambridge University Press, 1998), 112.

Index

In this index an "f" after a number indicates a separate reference on the next page, and an "ff" indicates separate references on the next two pages. A continuous discussion over two or more pages is indicated by a span of page numbers, e.g., "57–58." *Passim* is used for a cluster of references in close but not consecutive sequence.